A DIPLOMATIC HISTORY OF
THE AMERICAN REVOLUTION

A DIPLOMATIC HISTORY OF THE

AMERICAN
REVOLUTION

Jonathan R. Dull

Yale University Press • *New Haven and London*

Designed by Nancy Ovedovitz and set in Caledonia type by Eastern Graphics. Printed in the United States of America by Vail-
Ballou Press, Binghamton, N.Y.

Library of Congress Cataloging in Publication Data

Dull, Jonathan R., 1942–
  A diplomatic history of the American Revolution.
  Bibliography: p.
  Includes index.
  1. United States—Foreign relations—Revolution, 1775–1783.
I. Title
  E249.D859   1985   973.3'2   85–5306
  ISBN 0–300–03419–9 (alk. paper)

The paper in this book meets the guidelines for permanence and
durability of the Committee on Production Guidelines for Book
Longevity of the Council on Library Resources.

10 9 8 7 6 5 4 3 2

86000713

973.32
D 888

For Susan

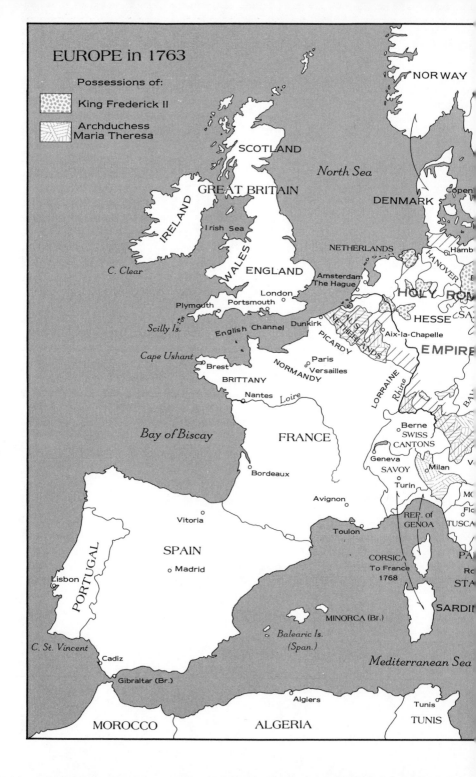

EUROPE in 1763

Possessions of:

King Frederick II

Archduchess
Maria Theresa

NORWAY

North Sea

SCOTLAND

GREAT BRITAIN

DENMARK

Copen

IRELAND

Irish Sea

NETHERLANDS

HANOVER

Hamb

Amsterdam
The Hague

HOLY ROM

WALES

ENGLAND

HESSE

C. Clear

London

AUSTRIAN
NETHERLANDS

CSA

Plymouth

Portsmouth

Aix-la-Chapelle

EMPIRE

Scilly Is.

English Channel

Dunkirk

PICARDY

Cape Ushant

Brest

Paris
Versailles

NORMANDY

LORRAINE

Rhine

BRITTANY

Nantes

Loire

BA

Berne
SWISS
CANTONS

Bay of Biscay

FRANCE

Geneva
SAVOY

Milan

V

Bordeaux

Turin

MO

Avignon

REP. of
GENOA

Fl

Vitoria

Toulon

TUSCA

PA

SPAIN

CORSICA
To France
1768

R

STA

PORTUGAL

Madrid

SARDI

Lisbon

MINORCA (Br.)

Balearic Is.
(Span.)

C. St. Vincent

Cadiz

Mediterranean Sea

Gibraltar (Br.)

Algiers

Tunis

MOROCCO

ALGERIA

TUNIS

CONTENTS

PREFACE

This book is written for undergraduate and graduate students, teachers and other historians, and general readers wishing an introduction to the diplomacy of the American Revolution. It is based on published sources, many of which have appeared within the last few years. This research, some of it my own, has questioned many aspects of Revolutionary diplomacy that we have taken for granted, such as the "idealism" of American diplomats or the significance of the Battle of Saratoga. It is time for a new synthesis; the most popular diplomatic history of the Revolution is a slightly revised version of a book published over fifty years ago, Samuel Flagg Bemis's *The Diplomacy of the American Revolution*. I attempt that synthesis, paying attention to the diplomacy of all the participants in the War for American Independence (the United States, Great Britain, France, Spain, and the Netherlands) and even to that of some of the onlookers, such as Russia. My interests are somewhat different from Bemis's; for example, I pay relatively more attention to the affairs of eastern Europe, relatively less to questions of neutral shipping and international law. Even within my field of concentration I cannot give adequate coverage to all the aspects of so complicated a story. I therefore provide a very lengthy annotated bibliography for those wishing to pursue particular topics in greater depth. My thanks go to my brother and sister historians who have provided the materials from which this book is built; my special thanks go to those of them who were kind enough to criticize my work in manuscript: Pat Coté of Natick High School, Natick, Massachusetts; Larry Kaplan of Kent State University; Hamish Scott of the University of St. Andrews; and Bill Willcox of the *Papers of Benjamin Franklin*. Finally, I would like to express my gratitude to Chuck Grench, Barbara Wells Folsom, and the other wonderful people at Yale University Press, as well as to my cartographer, Robert Williams.

PART ONE
Diplomatic Origins of the American Revolution

CHAPTER 1

The Prehistory of
American Diplomacy

American diplomacy was formally established in a simple manner. Unwilling as yet to send ambassadors abroad, the Continental Congress on November 29, 1775 voted to appoint a committee to correspond with "our friends" in Britain and elsewhere.[1] On the following day the new Committee of Secret Correspondence notified Arthur Lee, a former colonial agent in London, of its appointment; ten days later Benjamin Franklin, one of the committee members, wrote a similar letter to one of his correspondents in the Netherlands.[2] These letters are the first official pieces of American diplomatic correspondence. American relations with Britain technically were still those of fellow subjects of the same king, and America as yet had no formal contact with other states (although American merchants for many years had maintained extensive contacts with Dutch, French, and Spanish colonies in the West Indies).[3]

Although the history of American foreign relations thus techni-

1. Worthington Chauncey Ford et al., eds., *Journals of the Continental Congress, 1774–1789*, 35 vols. (Washington, D.C.: Government Printing Office, 1904–76), 3:392.

2. Leonard W. Labaree, William B. Willcox et al., eds., *The Papers of Benjamin Franklin*, 24 vols. to date (New Haven and London: Yale University Press, 1959–), 22:280–81, 287–91.

3. See Richard Pares, *Yankees and Creoles: The Trade between North America and the West Indies before the American Revolution* (Cambridge, Mass.: Harvard University Press, 1956), and Dorothy Burne Goebel, "The 'New England Trade' and the French West Indies, 1763–1774: A Study in Trade Policies," *William and Mary Quarterly*, 3rd ser., 20 (1963): 331–72.

cally begins in 1775, American diplomacy had a lengthy period of gestation. America was a long-standing factor in European diplomacy, and for many years Americans had been learning the techniques of diplomacy through their contacts with Parliament and various British administrative agencies. During the months following the Battles of Lexington and Concord (April 19, 1775) the Continental Congress assumed the character of a working government and began to treat Britain as a hostile foreign power. The decision to establish sources of communication and intelligence in Britain and the Netherlands was a part of that process. Thus, only by the most narrow of definitions can American diplomatic history be said to commence in November 1775.

In studying the origins of American diplomacy we as Americans must be careful, however, to avoid the all-too-human tendency to believe ourselves the central point around which the world revolves. It is true that the setting of boundaries in North America had for centuries been a matter for both soldiers and diplomats; New York, for example, was captured from the Dutch in 1664, and its retention by England was confirmed by the Anglo-Dutch Treaty of Breda of 1667.[4] America was of minor importance to European diplomacy, though, until the French and Indian War of 1754–63. Before then the ownership and boundaries of the various European colonies on the North American continent was for European statesmen a matter of less importance than the fate of minor Italian or German states, such as the Duchy of Parma or the Archbishopric of Cologne. True, in 1748 the French fort of Louisbourg on Cape Breton Island (now part of Canada) was returned to France as part of a complex peace settlement by which the French evacuated the Austrian Netherlands (now Belgium); this was not because the two were equivalent in value (whatever British public opinion might believe), but because the French had no hope of being allowed by the other powers of Europe to retain such a strategically and economically im-

4. Max Savelle, *The Origins of American Diplomacy: The International History of Angloamerica, 1492–1763* (New York: Macmillan Co., 1967), 56–57; Frances G. Davenport and Charles O. Paullin, eds., *European Treaties Bearing on the History of the United States and Its Dependencies*, 4 vols. (Washington: Carnegie Institute, 1917–37), 2:119–42.

portant acquisition as the Austrian Netherlands. This settlement, the Treaty of Aix-la-Chapelle, was particularly unstable because it failed to resolve the issues which had brought most of Europe to war between 1739/1740 and 1748. In the tense period that followed the treaty any of numerous issues could have rekindled war. It chanced that the spark was struck at a clearing in western Pennsylvania, where a French army detachment clashed with a party of Virginia militia commanded by Colonel George Washington.[5] That this clash led to a war between Britain and France was chiefly the result of miscalculations by British and French statesmen. Neither side wanted war, but as often happens, neither wanted to back down either, and the situation escalated until it was out of control.[6]

The mutual suspicion of Britain and France was duplicated elsewhere in Europe; in 1756 most of the other major powers of Europe began a huge war into which merged the hostilities between Britain and France. By that strange reversal of alliances called the Diplomatic Revolution, Britain henceforth was supported by France's former ally, Prussia, and France, by Britain's former allies, Austria and Russia (the latter only indirectly). This reversal was caused by considerations of the European balance of power (that is, the desire of the states of Europe that no single state become too strong); hence the resulting war, which historians of the wider conflict call the Seven Years' War, had relatively little to do with America. From a British standpoint, though, the fate of North America was a central concern. Statesmen on the European continent were more interested in the wealthy sugar-producing Caribbean islands or in offshore fisheries than they were in such economically unproductive outposts as Spanish

5. For the tense situation in Europe, see Rohan Butler, *Choiseul*, vol. 1: *Father and Son, 1719–1754* (Oxford: Clarendon Press, 1980), 800–21; for an account of the incident in Pennsylvania (from a Virginia standpoint), see Douglas Southall Freeman et al., *George Washington: A Biography*, 7 vols. (New York: Charles Scribner's Sons, 1948–57), 1:350–76.

6. Patrice Louis René Higonnet, "The Origins of the Seven Years' War," *Journal of Modern History* 40 (1968): 57–90; see also T. R. Clayton, "The Duke of Newcastle, the Earl of Halifax, and the American Origins of the Seven Years' War," *Historical Journal* 24 (1981): 571–603.

Texas or French Louisiana and Canada. British statesmen, however, viewed their colonies in North America as an integral part
of an interconnected empire. Americans purchased British manufactured goods, supplied raw materials (particularly from the
southern colonies), helped support the British West Indies, and
provided masts and naval stores for the British navy (although the
navy preferred the masts and naval stores of Scandinavia).[7] Furthermore, trade with America provided employment and training for the merchant seamen who in time of war would man the
navy's warships. The colonies of North America thus were vital
both to the health of the British economy and the strength of the
British navy, the country's first line of defense.[8]

The desire to protect the sources of this prosperity and power
does not fully justify, however, the British decision to send large
numbers of troops to America. In past wars they had not done so,
and as a consequence American wars had remained limited in nature and indecisive in results. Although they overestimated
French resources and misinterpreted French intentions, many
colonial and British leaders had come by 1754 to fear that the
French and their Indian allies posed a threat to future expansion,
to frontier settlements, and even to the colonies themselves. The
British government elected not only to defend the frontier but to
end permanently the French and Indian threat. This decision,

7. Daniel A. Baugh, *British Naval Administration in the Age of Walpole*
(Princeton, N.J.: Princeton University Press, 1965), 257, 279–81, discusses the
prejudice against American naval products. See also, however, Robert G. Albion,
Forests and Sea Power: The Timber Problem of the Royal Navy, 1652–1862
(Cambridge, Mass: Harvard University Press, 1926), and Herbert H. Kaplan,
"Russia's Impact on the Industrial Revolution in Great Britain during the Second
Half of the Eighteenth Century: The Significance of International Commerce,"
Forschungen zur Osteuropäischen Geschichte 29 (1981): 17–22. For a recent sur-
vey of America's economic role in the British Empire, see Jacob M. Price, "The
Transatlantic Economy" in Jack P. Greene and J. R. Pole, eds., *Colonial British
America: Essays in the New History of the Early Modern Era* (Baltimore and Lon-
don: Johns Hopkins University Press, 1984), 18–42.

8. For a fuller discussion of the supposed British dependence on America, see
Jonathan R. Dull, *The French Navy and American Independence: A Study of
Arms and Diplomacy, 1774–1787* (Princeton, N.J.: Princeton University Press,
1975), 36–44.

based partly on fears which in retrospect appear paranoid, had enormous consequences.

The first consequence was that French Canada was doomed. The French navy, vastly outnumbered and short of sailors, could not keep open supply lines between France and Canada. The inhabitants of Canada were not sufficiently numerous to provide adequate militia to reinforce the relatively few regiments of French regular troops. By late 1760 all of French Canada had been conquered, and in the 1763 Treaty of Paris that loss was confirmed. Moreover, France gave Louisiana to her ally Spain to compensate her for the loss of Florida to the British.[9] The French presence in North America was reduced to two small islands off Newfoundland, used to support their fishing fleet. The Mississippi became the boundary between British America and Spanish America (except for the city of New Orleans on the east side of the river, which was held by the Spaniards).

A second consequence was that the British were forced to decide what to do with their victorious army and newly conquered territory. They elected to keep a major portion of this army in America, to close the area west of the Appalachians to settlers from the established colonies, and to raise from the American colonies at least part of the revenue needed to pay for the army.[10] All three aspects of this decision aroused intense suspicion among Americans. In part the American fear was exaggerated, if not irrational. Suspiciousness about outside threats was and still is a prominent part of American political life; by removing the French threat the British transformed themselves from being the ultimate guarantors of American security to being pos-

9. A concise history of the French defeat can be found in W. J. Eccles, *France in America* (New York: Harper & Row, 1972), 178–208; a more complete account is Guy Frégault, *Canada: The War of the Conquest*, trans. Margaret M. Cameron (Toronto: Oxford University Press, 1969). For the transfer of Louisiana, see Arthur S. Aiton, "The Diplomacy of the Louisiana Cession," *American Historical Review* 36 (1930–31): 701–20. Fullest account of the treaty and its negotiation is Zenab Esmat Rashed, *The Peace of Paris, 1763* (Liverpool: Liverpool University Press, 1951).

10. John Shy, *Toward Lexington: The Role of the British Army in the Coming of the American Revolution* (Princeton, N.J.: Princeton University Press, 1965), 45–83, 192–204.

sible threats to it.[11] Moreover, Britain had become in many ways the most modernized country in the world; Americans, living in a generally rural, economically undeveloped society, perceived the growth of British government and changes in British society as "corruption," a moral as well as political danger.[12] British attempts to rationalize the administration of their colonial empire at the expense of local privileges (a movement that predated the recent war) needed to be implemented with great care after prior consultation with local leaders. The opposite occurred. During the dozen years which preceded the outbreak of revolution the British government made countless miscalculations, acting with an extraordinary mixture of insensitivity and vacillation. This story, with its famous highlights like the Stamp Act and the Boston Tea Party, has been more thoroughly studied than perhaps any other series of events in American colonial history.[13] With its breakdown of communications, its misunderstandings, its flares of temper and reconciliations, it is reminiscent of the breakdown of a marriage between spouses who no longer have enough in common to preserve their relationship. With few exceptions both Britons and Americans did try to preserve the bonds between them, but there was one irreconcilable difference—Americans wished to return the relationship to a former stage that most Britons could no longer accept, while the British wished to transform it in ways that most Americans could not tolerate.

11. See James H. Hutson, "The Origins of 'The Paranoid Style in American Politics': Public Jealousy from the Age of Walpole to the Age of Jackson," in David D. Hall, John M. Murrin, and Thad W. Tate, eds., *Saints and Revolutionaries: Essays on Early American History* (New York and London: W. W. Norton & Co., 1984), 332–72. For an opposing view, see John M. Murrin, "The French and Indian War, the American Revolution, and the Counterfactual Hypothesis: Reflections on Lawrence Henry Gipson and John Shy," *Reviews in American History* 1 (1973): 307–18.

12. For these fears, see Pauline Maier, *From Resistance to Revolution: Colonial Radicals and the Development of American Opposition to Britain, 1765–1776* (New York: Alfred A. Knopf, 1972).

13. For a bibliography, see Richard Dean Burns, ed., *Guide to American Foreign Relations since 1700* (Santa Barbara and Oxford: ABC-Clio, 1983), 90–92, 101–09.

A third consequence of the British absorption of Canada was that it helped transform America into an object of European, particularly French, diplomacy. The recent war had embittered Anglo-French relations, while the gradual process of estrangement between Britain and her American colonies left her vulnerable to an attack at what both Britons and French considered the most vital part of the British Empire. Between 1764 and 1768 the French sent secret agents to report on political developments in America and tried without success to cultivate the friendship of Benjamin Franklin.[14] The French abandoned their efforts after 1768, but as long as their relations with Britain remained poor they were not likely to remain bystanders in case of British difficulties.

The period of gradual estrangement from Britain after 1763 was also a critical stage in the preparation of American diplomacy. The necessity of taking common action in response to British provocation drew together the thirteen disparate colonies which hitherto had had, in many ways, closer links with Britain than with each other. By such institutions as committees of correspondence the colonies began what was, in effect if not in intention, the process of nation building. This, on the other hand, came to exclude other British colonies, which in spite of later American hopes did not become part of the United States — Quebec, Nova Scotia, West and East Florida, Bermuda, the Bahamas.

A side effect of common colonial action was the development of a rudimentary American foreign service. This foreign service or diplomatic corps was based on a transformation of the colonial agents. These agents, some English and others American, long had served individual colonies in their dealings with authorities in Britain, much as lobbyists today represent interested parties in

14. John Fraser Ramsey, "Anglo-French Relations, 1763–1770: A Study of Choiseul's Foreign Policy," *University of California Publications in History* 17 (1929–41), 164–65; Josephine F. Pacheco, "French Secret Agents in America, 1763–1778" (Ph.D. diss., University of Chicago, 1951); Friedrich Kapp, *The Life of John Kalb, Major-General in the Revolutionary Army*, trans. Charles Goepp (New York: privately printed, 1870), 34–73; Labaree, Willcox et al., *Papers of Benjamin Franklin* 14:244.

their dealings with Congress. Benjamin Franklin, for example, was sent to London in 1757 by the Pennsylvania Assembly to deal with the descendants of William Penn who, as proprietors of Pennsylvania, still appointed that colony's governor. For a dozen years Franklin tried unsuccessfully to remove Pennsylvania from proprietary control and to place it under direct rule of the king. With the Stamp Act crisis Franklin's role began to change. Gradually he (and to a lesser extent the more radical of his colleagues) came to represent the interests of America as a whole.[15] As a sign of this change more and more colonies selected Franklin to represent them. By 1774 he acted as spokesman for the assemblies of Georgia, New Jersey, and Massachusetts as well as Pennsylvania. That year saw the culmination of his efforts as the unofficial diplomatic agent of the colonies. For several months he secretly negotiated on his own authority with members of the British government in an attempt to prevent war between Britain and her colonies. Although he failed, he gained practical experience in diplomacy. America's first diplomatic mission (legation), the team of commissioners which assembled in Paris at the end of 1776, would be comprised of three reasonably experienced diplomats — Franklin; Arthur Lee, who, like Franklin, had been a colonial agent for the Massachusetts Assembly; and Silas Deane, who had spent the previous several months in France as a purchasing agent for Congress.[16]

The dozen years preceding the Revolution witnessed more than the progressive development of an American national identity and the training of her future first diplomats. The series of political crises during those years changed the way Americans viewed countries other than Britain. The wave of enthusiasm

15. The process of cooperation among colonial agents had, of course, long preceded the Stamp Act crisis. See Michael G. Kammen, *A Rope of Sand: The Colonial Agents, British Politics and the American Revolution* (Ithaca, N.Y.: Cornell University Press, 1968); Jack M. Sosin, *Agents and Merchants: British Colonial Policy and the Origins of the American Revolution, 1763–1775* (Lincoln: University of Nebraska Press, 1965); Lawrence S. Kaplan, *Colonies into Nation: American Diplomacy, 1763–1801* (New York and London: Macmillan, 1972), 1–84.

16. For Lee's activities in England, see Louis W. Potts, *Arthur Lee, a Virtuous Revolutionary* (Baton Rouge and London: Louisiana State University Press, 1981), 54–144. Deane and his mission will be discussed in chapter 6.

about the great victory over France subsided, and with it disappeared the view that Americans and Britons were partners. Many Americans came to see themselves as defenders of British political liberties that had been driven from Britain itself by corrupt politicians. Thus, ironically, American beliefs in British ideals served to separate America from Britain. At the same time the disappearance of the threat from France led to a diminution of the strong American hatred and fear of Catholics and Frenchmen. By the time the Anglo-American crisis came to bloodshed, many Americans had changed their attitudes toward other European states, particularly France.[17] Perhaps the oldest principle in diplomacy is "The enemy of my enemy is my friend." As long as France posed a threat, Americans shared a common strategic interest with Britain, as well as a common culture, religion, and language. Once Britain herself endangered British (i.e., American) liberties, could not Americans count on French help if it were needed?

While radical leaders like John Adams were willing to think this way, other Americans were more cautious. It took many months after the April 1775 battles of Lexington and Concord before the Continental Congress was ready for so bold a step as approaching France for assistance. Wisely, the radicals in Congress did not rush their more moderate brethren.[18]

First, Congress, which luckily was scheduled to convene in May 1775 to follow up the work of the first Continental Congress of 1774, had to establish its right to speak for America. Although representing only individual colonies, the members of Congress had to organize a national army and to improvise what were in actuality national institutions. In its dealings with Britain it turned first to the traditional methods used by the first Continental Congress: economic boycott to put pressure on British merchants and through them on Parliament, as well as the use of a petition to

17. Wonyung Hyun Oh, "Opinions of Continental American Leaders on International Relations, 1763–1775" (Ph.D. diss., University of Washington, 1963); Max Savelle, "The Appearance of an American Attitude toward External Affairs, 1750–1775," *American Historical Review* 52 (1946–47), 655–66.

18. Jack N. Rakove, *The Beginnings of National Politics: An Interpretive History of the Continental Congress* (New York: Alfred A. Knopf, 1979), 64–110.

the king and an address to the people of Britain to explain American grievances.[19] Meanwhile an army of militiamen continued to besiege the British army in Boston; soon these militiamen comprised a Continental army commanded by a Virginia colonel of militia aided by two former British army officers (Horatio Gates and Charles Lee).

Through the summer and fall of 1775, as Washington trained his army, Congress remained reluctant to internationalize the conflict. It shelved a proposal drafted by Franklin to open American trade to Britain's rivals. Instead it decided to admit only war materials, and in September it established a committee to obtain arms and ammunition for the Continental Army.[20]

As we shall see, this moderation was not matched by Britain. The British commitment to a military solution was in part a measure of Britain's frustration at a dozen years of failure in colonial policy. The British had met a similar failure in European diplomacy, which would soon offer America an opportunity to find foreign assistance. To understand that failure and its consequences, however, we must know something not only of British diplomacy but also of the European balance of power.

19. Ford et al., *Journals of the Continental Congress* 2:158–71.
20. Labaree, Willcox et al., *Papers of Benjamin Franklin* 22:126–28, 204–05.

CHAPTER 2

The European Balance of Power, 1763–1775

The "Balance of Power" is a theory of how independent states or countries conduct diplomacy. Because each state fears for its own security it theoretically will be impossible for any single state to dominate all the others; as soon as one state threatens to become too strong the others will combine forces to prevent its dominance. (This, of course, presumes that one state does not begin by being stronger than all of its rivals combined.) Supposedly the balance of power will confer a measure of security on even the weakest of states since it can call for help against a threatening neighbor whose growth would endanger the position of stronger states. The stronger states theoretically should come to the rescue of the weaker in order to protect their own position in the balance of power.

In eighteenth-century Europe, balance of power diplomacy was extremely complicated because of the number of major competing states.[1] In the preceding two centuries diplomacy had been dominated by the rivalry between France and the states ruled by the Habsburg family (including Spain, much of Italy, and Germany). By 1763 this simple division of "great powers" was long past; European diplomacy now balanced five great powers, ten or twenty states sufficiently powerful to claim a degree of independence in foreign policy and hundreds of states so inconsequential that they depended for protection on stronger states

1. The best survey of this subject is Derek McKay and H. M. Scott, *The Rise of the Great Powers, 1648–1815* (London and New York: Longman Group, 1983).

(or the balance of power itself). The division between states of the second and third orders was nebulous and alliances between the five great states shifted frequently. During the fifty years between 1713 and 1763 Britain, for example, had been allied at one time or another with each of the other four great powers. For an understanding of the subsequent workings of European diplomacy we must first know something of the various participants in this complex system.

The enjoyment of "great power" status was not based directly on a large population or even on a given level of economic development. The direct basis of such status was some form of military strength. Great Britain universally was regarded as a great power even though her army was relatively small. (The British army comprised only some 27,000 men in April 1775, 7,000 of which were in North America.)[2] Her power was based on several other factors. The first of these was her navy, the largest in the world. In time of war she could man nearly a hundred ships of the line, the gigantic battleships carrying fifty to a hundred cannon, upon whose number naval power was computed. (Even by the more demanding standard by which only ships with sixty-four or more guns were counted as ships of the line, Britain could command about eighty ships compared to sixty of France and fifty of Spain; lesser naval powers, in roughly descending order, were Russia, the Netherlands, Denmark, Turkey, Sweden, and Portugal.)[3] The second factor was Britain's ability to expand her military forces in time of war by recruiting additional regiments, using militia, purchasing foreign troops, and subsidizing the armies of her allies. In 1747, for example, Britain, in conjunction with the Netherlands, hired an army of 36,000 Russians to fight the French; in the Seven Years' War she was able to tie down a large

2. Piers Mackesy, *The War for America, 1775–1783* (Cambridge, Mass.: Harvard University Press, 1965), 524–25.
3. Jonathan R. Dull, *The French Navy and American Independence: A Study of Arms and Diplomacy, 1774–1787* (Princeton, N.J.: Princeton University Press, 1975), 98–99; Christopher Lloyd, "Armed Forces and the Art of War: Navies," in A. Goodwin, ed., *The New Cambridge Modern History*, vol. 8: *The American and French Revolutions, 1763–93* (Cambridge: Cambridge University Press, 1965), 190.

French army on the European continent by subsidizing the Prussian army and maintaining a mixed German-British army in western Germany.[4]

Britain was able to attain such power in spite of a relatively small population—some eight million people in England, Wales, and Scotland.[5] In large part this power was based on her huge colonial empire, which included Bombay and Bengal in India, Senegal and Gambia on the west coast of Africa, Ireland, Gibraltar, and Minorca in Europe, Jamaica and a dozen smaller islands in the Caribbean, the Bahamas, Bermuda, Quebec, Nova Scotia, Newfoundland, West and East Florida, and the thirteen North American colonies which later became the United States. Even though they were ultimately dependent on Parliament, many components of the empire had their own assemblies, although the British possessions in India were ruled through the East India Company and some other territories had only military governments. Her colonial trade helped make Britain the world's richest and most economically developed country, supporting on a population one-third that of France a comparable level of foreign trade and not greatly inferior government revenues.[6] No

4. For the circumstances leading to the hiring of the Russians, see Jack M. Sosin, "Louisburg and the Peace of Aix-la-Chapelle, 1748," *William and Mary Quarterly*, 3rd ser., 14 (1957): 530. A concise history of the army in Germany is given in Lawrence Henry Gipson, *The British Empire before the American Revolution*, 15 vols. (Caldwell, Idaho and New York: Caxton Printers and Alfred A. Knopf, 1936–70), 7:118–40 and 8:28–64; for more details, see Sir Reginald Savory, *His Britannic Majesty's Army in Germany during the Seven Years' War* (Oxford: Clarendon Press, 1966).

5. Population figures for this chapter, unless otherwise noted, are from H. J. Habakkuk, "Population, Commerce and Economic Ideas," in Goodwin, *American and French Revolutions*, 714–15.

6. For the British Empire in 1763, see Gipson, *British Empire before the American Revolution* 9:3–21. British government expenditure from 1764 to 1775 averaged in excess of £10,000,000: B. R. Mitchell, *European Historical Statistics, 1750–1975*, 2nd ed. (New York: Facts on File, 1981), 733; annual French government revenues in 1773–75 averaged in excess of 350,000,000 livres tournois (at 23.5 to £1): J. F. Bosher, *French Finances, 1770–1795: From Business to Bureaucracy* (Cambridge: Cambridge University Press, 1970), 90. British exports appear to have been somewhat higher than French, imports somewhat lower, although trade figures for the period are very unreliable. Compare B. R. Mitchell, *Ab-*

other state could match in trade or government revenue France and Britain, leaving them unique in having the resources to subsidize other governments and armies. Britain, however, enjoyed a great advantage over France. Partly because her businessmen and bankers helped share in governing the country (through their direct or indirect representation in the House of Commons), Britain found it much easier and less expensive to borrow the money needed to wage a protracted war. Thus Britain generally could outlast her enemies, who eventually spent themselves into bankruptcy.[7]

Britain was ruled by a king in conjunction with Parliament, comprised of the House of Commons and House of Lords. I shall speak later of the king in 1763, George III; let me briefly note here that by accident of inheritance he was simultaneously ruler of a medium-sized German principality, the electorate of Hanover, about which he was less concerned than had been his German-born grandfather and great-grandfather, King George II (reigned in Britain, 1727–60) and George I (reigned 1714–27). Britain's greatest weakness in 1763 was that for the first time in the eighteenth century she had no major ally on the European continent.

France had once been the most powerful state in Europe. She still possessed the largest population of any European state (24 million), trade and revenue comparable to Britain, and a peacetime army of 170,000 men, which could be doubled in time of war.[8] Her army and navy had performed poorly against Britain

---

stract of British Historical Statistics (Cambridge: Cambridge University Press, 1962), 279–81, to Ruggiero Romano, "Documenti e prime considerazioni intorno alla 'balance du commerce' della Francia dal 1716 al 1780," in Studi in onore di Armando Sapori, vol. 2 (Milan: Istituto Editoriale Cisalpino, 1957), 1266–1300. See also F. Crouzet, "Croissances comparées de l'Angleterre et de la France au XVIIIe siècle," Annales: Economies-Sociétés-Civilisations 21 (1966): 254–91.

7. For a French statesman's comment on the importance of that advantage, see Dull, French Navy and American Independence, 304.

8. Eric Robson, "The Armed Forces and the Art of War," in J. O. Lindsay, ed., The New Cambridge Modern History, vol. 7: The Old Regime, 1713–1763 (Cambridge: Cambridge University Press, 1963), 182; Lee B. Kennett, The French Armies in the Seven Years' War: A Study in Military Organization and Administration (Durham, N.C.: Duke University Press, 1967).

and Prussia in the Seven Years' War, however. France was allied with Austria and Spain, but she also protected numerous small states along her eastern border such as Genoa, the Swiss cantons, and the many principalities of Germany (whose virtual independence was guaranteed by France under the terms of the 1648 Peace of Westphalia). She also sought to block the expansion of unfriendly states like Russia and Prussia by supporting the independence of the large but weak states of Sweden, Poland, and Turkey.

Eastern Europe contained three "great powers" which owed their position not to their economic strength but to the size of their armies. The most recently recognized great power was Prussia, formerly a mere medium-sized German state. In 1740 Prussia's new king, Frederick II (1712–86), seized the rich Austrian province of Silesia in a surprise attack. During two ensuing wars, the War of the Austrian Succession (1740–48) and the Seven Years' War (1756–63), Austria attempted in vain to regain the province. After 1763 she gave up the attempt, leaving Germany in temporary equilibrium. Frederick's position nevertheless remained precarious; his splendid army was soon rebuilt to 200,000 men,[9] but Prussia, a poor and still economically undeveloped state of three and a half million people, had been virtually bankrupted by the two recent wars. Prussia's diplomatic position improved dramatically in April 1764 when Frederick signed a treaty of alliance with Russia.

Austria differed in many ways from Prussia. Indeed, the name itself is merely shorthand for the possessions of the archduchess of Austria, Maria Theresa (1717–80, reigned from 1740). Maria Theresa is usually titled empress, since her husband, Francis (1708–65), held the largely ceremonial title of Holy Roman Emperor, by which he was the titular ruler of all Germany (as will be discussed shortly). Maria Theresa, a strong, intelligent, and conscientious monarch, herself ruled the Habsburg family dominions, which extended across much of Europe: Austria, Bohemia

9. Gerhard Ritter, *Frederick the Great: A Historical Profile*, trans. Peter Paret (Berkeley and Los Angeles: University of California Press, 1968), 185. For further details on the Prussian army, see Christopher Duffy, *The Army of Frederick the Great* (Newton Abbot, Eng. and elsewhere: David & Charles, 1974).

and Hungary (over both of which Maria Theresa reigned as queen), Milan, and the Austrian Netherlands (now Belgium). These diverse areas were unwieldy to rule and for the most part economically backward, but they contained more than 15 million inhabitants and supported a respectable army comparable in size to that of Prussia. Since 1756 Austria had been allied to her former bitter enemy, France. Maria Theresa, still fearing Prussia, was anxious enough to preserve the alliance to send her daughter, Marie Antoinette, as bride to the heir to the French throne in 1770.[10]

The most powerful state in eastern Europe was Russia. Although still economically undeveloped, her population of perhaps 19 million inhabitants and her centralized government permitted her to maintain an army of 280,000, the largest peacetime army of any of the great powers.[11] Temporarily, Russian foreign policy was cautious; Empress Catherine II (1729–96) had seized power in 1762 in a coup d'état in which her husband Emperor Peter III was murdered, so she still needed to consolidate her political position.[12] Catherine eventually proved to be a ruler of exceptional imagination, strength, courage, and, at least in foreign policy, ruthlessness. In 1764–65 Catherine made her first moves to strengthen Russia's diplomatic position by contracting alliances with Prussia and Denmark.

Another group of states played an important, although lesser, role in European diplomacy. Some, like Spain and the Netherlands, had formerly been great powers but had failed to keep pace with the growing power of their rivals. Others, like Denmark and Portugal, lacked the population to play a major

10. Albert Sorel, *The Eastern Question in the Eighteenth Century: The Partition of Poland and the Treaty of Kainardji*, trans. F. C. Bramwell (London: Methuen & Co., 1898), 104. For a recent biography in English of Maria Theresa, see Edward Crankshaw, *Maria Theresa* (New York: Viking Press, 1969).

11. Army strength is that of 1767: Isabel de Madariaga, *Russia in the Age of Catherine the Great* (New Haven and London: Yale University Press, 1981), 206–07.

12. Ibid., 21–37. For a reappraisal of Peter's character and abilities, see Karl W. Schweizer and Carol S. Leonard, "Britain, Prussia, Russia and the Galitzin Letter: A Reassessment," *Historical Journal* 26 (1983): 531–56.

role, while still others, like Poland and the Ottoman Empire (Turkey) were too politically or economically backward.

Portugal was Britain's only real European ally, an alliance based for the Portuguese on necessity. This small nation of two million people shared a lengthy border with Spain, which possessed four to five times her population. In 1762 British troops had helped defend Portugal from the Spaniards. The Portuguese king, Joseph I (1714–77, reigned from 1750), was a nonentity who delegated all real power to his chief minister, the count de Oeiras (known after 1770 as the marquis de Pombal).[13]

Spain was France's closest ally. The Spanish king, Charles III (1716–88, reigned from 1759), was distantly related to King Louis XV of France; the alliance between their countries, which Charles renewed shortly after his accession, was called the Family Compact. (The two kings were members of the house or family of Bourbon and are jointly known as "the Bourbons.") In 1762 Charles brought Spain into the Seven Years' War, but this intervention was disastrous; Britain soon won away from her Cuba, the Philippines, and Florida, keeping the last when peace was concluded the following year. In spite of this initial setback in foreign policy, Charles eventually proved the most successful and popular monarch of eighteenth-century Spain, partly because Spain underwent an economic boom under such reformist ministers as the count de Aranda. Spain possessed a large navy, which was to play a major role in the War for American Independence, but her army was generally considered second-rate.[14] Her main claim to greatness was her possession of a gigantic colonial empire, including most of the Western Hemisphere.

The United Provinces of the Netherlands, like Spain, had once been among the most powerful states of Europe. The Netherlands did still possess a large colonial empire, which included the Cape colony at the southwestern tip of Africa, Ceylon, and the Dutch East Indies (now Indonesia), but her once great army and

13. H. V. Livermore, *A New History of Portugal*, rev. ed. (Cambridge: Cambridge University Press, 1976), 212–38.

14. An excellent survey of Charles III's accomplishments is Richard Herr, *The Eighteenth-Century Revolution in Spain* (Princeton, N.J.: Princeton University Press, 1958).

navy had sharply declined. Her economic strength had been surpassed by Britain and France and her complicated political system was a drawback in diplomatic and commercial competition. The States General, Netherlands' parliament, was a battleground for the seven provinces comprising the country—provinces which retained a great deal of autonomy and were the final arbiters of legislation. In 1747 the Dutch, fearing French invasion, had restored the power of the chief of state or stadholder, the hereditary ruler of the Netherlands. Although technically an ally of Britain, the Netherlands had remained neutral during the Seven Years' War. The present stadholder was William V (1748–1806, served from 1751), who was pro-British but ineffectual, giving the States General an opportunity to recover some of its lost power.[15]

Germany was divided into hundreds of petty states whose autonomy had been preserved by the Peace of Westphalia. That peace ended the Thirty Years' War (1618–48), during which the titular rulers of Germany, Emperors Ferdinand II and Ferdinand III, tried unsuccessfully to establish their dominions as a unified, centralized state. (These dominions were called the Holy Roman Empire, "Germany" being a cultural and linguistic term.) For the remainder of its existence the Holy Roman Empire existed chiefly to arbitrate disputes between member principalities and the emperors' power was chiefly moral. The present emperor, Francis I (elected in 1745), held far less power than did either his wife, Maria Theresa, archduchess of Austria, or their archenemy King Frederick II of Prussia, although both were nominally subject to the emperor's authority. The emperor was elected by nine electors, themselves rulers of some of the most important principalities within the empire. In addition to Austria and Prussia, several principalities within the empire had a given amount of importance in European affairs, chiefly Saxony (whose present ruler simultaneously was the elected king of Poland), Hanover (whose ruler was king of Britain and Ireland), and Bavaria.[16]

---

15. A brief introduction to Dutch foreign policy is Alice Clare Carter, *Neutrality or Commitment: The Evolution of Dutch Foreign Policy, 1667–1795* (London: Edward Arnold, 1975).

16. John G. Gagliardo, *Reich and Nation: The Holy Roman Empire as Idea and Reality, 1763–1806* (Bloomington and London: Indiana University Press, 1980).

Italy, like Germany, was not unified until the latter half of the nineteenth century. It was divided into a dozen states: the Kingdom of Sardinia (which included Savoy), the Kingdom of the Two Sicilies (which included Naples and was ruled by a son of King Charles III of Spain), the Grand Duchy of Tuscany (ruled by one of Maria Theresa's sons), Milan (administered directly by Austria), the republics of Venice and Genoa, the Papal States, and several smaller principalities. In 1752 Spain and Austria, which hitherto had contested for primacy in Italy, agreed to end their rivalry.[17] Italy became diplomatically one of the quietest parts of Europe, and for some forty years Italians were spared from war.

Another fortunate people were the Danes, who also enjoyed a long period of peace. Denmark, however, was menaced by Swedish designs on Norway, which was ruled by the Danes. In 1765 Denmark sought safety by concluding a defensive alliance with Russia and soon thereafter arranged a future exchange of territory with Catherine's son, the crown prince of Russia, and his German relatives by which Denmark eventually would receive the German principality of Holstein along the Danes' southern border. This further tied together Denmark and Russia. Danish diplomacy was in the exceptionally capable hands of a German-born foreign minister, Count Johan Hartwig Ernst von Bernstorff.[18]

Along the borders of Russia lay three extensive states, each of them dangerously weakened by obsolete political institutions. These dinosaurs had once been mighty; now they were threatened by rapacious new predators. For the two decades before 1763, central Europe had been the great area of European diplo-

---

The king of Prussia and archduchess of Austria also held territories outside the empire.

17. For a short description of the Treaty of Aranjuez of 1752, see Rohan Butler, *Choiseul*, vol. 1: *Father and Son, 1719–1754* (Oxford: Clarendon Press, 1980), 983–86.

18. Michael Roberts, "Great Britain, Denmark and Russia, 1763–1770," in Ragnhild Hatton and M. S. Anderson, eds., *Studies in Diplomatic History: Essays in Memory of David Bayne Horn* (London: Longman, 1970), 236–67; Lawrence J. Baack, "State Service in the Eighteenth Century: The Bernstorffs in Hanover and Denmark," *International History Review* 1 (1979): 323–48; Madariaga, *Russia in the Age of Catherine the Great*, 192–93, 260–61.

matic instability; once equilibrium had been restored, the scene of struggle moved to eastern Europe, where Russia menaced these three states: Poland, the Ottoman Empire (known also as Turkey), and Sweden.

Poland, with a population of 11 million, was the weakest of the three. Its elected king, Augustus III (1696–1763, elected 1733), possessed neither political authority within Poland nor an army to defend her borders. Poland consequently was a Russian satellite, possessing nominal autonomy but having no real independence in foreign affairs.[19]

The Ottoman Empire had a population of 28 to 30 million, one-third of it in Europe,[20] and a huge army, in theory 600,000 strong.[21] Although once able to menace even Vienna, this army had become increasingly obsolete and the Turks had had the good sense to remain neutral during the Seven Years' War. Though not formally allies, the Turks looked chiefly to France for protection against Austria and Russia. The present sultan, Mustafa III (1717–74, reigned from 1757) was eager to restore Turkish prestige and was less cautious than his immediate predecessors.

Sweden was more developed economically than either Poland or Turkey but far smaller in population—two and a half million, counting Finland, then a part of Sweden. Its army and navy were small and its monarch limited in power. Real power was exercised by the Swedish parliament, the Diet, where the pro-French "Hat" party and the pro-British and Russian "Cap" party fought for dominance (with King Adolphus Frederick [1710–71, reigned from 1751] a mere onlooker).[22]

The diplomatic troubles of the 1760s developed gradually. In October 1763 King Augustus III of Poland suddenly died. Empress Catherine, wishing to continue Russian control over Po-

19. For a survey of Polish history, including the insurrection subsequently mentioned, see Norman Davies, *God's Playground: A History of Poland*, 2 vols. (Oxford: Clarendon Press, 1981), esp. 1: 511–26.

20. Colin McEvedy, *The Penguin Atlas of Modern History (to 1815)* (Harmondsworth, Eng. and Baltimore: Penguin Books, 1972), 57, 87.

21. Madariaga, *Russia in the Age of Catherine the Great*, 207.

22. See Michael Roberts, *British Diplomacy and Swedish Politics, 1758–1773* (Minneapolis: University of Minnesota Press, 1980).

land, forced the Polish Diet into electing her former lover Stanislas Poniatowski as King Stanislas Augustus and made recognition
of the new Polish king a part of her alliance with Prussia.
Catherine and Frederick also forced the Diet to recognize Russia
and Prussia as guarantors of the rights of Polish "dissidents," that
is, members of the Protestant and Orthodox faiths. This protection was not accorded merely out of concern for religious toleration but also to give Prussia and Russia an excuse to intervene in
Polish domestic affairs. This interference was regarded by most
Poles as an affront to their Catholicism, and in early 1768 a rebellion broke out at the town of Bar in southern Poland. Russian
troops marched against the Confederates of Bar, and when fighting spilled across the border of the Ottoman Empire, the Turks
(in October 1768) declared war against Russia.[23]

The Russians proved capable of dealing simultaneously with
Turks and Poles. Part of their Baltic fleet sailed via England to
the Aegean Sea, where in July 1770 it annihilated a larger Turkish fleet.[24] Russian armies were also victorious, penetrating
deep into the Ottoman Empire. Meanwhile, as the Polish rebels
received no outside assistance except for a few French officers
and some French financial help, their uprising degenerated into
a protracted guerrilla war.

Russia now threatened to become master not only of Poland
but also of the Balkans. Even Constantinople was endangered.
This posed an enormous threat to Austria. Emperor Francis died
in 1765, upon which his son Joseph (1741–90) was elected Holy
Roman Emperor and was named by his mother coregent of Austria (although she reserved final authority for herself). In 1769
and 1770 Joseph met with King Frederick II of Prussia. The two
agreed that Germany would remain neutral even if hostilities
broke out between Austria and Russia.[25] The Austrians then
signed a treaty of alliance with the Ottoman Empire (July 1771),

23. Madariaga, *Russia in the Age of Catherine the Great*, 11–16, 188–204;
Herbert H. Kaplan, *The First Partition of Poland* (New York and London: Columbia University Press, 1962), 1–105.

24. M. S. Anderson, "Great Britain and the Russian Fleet, 1769–70," *Slavonic
and East European Review* 31 (1952–53), 148–63.

25. The fullest diplomatic history of the crisis is still Sorel, *Eastern Question in
the Eighteenth Century*, but see also Kaplan, *First Partition of Poland*, and Karl

but waited to ratify it in hopes they could still avoid war with Russia. It was Frederick who devised the solution by which an Austro-Russian war was averted. He proposed that Russia limit the Turkish territory she would keep at the end of hostilities, taking instead part of Poland. Austria and Prussia would take equivalent slices from Poland, thus preventing any of the three great powers from growing more than the others. Reluctantly Maria Theresa agreed in February 1772; Catherine overruled the advice of her foreign minister to do so as well, and in July the treaties were signed. The following year the Polish Diet, under duress, ratified the partition; by this time the rebellion had died out. Poland lost to her neighbors 29 percent of her territory and 35 percent of her population.[26] The most strategically important territory, the Baltic coast, went to Prussia, although her attempts to include the port of Danzig in her share were rebuffed by Russia. Russian gains in population and territory were larger, but by weakening a state already under her domination Russia really gained little. The biggest loser was Austria. Although she gained 2,500,000 new subjects (more than Prussia and Russia combined), she had betrayed Turkey and Poland, who posed no threat to her, and had strengthened Prussia and Russia, two potential enemies.

The war between the Russians and Turks, suspended by a series of armistices in 1772 and early 1773, resumed in March 1773 and lasted another sixteen months. It was ended by the Treaty of Kuchuk Kainarji, through which the victorious Russians took little territory but gained two great advantages: they forced the Turks to turn the Crimean peninsula and the surrounding territory into a Russian satellite like Poland and procured the right subsequently to intervene in Turkish internal affairs as the protector of the rights of Orthodox Christians. Austria took a small piece of Turkish territory as well—in payment for the aid she had rendered her Turkish allies![27]

A. Roider, Jr., *Austria's Eastern Question, 1700–1790* (Princeton, N.J.: Princeton University Press, 1982), 1–149.

26. N. J. G. Pounds, *An Historical Geography of Europe, 1500–1840* (Cambridge: Cambridge University Press, 1979), 104; Kaplan, *First Partition of Poland*, 188–89.

27. Sorel, *Eastern Question in the Eighteenth Century*, 247–55.

States other than Poland and Turkey were appalled by these developments. As we shall see, the British government was opposed to the partition of Poland. For France, however, the events of these years were a disaster. During the preceding century she had regarded herself (in spite of her failures) as the protector of the Ottoman Empire and Poland. Now the Turks and Poles had been betrayed by France's own ally, Austria, while France watched helplessly. Would the small states along France's borders continue to look to her for protection and remain a shield against invasion? Would the great powers of eastern Europe continue their expansion, perhaps dividing among themselves the small principalities of Germany, whose protection had been the cornerstone of French foreign policy for 125 years?

For Sweden the threat was even more immediate. Upon King Adolphus Frederick's death in 1771, the dynamic and ambitious Crown Prince Gustavus (1746–92) became king. Fearing Sweden would suffer the same fate as Poland, he led a bloodless coup d'état against the Swedish Diet in August 1772. His enemies were temporarily banished and Gustavus III unilaterally revised the constitution to make himself an absolute monarch.[28] His actions, though, brought the threat of Russian retaliation, since the protection of the Swedish constitution (which left Sweden defenseless) was a key element in Catherine's diplomacy.

Gustavus's coup was also a setback for British diplomacy. For years the British had been helping the Russians support the Cap party in hopes of winning Russian friendship. This setback, moreover, was merely the latest in a series of failures suffered by British diplomacy. Before we discuss the outcome of the coup, let us turn back to the impact of earlier events on British diplomacy.

28. Roberts, *British Diplomacy and Swedish Politics*, gives an excellent account of the coup and its background.

CHAPTER 3

The Failure of
British Diplomacy after
the Seven Years' War

The virtues of King George III (1738–1820, reigned from 1760) were not dissimilar to those of Winston Churchill. Both these leaders were principled, courageous, indomitable, and supremely confident that their beloved country could overcome even the greatest of trials, if necessary by acting alone against all of Europe. Unlike Churchill, though, George for all his virtues proved the wrong man for his time, for his was an age of limited war, changing alliances, and shifting objectives. George was not well equipped for such a world, as he had the vices often found in those having his virtues—stubbornness, overconfidence, and a reluctance to make compromises. These vices contributed to the crisis with the American colonists. They also bedeviled British diplomacy.[1]

In diplomacy as in other areas George lacked the power of a Russian empress or a French king. Dependent on Parliament for his finances, George could not initiate policy by himself; instead he had to rule through a prime minister (more properly called at this time a "chief minister") and his cabinet. The chief minister

1. For George's virtues, see Piers Mackesy, *The War for America, 1775–1783* (Cambridge, Mass.: Harvard University Press, 1965), 23 and passim, and John Brooke, *King George III* (London: Constable & Co., 1972). A more critical view of his character can be found in J. Steven Watson, *The Reign of George III, 1760–1815* (Oxford: Clarendon Press, 1960), 1–9.

in turn was responsible for maintaining a parliamentary majority, particularly in the House of Commons. As we shall see, this greatly circumscribed the monarch's choices of both men and measures. That the choices in both proved unfortunate thus was not totally George's fault.

During the first twenty years of his reign neither George nor Britain was well served by the chief ministers who directed the British government. Hardly more successful were the secretaries of state who, as members of the chief minister's cabinet, directed the operations of British diplomacy (and, in wartime, British military operations). During his first decade of rule, the 1760s, George had six chief ministers, none of whom had a firm hold on Parliament, none of whom held their office for more than twenty-seven months. For the next dozen years the chief minister was Frederick, Lord North, who was a brilliant parliamentary leader, an excellent First Lord of the Treasury, and a kindly and humane man, but who did not usually consider as his personal charge the direction of diplomacy or warfare.[2]

Few of the secretaries of state of the period were much better. Before 1782 responsibility for foreign affairs was divided among the secretary of state for the northern department (who dealt with the states of *eastern* Europe), the secretary of state for the southern department (who dealt with the states of *western* Europe), and (between 1768 and 1782) the secretary of state for the American colonies. Between George's accession and the outbreak of the American War, ten men served as secretaries for the northern department (two of them twice), eight as secretary for the southern department (including four who also served in the northern department), and two as secretary for the American colonies. Except for the elder William Pitt, dismissed in October 1761, these sixteen secretaries were an unimpressive lot, ranging from the competent but flawed (for example, the earl of Rochford, whom we shall meet shortly) to the inexperienced, inflexi-

2. A good short biography is Peter D. G. Thomas, *Lord North* (London: Allen Lane, 1976). See also Mackesy, *War for America*, passim. The relationship between King George III and his chief ministers is discussed in Ian R. Christie, *Myth and Reality in Late-Eighteenth-Century British Politics and Other Papers* (London: Macmillan and Co., 1970), 55–108.

ble, or incompetent political hacks who unfortunately were closer to the norm than to the exception.[3] The rapid turnover prevented even the better secretaries from making a long-term impact; moreover, part of the erratic nature of British diplomacy came from differences in policy among the secretaries on such issues as whether British should seek an Austrian alliance or a Prussian alliance. Nevertheless, the major failure of British diplomacy lay not in personnel, but in policy. This failure, paralleling the failure of British's colonial policy, can be seen predominantly in two areas: (1) the series of sterile confrontations with Britain's colonial rivals, France and Spain; and (2) Britain's failure to find a major ally on the European continent.

As already mentioned, the Treaty of Paris of 1763 which ended the Seven Years' War enriched the British Empire at the cost of France and Spain.[4] France's loss of Canada, the African colony of Senegal, and influence in India, and Spain's loss of West and East Florida were not in themselves economically or strategically crippling. The loss of Florida did put at risk, however, Spain's remaining possessions in North America, as the superb port of Pensacola gave the British access to Spanish Louisiana for purposes of smuggling or even military operations. It also could permit the British to intercept shipping from Spanish Cuba. Likewise, the British conquest of Canada not only cost the French the Canadian fur trade, but also put at risk the far more valuable French share of the Newfoundland fishery, France now being dependent for bases on the tiny islands of Miquelon and St. Pierre. Even before the war ended France and Spain began a major naval rebuilding program in preparation for an eventual war of revenge

3. For a history of the office, see Mark A. Thomson, *The Secretaries of State, 1681–1782* (Oxford: Clarendon Press, 1932); pp. 180–85 list the holders of the office. Their personalities and policies have been best sketched by the great diplomatic historian Michael Roberts; see especially his *British Diplomacy and Swedish Politics, 1758–1773* (Minneapolis: University of Minnesota Press, 1980) and his *Splendid Isolation, 1763–1780* (Reading, Eng.: University of Reading, 1970). Although my conclusions are somewhat at variance from his, this chapter is greatly indebted to him.

4. See chapter 1 for France's losses, chapter 2 for Spain's.

against Britain.[5] As we shall see, the Franco-Spanish rearmament program failed and the war was postponed indefinitely. Nonetheless the period of 1763 through 1770 was one of recurrent confrontation between Britain and the Bourbon powers (France and Spain) over a variety of issues: the extent of French fishing rights off Newfoundland and of British timbercutting rights in Spanish Central America; the payment of a Spanish war indemnity; the French purchase of the Mediterranean island of Corsica from the Republic of Genoa; and, most threateningly, the presence of a British settlement in the Falkland Islands off Spanish South America.[6] In 1770 a crisis over the last issue briefly seemed likely to lead to war; King Louis XV of France went so far as to dismiss his foreign minister as a sign of his desire for peace. There was considerably less to these crises than appeared on the surface; France and Spain were not in a position to fight Britain (and, in the case of Corsica, Britain was not ready to fight them). Instead, the various crises were a test of will in which each party attempted to gain advantage from forcing the other to back down. This kind of posturing can lead to accidental wars over trivial objects and is a distraction from more legitimate

5. Ramón E. Abarca, "Classical Diplomacy and Bourbon 'Revanche' Strategy, 1763–1770," *Review of Politics* 32 (1970): 313–37; Margaret Cotter Morison, "The Duc de Choiseul and the Invasion of England, 1768–1770," *Transactions of the Royal Historical Society*, 3rd ser., 4 (1910): 83–115; H. M. Scott, "The Importance of Bourbon Naval Reconstruction to the Strategy of Choiseul after the Seven Years' War," *International History Review* 1 (1979): 17–35; Nicholas Tracy, "British Assessments of French and Spanish Naval Reconstruction, 1763–1768," *Mariner's Mirror* 61 (1975): 73–85.

6. Julius Goebel, Jr., *The Struggle for the Falkland Islands: A Study in Legal and Diplomatic History* (New Haven: Yale University Press, 1927), 278–363; Thadd E. Hall, *France and the Eighteenth-Century Corsican Question* (New York: New York University Press, 1971); John Fraser Ramsey, "Anglo-French Relations, 1763–1770: A Study of Choiseul's Foreign Policy," *University of California Publications in History* 17 (1929–41): 143–263; Geoffrey W. Rice, "Great Britain, the Manila Ransom and the First Falkland Islands Dispute with Spain, 1766," *International History Review* 2 (1980): 386–409; Nicholas Tracy, "The Administration of the Duke of Grafton and the French Invasion of Corsica," *Eighteenth-Century Studies* 8 (1974–75): 169–82; Nicholas Tracy, "The Falkland Islands Crisis of 1770: Use of Naval Force," *English Historical Review* 90 (1975):

concerns. After 1770 British attention turned elsewhere, but the confrontations of the preceding decade had left a legacy of mistrust that prevented the normalization of relations with France and Spain.

Part of the reason the British were so concerned to show their resolve was Britain's diplomatic isolation. This isolation began in 1762 when the British balked at renewing their subsidy to their ally, Prussia. King Frederick was subsequently able to extricate himself from the war (the Russians no longer being among his enemies), but relations between Britain and Prussia henceforth were chilly.[7] Once he had made an alliance with the Russians, Frederick opposed even a joint Russo-Prussian alliance with the British. Many historians have viewed this opposition as motivated by Frederick's resentment at how he was treated in 1762; more likely the cynical Frederick opposed the alliance because he no longer needed British support and feared being drawn into an Anglo-French war.[8]

Britain had little more hope of renewing its old alliance with Austria, broken by the Diplomatic Revolution of 1756. This alliance, favored by King George III, was pursued sporadically, in particular by the earl of Sandwich, secretary of state for the northern department in 1763–65, but nothing came of the attempts. The Austrians, still fearing Prussia, clung to their alliance with France. Not only did France have a large army, but also the French alliance freed Austria from having to worry about her possessions in the Netherlands and Italy.[9]

40–75; Nicholas Tracy, "The Gunboat Diplomacy of the Government of George Grenville, 1764–1765: The Honduras, Turks Island and Gambian Incidents," *Historical Journal* 17 (1974): 711–31.

7. Herbert Butterfield, "Review Article: British Foreign Policy, 1762–5," *Historical Journal* 6 (1963): 131–40; Karl W. Schweizer, "The Non-renewal of the Anglo-Prussian Subsidy Treaty, 1761–1762: A Historical Revision," *Canadian Journal of History* 13 (1978): 384–96; Karl W. Schweizer and Carol S. Leonard, "Britain, Prussia, Russia and the Galitzin Letter: A Reassessment," *Historical Journal* 26 (1983): 531–56; Karl W. Schweizer, "Lord Bute, Newcastle, Prussia, and the Hague Overtures: A Re-Examination," *Albion* 9 (1977): 72–97.

8. Horst Dippel, "Prussia's English Policy after the Seven Years' War," *Central European History* 4 (1971): 195–214; Roberts, *Splendid Isolation*, 21–23.

9. Frank Spencer, ed., *The Fourth Earl of Sandwich: Diplomatic Correspon-*

The major British postwar diplomatic effort was directed at obtaining an alliance with Russia, either directly or through a joint alliance with Sweden. These efforts failed, although in 1766 Britain signed a commercial treaty with Russia (and, the same year, a rather meaningless treaty of friendship with Sweden). The reason for the failure was Britain's refusal to offer any substantive advantages to Empress Catherine II. Britain could probably have had the alliance in exchange for (in roughly chronological order) (1) a subsidy to the Russians to support their clients in Poland, (2) acceptance of Russian demands for a promise of support in case of a Turkish war, or (3) a subsidy to the Swedish government to keep Sweden permanently tied to Russia and Britain. Britain helped the Russian navy during the Turkish war of 1768–74 and contributed substantial amounts to the election expenses of the Swedish Cap party, but she refused to commit herself to guaranteeing support in a Turkish war or to subsidizing other states in peacetime.[10] In mid-1771 negotiations for an alliance broke off as Catherine turned her attention to resolving the crisis in eastern Europe. In spite of British wishes she soon reached agreement with the Austrians and Prussians to partition Poland; the British government, although unhappy, acquiesced rather than defy public opinion by taking joint action with France on behalf of the Poles. Catherine's actions, however, temporarily cooled British interest in a Russian alliance.[11]

---

dence, 1763–1765 (Manchester, Eng.: Manchester University Press, 1961; Roberts, Splendid Isolation, 20–21.

10. M. S. Anderson, "Great Britain and the Russo-Turkish War of 1768–74," English Historical Review 69 (1954): 39–58; Roberts, British Diplomacy and Swedish Politics, passim; Roberts, Splendid Isolation, 24–32; Michael Roberts, "Great Britain and the Swedish Revolution, 1772–73," Historical Journal 7 (1964): 1–46; Michael Roberts, "Great Britain, Denmark and Russia, 1763–1770," in Ragnhild Hatton and M. S. Anderson, eds., Studies in Diplomatic History: Essays in Memory of David Bayne Horn (London: Longman, 1970): 236–67; Michael Roberts, "Macartney in Russia," English Historical Review, supplement 7 (1974); H. M. Scott, "Great Britain, Poland and the Russian Alliance, 1763–1767," Historical Journal 19 (1976): 53–74; Isabel de Madariaga, Russia in the Age of Catherine the Great (New Haven and London: Yale University Press, 1982), 187–236.

11. Roberts, British Diplomacy and Swedish Politics, 366–67; Roberts, Splen-

Would a Russian alliance have helped the British in the American War? Russia probably would not have provided substantial direct aid, beyond perhaps furnishing some auxiliary troops. Moreover, a Russo-British alliance probably would not have deterred French intervention on behalf of the Americans, although this is less than certain. Russia, however, would have made it more difficult for the French navy to obtain naval stores from the Baltic. More importantly, a Russo-British alliance might have been a deterrent to the pro-American policy pursued by the Dutch. As we shall see later, the Dutch navy, small as it was, played a significant role in the campaign of 1781, in which the outcome of the war hung in delicate balance—so delicate a balance that the smallest of weights was critical. No matter what help the Russians could have provided, it is evidence of British shortsightedness about the dangers in America that they were so reluctant to pay the relatively low price for an alliance—once war had begun, British attempts to purchase an alliance proved hopeless.[12]

There is a yet more damning indictment of British shortsightedness. On the eve of the final crisis in America, Britain wasted her last and most surprising opportunity to escape her diplomatic isolation and foreclose any outside help for the Americans. This opportunity was to reach an accommodation with France.

---

did Isolation, 37–38; Anderson, "Great Britain and the Russo-Turkish War," 53–54; Albert Sorel, *The Eastern Question in the Eighteenth Century: The Partition of Poland and the Treaty of Kainardji,* trans. F. C. Bramwell (London: Methuen & Co., 1898), 216; David Bayne Horn, *British Public Opinion and the First Partition of Poland* (Edinburgh and London: Oliver and Boyd, 1945).

12. For the opposing argument—that Britain did not need the Russian alliance, particularly at the price demanded—see Roberts, *Splendid Isolation,* 33–36.

CHAPTER 4

French Foreign Policy
during the Reign of Louis XV

Between 1689 and 1815 Britain and France fought seven wars. These wars, marked by naval battles and attacks on colonial possessions, tended to be similar, leading many historians now to see them as the inevitable result of France's and Britain's competition for colonial empire. This theory of inevitability, however, leaves unanswered the shift which occurred in 1815. Since that date there have been no wars between the two countries, even though they remained until the 1950s the world's two greatest colonial powers. Indeed, they were allies (in spite of considerable reciprocal dislike and mistrust) in the First and Second World Wars. The chief reason for this collaboration has been, I believe, their discovery of a mutual interest in protecting the European balance of power. The map of today's Europe looks vastly different from the Europe of 1815, yet the borders of France and the United Kingdom (as Britain became in 1801 by the union with Ireland) have changed little, except for the independence of the Irish Republic. Both France and Britain have feared the growth of large states in central and eastern Europe as threats to their security and, in spite of colonial rivalry and cultural dissimilarities, have found a common interest in resisting changes in the European balance of power.

The same common interest existed for much of the eighteenth century, in spite of the British public's obsession with colonial issues. Neither country's economy could absorb both its own and the other's colonial trade; in other words, the total volume of colonial trade was big enough for the two countries to share. Moreover, during the period between the expansionism of King Louis XIV and the expansionism of the French Revolution, France was ruled by two weak kings, Louis XV (1710–74, reigned from 1715) and Louis XVI (1754–93, reigned from 1774). The French diplomacy of this time generally was centered on the preservation of a divided Germany, maintenance of the balance of power, and protection of weaker states such as Turkey, Poland, and Sweden (or, even more directly, the small states along the French border, such as the cantons of Switzerland). Britain, too, sought the preservation of the status quo in Germany (in order to protect Hanover) and the prevention of a strong state's gaining control of the North Sea coast (where Austria ruled with reassuring indifference the Austrian Netherlands). Given their common interests why, then, were not Britain and France allies during the eighteenth century?

Initially they were. Because Louis XV was only five years old when he succeeded his great-grandfather as king, France was governed for more than two decades by Louis's older relatives, the duke d'Orléans (regent, and later, chief minister, 1715–23) and the duke de Bourbon (chief minister, 1723–26), and his tutor, the cardinal de Fleury (effective chief minister, 1726–43). In 1716 Britain and France concluded an alliance that technically lasted until 1744. During the 1720s the two countries were firm allies and prevented a series of diplomatic crises from resulting in war.[1]

Relations between them cooled in the 1730s, becoming threatening by the end of that decade. In 1739 Britain went to war with France's close ally, Spain, and the following year France, over the objections of Fleury, attacked Austria. Britain sent troops to Germany to act as auxiliaries to help the Austrians and in 1744 went to war against France. Part of the blame for the war be-

---

1. For Anglo-French relations and European diplomacy from 1714 to 1740, see Derek McKay and H. M. Scott, *The Rise of the Great Powers, 1648–1815* (London and New York: Longman Group, 1983), 94–158; Paul Langford, *The Eighteenth Century, 1688–1815* (London: Adam and Charles Black, 1976), 71–118; Arthur McCandless Wilson, *French Foreign Policy during the Administration of Cardinal Fleury, 1726–1743: A Study in Diplomacy and Commercial Development* (Cambridge, Mass.: Harvard University Press, 1936).

tween Britain and France lies with King Louis XV, who, in spite of considerable intelligence and personal charm, proved to be a superstitious, petty, weak person and an inept ruler.[2] Part of the blame, however, lies with the errors of British statesmen, who had their own grandiose ambitions on the European continent and who succumbed to the anti-Spanish hysteria of British public opinion.

The War of the Austrian Succession, which ended in 1748, theoretically should not have destroyed all chances of an Anglo-French reconciliation—at war's end Britain and France relinquished their conquests—but relations between them were tense, and mutual distrust soon led to new hostilities. The Seven Years' War further damaged relations. Even before the war ended the French foreign minister, the duke de Choiseul,[3] began planning retaliation. In 1761 he gave his post at the foreign ministry to his cousin the duke de Choiseul-Praslin and became naval minister so as to direct the rebuilding of the Frency navy. We have already seen that the 1760s marked a series of confrontations with Britain.[4] What the British failed to realize was that the same period saw a major change in the orientation of French diplomacy. This was caused both by the slowness of the parallel naval reconstruction program of France's ally Spain (which forced an indefinite suspension of the planned joint war against Britain) and by the developments in Poland. Choiseul, a bitter enemy of Empress Catherine II of Russia, watched with enormous concern the growth of Russian power. In 1766 he reassumed his position as secretary of state for foreign affairs (his cousin taking over the navy).[5] While still hostile to Britain, French diplomacy became increasingly anti-Russian, particularly after the Turks and Rus-

2. For a character sketch of Louis XV, see Rohan Butler, *Choiseul*, vol. 1: *Father and Son, 1719–1754* (Oxford: Clarendon Press, 1980), 376–86.

3. There is as yet no adequate biography of Choiseul. Butler's projected three-volume biography should help remedy the deficiency, but as yet only the first volume has appeared.

4. See above, chapter 3, note 6.

5. H. M. Scott, "The Importance of Bourbon Naval Reconstruction to the Strategy of Choiseul after the Seven Years' War," *International History Review* 1 (1979): 17–35.

sians went to war in 1768. The changed emphasis can be seen in the virtual ending of the naval rearmament program. The French navy had risen in strength from 47 ships of the line in 1762 to 62 ships of the line in 1766 (18 fewer than Choiseul's target); for the remainder of Louis XV's reign it fluctuated between 59 and 63 ships of the line. The number of masts on hand, a good measure of preparedness, declined after 1766 (although the supply of timber continued to increase until 1770).[6] By the time of the great Falkland Islands crisis of 1770 the Franco-Spanish war of revenge against Britain had become largely a hollow threat.

The anti-British Choiseul nevertheless was dismissed by Louis XV in December 1770 to defuse the threat of war. For several critical months France was without a foreign minister. Finally, in the following June, Louis chose the duke d'Aiguillon, a loyal supporter of the king's attempts to reassert his power in French domestic politics, fiercely anti-Russian, but with very little direct experience of diplomacy.[7] Significantly, the king rejected the count de Broglie, a violent opponent of Britain who headed the king's own secret diplomatic service, the *secret du Roi*.[8] Aiguillon failed to prevent the partition of Poland, but as a small compensation he gained a new ally—King Gustavus III of Sweden, whose revolution was aided by French money and advice. With the Swedish revolution arose the possibility of Russian in-

6. Information is from a 1775 list entitled "Tableau des forces navales du roi dans le courant des treize années," Archives de la Marine (at the Archives Nationales, Paris), series B^5, box 10.

7. For Aiguillon's ministry, see Lucien Laugier, *Un Ministère réformateur sous Louis XV: Le Triumvirat (1770–1774)* (Paris: La Pensée Universelle, 1975), 346–502; there is a superb sketch of his anti-Russian policies in Michael Roberts, *British Diplomacy and Swedish Politics, 1758–1773* (Minneapolis: University of Minnesota Press, 1980), 370–71.

8. For Broglie and the *secret du Roi*, see Albert, duc de Broglie, *The King's Secret: Being the Secret Correspondence of Louis XV with His Diplomatic Agents from 1752 to 1774*, trans. unidentified, 2 vols. (London, Paris, and New York: Cassell, Pelter and Galpin, 1879); Didier Ozanam and Michel Antoine, eds., *Correspondance secrète du comte de Broglie avec Louis XV (1756–1774)*, 2 vols. (Paris: C. Klincksieck, 1956–61); and Edgard Boutaric, ed., *Correspondance secrète inédite de Louis XV sur la politique étrangère avec le comte de Broglie, Tercier, etc.*, 2 vols. (Paris: Henri Plon, 1866).

tervention and a war into which France might be drawn. Anxious to avoid this, Aiguillon turned to Britain for help.[9]

Although the British had earlier rebuffed his appeals for a common front on behalf of Poland,[10] Aiguillon had some reason for optimism. Two British leaders had come to realize that the rise of Russia had made the Franco-British antagonism an anachronism. One was the earl of Rochford, a professional diplomat and secretary of state who had recently been switched from the northern to the southern department.[11] Another was King George III, who secretly encouraged Aiguillon's advances. (Lord North may also have been involved.) In April 1773, when a Russian attack on Sweden seemed imminent, Rochford even hinted to Aiguillon (via a secret agent the French foreign minister had sent to London) that Britain would delay countermeasures should France send troops to help Sweden. Seemingly Britain was now ready to end her sterile confrontations with France.

The opportunity, however, quickly passed. George and Rochford proved unwilling to defy the almost universal public hostility toward France. Worse still, they added insult to injury. France planned to arm a squadron in the Mediterranean to menace the Russian naval forces in the Aegean Sea as an indirect support for

9. For the French initiative and British response, see Michael Roberts, "Great Britain and the Swedish Revolution, 1772–73," *Historical Journal* 7 (1964): 1–46. See also Bertrand de Fraguier, "Le duc d'Aiguillon et l'Angleterre (juin 1771-avril 1773)," *Revue d'histoire diplomatique* 26 (1912): 607–27; David Bayne Horn, *British Public Opinion and the First Partition of Poland* (Edinburgh and London: Oliver and Boyd, 1945), 2–13; Marie-Antoine Bouët de Martange, *Correspondance inédite du Général-Major de Martange, aide de camp du Prince Xavier de Saxe, Lieutenant Général des Armées (1756–1782)* (Paris: A. Picard et fils, 1898); Sir John Fortescue, *The Correspondence of King George the Third from 1760 to December 1783*, 6 vols. (London: Macmillan and Co., 1927–28), 2:428–29; Derek McKay and H. M. Scott, *The Rise of the Great Powers, 1648–1815* (London and New York: Longman Group, 1983), 256; Isabel de Madariaga, *Russia in the Age of Catherine the Great* (New Haven and London: Yale University Press, 1981), 231, 616.

10. See above, chapter 3, note 11.

11. Roberts, *British Diplomacy and Swedish Politics*, 278, discusses Rochford's background and abilities; for other work on Rochford including work in progress, see H. M. Scott, "Review Article: British Foreign Policy in the Age of the American Revolution," *International History Review* 6 (1984): 113–25.

the Swedes; Britain forced the French government to counter-
mand the mobilization. Luckily for Sweden, Empress Catherine
was concerned by the possibility of a Franco-British reconciliation, and by the time she learned the truth the armistice that she
had concluded with the Turks at the time of the Polish partition
had broken down. Russia, already exhausted by five years of hostilities, now needed all her resources for the renewed war with
the Turks; and so the Swedish crisis passed.

This crisis, however, would prove to be a critical factor in the
diplomatic origins of the American Revolution. By passing up
Aiguillon's offer of cooperation, Britain lost her last chance to de-
prive the Americans of outside support in case of a future rupture
between the mother country and her colonies. In mid-1773 British statesmen expected no further trouble in America that would
dictate such precautions. In May, just as the Swedish crisis was
ending, Parliament approved without any real opposition the Tea
Act, largely oblivious to the threat it posed to the political truce
in America.[12]

For the French the crisis completely discredited Aiguillon's
policy of reconciliation with Britain. Although the British gained
little credit with Empress Catherine, their humiliation of France
seemed to give credence to Choiseul's belief that Britain was behind Russia's dominance of eastern Europe.[13] At the very least
it confirmed Britain as being essentially pro-Russian and as providing at least passive support to Catherine's expansionist policies.
In May 1774 King Louis XV died unexpectedly and Aiguillon was
subsequently dismissed from office. His replacement was
Charles Gravier, count de Vergennes (1719–87), who had been
Choiseul's ambassador to the Turks and Aiguillon's ambassador
to the Swedes. He had urged the Turks to war against Russia; in
Stockholm he had observed the Russian and British support of
the Cap party and had provided last-minute help to Gustavus in

    12. Bernhard Knollenberg, *Growth of the American Revolution, 1766–1775*
(New York: Free Press, 1975), 90–94; Benjamin Woods Labaree, *The Boston Tea
Party* (New York: Oxford University Press, 1964), 58–79.
    13. Orville T. Murphy, *Charles Gravier, Comte de Vergennes: French Diplo-
macy in the Age of Revolution, 1719–1787* (Albany: State University of New York
Press, 1982), 151.

preparing his coup d'état.[14] In 1771 both the anti-Russian Austrians and the anti-British Spaniards had hoped to see him named as Choiseul's replacement.[15] He was, in spite of his well-deserved reputation for caution, not the man to pass up an opportunity to weaken either of France's rivals.[16]

He was soon presented the opportunity. The Russian war against the Turks ended successfully in July 1774, but the Russian need to restore their finances gave France a few years in which to act elsewhere. The British meanwhile presented France with a field for action. In December 1773, just eight months after it had humiliated the French, the British government was defied by the citizens of Boston. The Boston Tea Party of that month was followed by a year's escalating crisis until in April 1775 armed rebellion ensued.[17] That rebellion gave France, temporarily free from worry about Russia, the chance to deal a blow to Britain.

14. For Vergennes, see ibid, passim; Roberts, *British Diplomacy and Swedish Politics*, 340–403; Louis Bonneville de Marsangy, *Le Chevalier de Vergennes, son ambassade à Constantinople*, 2 vols. (Paris: Plon, Nourrit, 1894), and *Le Comte de Vergennes, son ambassade en Suède, 1771–1774* (Paris: Plon, Nourrit, 1898).

15. Arthur S. Aiton, "Spain and the Family Compact, 1770–1773," in A. Curtis Wilgus, ed., *Hispanic American Essays: A Memorial to James Alexander Robertson* (Chapel Hill: University of North Carolina Press, 1942), 141.

16. Murphy, *Charles Gravier, Comte de Vergennes*, 217, quotes Vergennes on the humiliations, including that of 1773, suffered from Britain.

17. A good summary of the escalation is David Ammerman, *In the Common Cause: American Response to the Coercive Acts of 1774* (Charlottesville: University Press of Virginia, 1974). Neil R. Stout, *The Perfect Crisis: The Beginning of the Revolutionary War* (New York: New York University Press, 1976), is an alternate account.

PART TWO
Responses to the Revolution

CHAPTER 5

British Reaction to
the American Rebellion

The British government, blind to the danger of an American rebellion, failed to provide itself in advance with allies or to compromise with its enemies. It also failed to establish in America an
effective military base of operations and sufficient troops to suppress a rebellion. In January 1775 it issued orders to arrest the
leaders of the Massachusetts radicals; but to carry out its orders it
had less than five thousand troops in the thirteen American colonies. Assuming that its problems could be restricted to Massachusetts, the preponderance of its troops were in Boston—
nearly four thousand of them crowded into a city which could
easily be bombarded from the surrounding hills and which was
connected only by a narrow causeway to an easily defended countryside.[1] It is hardly surprising that General Thomas Gage, the
British commander, found it difficult to conduct military operations, even against untested American militia. His army suffered
two hundred and fifty casualties when it tried to penetrate the
countryside in April (Battles of Lexington and Concord) and over

1. Clarence Edwin Carter, ed., *The Correspondence of General Thomas Gage
with the Secretaries of State, and with the War Office and the Treasury,
1763–1775*, 2 vols. (New Haven and London: Yale University Press and Oxford
University Press, 1931–33), 2:179–83; John Shy, *Toward Lexington: The Role of
the British Army in the Coming of the American Revolution* (Princeton, N.J.:
Princeton University Press, 1965), 375–424. Total strength in North America, including Florida and Canada, was about seven thousand: Piers Mackesy, *The War
for America, 1775–1783* (Cambridge, Mass.: Harvard University Press, 1965),
524–25.

a thousand when in June it tried to drive the Americans from the hills commanding Boston (Battle of Bunker Hill). The British lack of foresight left a demoralized army in a surrounded city, while the Americans were given an entire year to transform a collection of militia units into a unified army. The campaign of 1775 developed into a stalemate; the American army lacked the artillery to destroy Boston, the British lacked enough troops to push beyond it. The stalemate ended in March 1776 when the Americans finally assembled the necessary artillery, provided for them by British stupidity. (The British had left it in the huge, virtually undefended fort of Ticonderoga, two hundred miles from Boston.) Once the Americans had transported the artillery to the hills overlooking Boston, the British had no choice but to evacuate the city. In early July 1776 the British began the war anew, landing an army on Staten Island in preparation for an attack on New York, the strategic center of the thirteen rebellious colonies.[2]

The British army that fought the New York campaign of 1776 was gigantic by American standards. By mid-August it comprised almost twenty-five thousand professional soldiers.[3] To assemble and transport it to America had been the major task facing Lord North and his government in 1775 and early 1776.

Lord North left the responsibility for war and diplomacy largely to his cabinet—he would maintain the government's majority in Parliament and find the money to finance the war, but others would have to provide the energy and technical skill to fight it.[4] Within the cabinet the waging of war characteristically was a joint responsibility, the First Lord of the Admiralty controlling naval operations, while the secretaries of state made military and diplomatic decisions. News of Lexington, Concord, and Bunker Hill, received in the summer of 1775, led in the autumn to a change of personnel in these offices. Two of the three secretaries of state were replaced. Lord Dartmouth, the conciliatory

2. Ibid., 80–87.
3. Ira D. Gruber, *The Howe Brothers and the American Revolution* (New York: W. W. Norton & Co., 1972), 101.
4. Mackesy, *War for America*, 20–24.

secretary for American affairs, gave way to Lord George Germain, a man who it was felt could be counted on for firmness. Fifteen years earlier Germain had been unjustly dismissed from the British army for supposedly disobeying orders in combat.[5] He now wanted to prove himself and hence was not likely to settle for anything less than victory over the rebels. Rochford, who as southern secretary had to deal with the French, was also replaced, but for reasons not of policy but of politics.[6] Viscount Weymouth, a hardliner on American issues with excellent political connections in Britain, was brought into the cabinet to broaden its political base of support. Ironically, Rochford in 1770 had replaced Weymouth, who had resigned in protest over the government's unwillingness to use force in the Falkland Islands crisis. As a secretary of state, Weymouth previously had acquired a reputation for laziness, drunkenness, and reluctance to correspond with his own ambassadors.[7] The northern department was left in the hands of the earl of Suffolk, who was far more capable (and whose expressed feelings about the rebellion, however rhetorical, verged on bloodthirstiness). Suffolk, however, was frequently incapacitated by gout and after June 1778 was almost completely disabled.[8] The most capable diplomat in the cabinet probably was the earl of Sandwich, who twice before had been a secretary of state. Sandwich now was responsible not for diplomacy, but for the navy. An able naval administrator, Sandwich

5. Piers Mackesy, *The Coward of Minden: The Affair of Lord George Sackville* (London: Allen Lane, 1979).

6. Charles R. Ritcheson, *British Politics and the American Revolution* (Norman: University of Oklahoma Press, 1954), 200. Also, Rochford was in ill health: Peter D. G. Thomas, *Lord North* (London: Allen Lane, 1976), 89.

7. Michael Roberts, *British Diplomacy and Swedish Politics, 1758–1773* (Minneapolis: University of Minnesota Press, 1980), 278–79, 336–37; Michael Roberts, *Splendid Isolation, 1763–1780* (Reading, Eng.: University of Reading, 1970), 6–7; Henri Doniol, ed., *Histoire de la participation de la France à l'établissement des Etats-Unis d'Amérique: Correspondance diplomatique et documents*, 5 vols. and supplement (Paris: Imprimerie Nationale, 1886–99) 1:236–37.

8. Ritcheson, *British Politics and the American Revolution*, 192–93; Mackesy, *War for America*, 38, 246; Alan Valentine, *The British Establishment, 1760–1784: An Eighteenth-Century Biographical Dictionary*, 2 vols. (Norman: University of Oklahoma Press, 1970), 1:471–72.

nevertheless would have been far better placed in either Weymouth's or Suffolk's post, as his grasp of naval strategy was seriously deficient and his nerve weak—his fear of Britain's being
invaded repeatedly deprived British fleets in the Western
Hemisphere of vital reinforcements.[9] Germain, left in control of
Britain's armies by Suffolk's deficiencies of body and Weymouth's of character, came eventually to hate him.[10]

The new cabinet's first responsibility was that of providing an
army to crush the American rebellion. To do so was a matter not
of domestic policy but of diplomacy. The British army was composed of paid professionals rather than conscripts, and the raising
of regular regiments would have been too lengthy and expensive.
The army of Hanover provided five regiments (3,500 men) to garrison Gibraltar and Minorca and another five regiments were
transferred from Ireland to America, but the bulk of the reinforcements for America had to be hired abroad.[11] British diplomats sought these auxiliary troops from several traditional
sources.

One source was the Scots Brigade (of somewhat less than 2,000
men), then in the service of the Netherlands, which technically
was a British ally. Sir Joseph Yorke, the British ambassador, requested the temporary use of the brigade; the Dutch demanded
that it be used only in Europe and paid for in full. The British
then dropped their request, which had merely embittered
Anglo-Dutch relations.[12]

Another and potentially much larger source was Russia, from
which, as we have seen, Britain had hired troops thirty years previously. Suffolk's attempts to hire 20,000 troops now were firmly

9. Jonathan R. Dull, *The French Navy and American Independence: A Study
of Arms and Diplomacy, 1774–1787* (Princeton, N.J.: Princeton University
Press, 1975), 107, 192, 237, 263.

10. Mackesy, *War for America*, 451.

11. Ibid., 39–40.

12. Jan Willem Schulte Nordholt, *The Dutch Republic and American Independence*, trans. Herbert H. Rowen (Chapel Hill and London: University of North
Carolina Press, 1982), 19–21; Friedrich Edler, *The Dutch Republic and the
American Revolution* (Baltimore: Johns Hopkins Press, 1911 [*Johns Hopkins University Studies in Historical and Political Science*, ser. 29, no. 2]), 28–32.

rejected, however, by Empress Catherine II.[13] This left as the only possible source the smaller princes of the Holy Roman Empire, who had provided many of the troops for the Anglo-German army during the Seven Years' War. Here Britain was successful, signing treaties with the rulers of four small German principalities in early 1776 to provide approximately 18,000 troops. Almost 13,000 troops from Hessen-Kassel alone were sent to North America in 1776; by the end of the war some 30,000 Germans from six different principalities had entered British service. The British army in America henceforth always derived at least a third of its strength from German auxiliaries; without them the effort to suppress the American rebellion could hardly have been attempted.[14]

To command the army and navy in North America the cabinet appointed two brothers, Major General William Howe and Vice Admiral Richard Howe. It also named them as peace commissioners to accept America's submission to British authority and then to open negotiations on political reforms. This dual mission, however, was probably an error. At the very least, the responsibility of being both warriors and diplomats proved a distraction to the Howes; at worst, it caused them to proceed more gingerly than otherwise they might. Admiral Richard Howe had negotiated with Franklin in the winter of 1774–75, and he in particular took his diplomatic responsibilities far more seriously than the government realized.[15]

The main task of the cabinet once the army had been dis-

13. Nikolaĭ N. Bolkhovitinov, *Russia and the American Revolution*, trans. C. Jay Smith (Tallahassee, Fla.: Diplomatic Press, 1976), 6–12; *Sbornik Imperatorskago russkago istoricheskago obshchestva* [Collection of the Imperial Russian Historical Commission], 148 vols. (St. Petersburg: Imperial Russian Historical Commission, 1867–1916), 19:471–505.

14. Rodney Atwood, *The Hessians: Mercenaries from Hessen-Kassel in the American Revolution* (Cambridge and elsewhere: Cambridge University Press, 1980); Max von Eelking, *The German Allied Troops in the North American War of Independence, 1776–1783*, trans. J. G. Rosengarten (Albany: Joel Munsell's Sons, 1893).

15. Gruber, *Howe Brothers and the American Revolution*, 350–65, and passim, argues that the Howe brothers' hopes of conciliation were primarily responsible for British military failure in 1776.

patched was to prevent any European power from providing help to the Americans. In August 1775 it declared the Americans in a state of rebellion and in December announced the impending closure of American ports to all commerce. British attempts to intercept arms shipments to America, however, were less than successful. One of the main sources of arms and powder was the small Caribbean island of St. Eustatius, a Dutch colony used as a gigantic warehouse for arms smuggling. Sir Joseph Yorke's repeated attempts to stop this clandestine trade failed; the Dutch government prohibited it but failed to enforce the law. Eventually the Dutch at St. Eustatius went so far as to exchange salutes with an American warship entering their port, drawing even more violent protests from Yorke.[16]

Another major route of arms supplies was through the French Caribbean colonies of Martinique, Guadeloupe, and St. Domingue (now Haiti).[17] France was for Britain a greater concern than was the Netherlands, as in her case arms smuggling might eventually lead to more direct aid. Counterbalancing these fears, however, were the characters of the new leaders of the French government. The idealistic new king, Louis XVI (1754–93, reigned from May 1774), was chiefly concerned about bettering the lives of his subjects and believed his foreign policy should be based on honesty and restraint.[18] In addition, his foreign minister, the count de Vergennes, and his chief minister, the elderly count de Maurepas (1701–81), were known for their caution. Maurepas, intelligent but cynical and self-centered, was a master of court politics; Vergennes, sober, industrious, and devoted to his family, deferred to Maurepas's authority and was left considerably latitude in making foreign policy.

16. J. Franklin Jameson, "St. Eustatius in the American Revolution," *American Historical Review* 8 (1902–03): 683–708; Daniel A. Miller, *Sir Joseph Yorke and Anglo-Dutch Relations, 1774–1780* (The Hague and Paris: Mouton, 1970), 37–55.

17. Robert Rhodes Crout, "The Diplomacy of Trade: The Influence of Commercial Considerations on French Involvement in the Angloamerican War of Independence, 1775–78" (Ph.D. diss., University of Georgia, 1977), 37–65.

18. Robert Rhodes Crout, "In Search of a 'Just and Lasting Peace': The Treaty of 1783, Louis XVI, Vergennes, and the Regeneration of the Realm," *International History Review* 5 (1983): 366–72.

The British made little effort to offer concessions to France on the various issues affecting their diplomatic relations. Instead they relied on persuasion: downplaying the extent of their problems in America, offering friendly advice on the danger that a contagious rebellion might spread to France's own colonies, and firmly but politely protesting reports of arms smuggling.[19] Initially these tactics seemed to work well enough. As a defensive measure the French in the autumn of 1775 sent 3,000 reinforcements to their West Indian colonies, but these were announced in advance to the British. Indeed, less concern about French intentions was shown by the British than was shown by American leaders, who were unsure about the purpose (and the size) of the French reinforcements and who feared a clandestine agreement between Britain and France.[20]

All, however, was not as it appeared. In August 1775 Vergennes, acting on the advice of his ambassador in London, approved the sending of a secret messenger to the American Continental Congress. The ambassador's choice was a young nobleman named Julien-Alexandre Achard de Bonvouloir, who had formerly been stationed in St. Domingue and claimed to have visited America.[21] Bonvouloir's mission was a major turning point in both American and French diplomacy. When he reached Philadelphia in December 1775 he found as a ready audience the newly appointed Committee of Secret Correspondence.

19. Crout, "Diplomacy of Trade," 70–71, 75–82; Orville T. Murphy, *Charles Gravier, Comte de Vergennes: French Diplomacy in the Age of Revolution, 1719–1787* (Albany: State University of New York Press, 1982), 232.

20. Dull, *French Navy and American Independence*, 27; James H. Hutson, "The Partition Treaty and the Declaration of American Independence," *Journal of American History* 58 (1971–72): 877–96.

21. Cornelis-Henri de Witt, *Thomas Jefferson: Etude historique sur la démocratie américaine* (Paris: Librairie Académique, Didier, 1861), 465–87; Joseph Hamon, *Le Chevalier de Bonvouloir, premier émissaire secret de la France auprès du Congrès de Philadelphie avant l'indépendance américaine* (Paris: Jouve, 1953).

CHAPTER 6

The Development of
American Diplomacy

Bonvouloir's arrival in Philadelphia could not have been more fortunately timed. The Committee of Secret Correspondence on December 12, 1775, requested Arthur Lee to ascertain the disposition of foreign powers toward America;[1] on the same day Franklin wrote the scholarly youngest son of King Charles III of Spain to thank him for the gift of a book he had translated and to suggest America's desire for friendship with his country.[2] Within days the committee began a series of meetings with the newly arrived Bonvouloir, held secretly by night in Carpenters' Hall. The committee asked if France were disposed favorably toward the Americans, if she would send them two good army engineers, and if she would sell them arms and war supplies in her ports. Bonvouloir, in accordance with his orders, maintained the transparent fiction that he was acting on his own authority, but gave favorable responses to all the questions.[3]

The committee had admitted America's need of naval protection but hesitated to ask help for fear that public opinion was still unready for foreign involvement in American affairs.[4] In January 1776 Thomas Paine's *Common Sense* was published to great ac-

1. Leonard W. Labaree, William B. Willcox et al., eds., *The Papers of Benjamin Franklin*, 24 vols. to date (New Haven and London: Yale University Press, 1959–), 22:296–97.
2. Ibid., 298–99.
3. Ibid., 310–18.
4. Ibid., 314.

claim and formerly radical ideas became acceptable. The committee soon was given an opportunity to test French good will. At this moment foreign diplomacy chanced to intersect with a more primitive kind of diplomacy. Another congressional committee, the Secret Committee (which arranged for arms purchases) decided to purchase in France goods to bribe American Indian tribes.[5] It selected as its purchasing agent Silas Deane, a former congressional delegate from Connecticut. In addition to serving the Secret Committee, Deane entered into a commercial partnership with several of its most important members. The Committee of Secret Correspondence now asked Deane to serve also as *its* representative. It instructed Deane to sound French intentions and to purchase from the French government uniforms and arms for 25,000 soldiers plus a hundred pieces of field artillery.[6]

Deane was unable to find credit in order to purchase most of the goods wanted for the Indians.[7] It was generally a losing cause anyway; most tribes distrusted Americans even more than they did Britons. (In 1779 the problem of the Iroquois, the most important group of northern tribes, was resolved by a type of diplomacy Americans traditionally have used with Indian nations—a large detachment from the Continental Army was sent to destroy their crops; militia were employed against hostile southern tribes like the Creek and Cherokee.)[8] Deane was more successful, however, with the other parts of his mission. He arrived in France in June 1776 and early the following month reached Paris, where he immediately put himself in touch with Vergennes.[9] As we shall see later, he met with a friendly reception,

5. Ibid., 354.

6. Ibid., 369–74.

7. Charles Isham, ed., *The Deane Papers*, 5 vols. (New York: New-York Historical Society 1887–1891 [*Collections*, vols. 19–23]), 2:20.

8. Barbara Graymont, *The Iroquois in the American Revolution* (Syracuse: Syracuse University Press, 1972); Jack M. Sosin, *The Revolutionary Frontier, 1763–1783* (New York and elsewhere; Holt, Rinehart and Winston, 1967); Isabel Thompson Kelsay, *Joseph Brant, 1743–1807: Man of Two Worlds* (Syracuse: Syracuse University Press, 1984).

9. Labaree, Willcox et al., *Papers of Benjamin Franklin*, 22:487–90; Isham, *Deane Papers*, 1:195–201.

although Congress did not learn this for many months (since none of his early letters from Paris were received).[10]

Even before Deane reached France some congressional delegates had come to believe his mission inadequate to America's diplomatic needs. In early June, Virginia delegate Richard Henry Lee (a brother of the American agent in London) proposed that Congress declare American independence, draft a commercial treaty to propose to foreign nations, and prepare a plan of confederation for the American states.[11] There was coming to be only one major issue dividing Americans, loyalty to Britain or loyalty to the new nation, the United States. Among those who chose the latter loyalty, a remarkable consensus was developing, particularly on questions of foreign affairs.[12] This emerging consensus included several key points.

The first point was that America should declare its independence from Britain. By July only the most cautious of congressional delegates remained hesitant to acknowledge what to most had become obvious—that the war had irreparably severed America from Britain. When New York's delegation abstained from the vote on independence the final obstacle was removed. The Declaration of Independence was largely a foreign-policy statement; without it America hardly could appeal for foreign assistance against the great army gathering to attack New York and the navy blockading its ports. The Declaration also may have been, at least in part, a reaction to fears that the French reinforcements to the West Indies were destined for use in cooperation with Britain against the American cause. It is difficult, however, to ascertain precisely how widespread or serious such fears were.[13]

10. Larabee, Willcox et al., *Papers of Benjamin Franklin*, 22: 487n.

11. For the development of consensus on independence, see Jack N. Rakove, *The Beginnings of National Politics: An Interpretive History of the Continental Congress* (New York: Alfred A. Knopf, 1979), 79–110.

12. The remainder of this chapter is a restatement of part of my earlier article, "Benjamin Franklin and the Nature of American Diplomacy," *International History Review* 3 (1983): 346–63.

13. James H. Hutson, "The Partition Treaty and the Declaration of American Independence," *Journal of American History* 58 (1971–72): 877–96, argues the importance of such fears.

A second part of the consensus was that any British peace offer that did not acknowledge American independence would be unacceptable. A committee of three delegates, Benjamin Franklin, John Adams, and Edward Rutledge, did meet with Admiral Howe in September 1776 to hear his proposals. The meeting was fruitless and the general feeling persisted in Congress that the time was past for considering submission to British authority under any conditions whatsoever.[14]

There was also a consensus that in order to maintain her independence the United States would need foreign military supplies (and possibly naval escort), but that to obtain such help America need not and should not offer more than her trade. This reluctance to offer a military alliance in exchange for foreign assistance was based on both the fear of such alliances and the belief that they would be unnecessary. The fear of military alliances is hardly surprising. Both Paine and Franklin had claimed that it was America's ties with Britain which were responsible for involving her in European wars;[15] independence was desirable as a way of escaping entrapment in the European balance of power. Moreover, most Americans had been trained from childhood to distrust Catholic France and its absolutist government. John Adams, a leader in the effort to involve France in the American war, hardly was unusual in distrusting France as much as he did Britain.[16] What is more surprising is America's unrealistic expectation that the mere offer of a commercial alliance would be sufficient to secure from France open assistance and an acknowledgment of American independence—actions that would surely lead to a British declaration of war. In case of such a war Congress was prepared to offer little more than American neutrality.

14. Labaree, Willcox et al., *Papers of Benjamin Franklin*, 22:565–66, 575, 591–93, 597–605; Paul H. Smith, ed., *Letters of Delegates to Congress, 1774–1789*, 10 vols. to date (Washington, D.C.: Library of Congress, 1976–), 5: passim.

15. Labaree, Willcox et al., *Papers of Benjamin Franklin*, 21:509, 603–04; Philip S. Foner, ed., *The Complete Writings of Thomas Paine*, 2 vols. (New York: Citadel Press, 1945), 1:18–19.

16. See, for example, Robert Taylor, ed., *Papers of John Adams*, 6 vols. to date (Cambridge, Mass.: Belknap Press of Harvard University Press, 1977–), 4:122–23.

Such facile optimism about the attractiveness of a commercial alliance was based on a naïve overestimation of the importance of
American trade. Most American statesmen believed that this
trade would become, if it were not already, the dominant element in the European balance of power. They soon were disillu-
sioned, and the events of war produced a shift in the consensus.
Congress was taught the necessity of compromise by a series of
terrible military defeats that cost it New York and brought
Howe's army to the banks of the Delaware. By late December of
1776, Congress was willing to offer not only a military alliance
but also the promise of American cooperation if Spain and France
wished to conquer Florida or the British West Indies.[17]

The part of the consensus which first developed, however, was
that Canada should be part of the American union. Long before
Congress had even begun to debate independence, American armies were en route to liberate what it was thought would be
grateful Canadians. The American tradition of invading other
countries for their own good, seen often in the Caribbean and in
central America, thus dates from 1775. The supposed liberators
of Canada were met with hostility on the part of the predominantly Catholic inhabitants and the invasion ended in total failure.[18] For the remainder of the war most, if not virtually all,
Americans continued to agree on the desirability of adding Canada to the United States and, of course, on America's right under
colonial charters to the lands between the Appalachian moun-
tains and the Mississippi River, no matter how few the American
settlers or how tenuous the American military presence in the
area.

The foreign-policy consensus of 1776 proved temporary. Beneath the unity forged by military danger—a unity resembling
that of the period following Pearl Harbor—lay deep divisions.

17. Worthington Chauncey Ford et al., eds., *Journals of the Continental Congress, 1774–1789*, 35 vols. (Washington, D.C.: Government Printing Office,
1904–76), 6:1054–58; Labaree, Willcox et al., *Papers of Benjamin Franklin*,
23:96–100.

18. See Gustave Lanctot, *Canada and the American Revolution*, trans. Margaret M. Cameron (Cambridge, Mass.: Harvard University Press, 1967).

Some of the divisions were sectional: southerners had little more interest in contending for New England's fishing rights off Newfoundland than northerners did for accommodating western and southern desires for navigation rights on the Mississippi.[19] Some of the divisions were philosophical. Radicals, who distrusted wealth and commerce, tended also to distrust the French, even after the alliance.[20] Within a few years congressional unity would be shattered by these underlying divisions, manifesting themselves in disputes over peace terms and the propriety of America's diplomatic representatives in Europe; in 1776 Americans were still unified by the dangers posed by General Howe's army and the need to find foreign help in breaking the British naval blockade.

The Continental Congress, hoping for such help, spent from mid-June to mid-September preparing a model treaty of amity and commerce to offer France and Spain.[21] A day or two before the final approval Franklin learned from a friend in Paris that the French government was anxious to aid the Americans.[22] Quickly Congress approved the draft treaty and decided to forward it to France. Congress then elected Franklin and Thomas Jefferson as co-commissioners with Deane to negotiate its acceptance.[23] When Jefferson declined, Arthur Lee, the American agent in London, was elected in his place. The commissioners' instructions, approved on September 24, authorized them to promise that America would notify France before making any peace but did not yet authorize the offer of an alliance in exchange for France's assuming the risk of war. Supplementary instructions over the next month gave the commissioners the authority to ne-

19. Rakove, *Beginnings of National Politics*, 243–74.

20. Edmund S. Morgan, "The Puritan Ethic and the American Revolution," *William and Mary Quarterly*, 3rd ser., 24 (1967): 33.

21. Taylor, *Papers of John Adams*, 4:260–302; William C. Stinchcombe, "John Adams and the Model Treaty," in Lawrence S. Kaplan, ed., *The American Revolution and "A Candid World"* (Kent, Ohio: Kent State University Press, 1977), 69–84.

22. Labaree, Willcox et al., *Papers of Benjamin Franklin*, 22:453–71.

23. Ford et al., *Journals of the Continental Congress*, 5:813–17, 827; 6:897.

gotiate commercial treaties with other European states and ordered them to procure, if possible, the loan or sale of eight French ships of the line.[24] On October 26, Benjamin Franklin embarked on an American warship in the Delaware to join his colleagues in Europe.

24. Labaree, Willcox et al., *Papers of Benjamin Franklin*, 22:624–30.

CHAPTER 7

France Offers Secret Aid

Bonvouloir's mission was a turning point in French as well as American diplomacy.[1] As soon as Vergennes received the report of Bonvouloir's meetings with the Committee of Secret Correspondence, he proposed a major shift in French policy toward the American Revolution. He presented to King Louis XVI a memoir, labeled "Considerations," warning that Britain and America might end their war and then attack the French West Indies and proposing that France provide secret arms aid to the rebels in order to keep the Revolution alive for another year.[2] This would give France and Spain time to strengthen the defenses of their colonies in the Western Hemisphere.

The memoir was directed more at soothing the king's conscience than at averting any real danger. There were few, if any, indications that the French possessions in the Caribbean faced a threat. Moreover, these colonies had already been sent major reinforcements. The lack of danger in 1776 is evidenced by the facts that no more reinforcements were sent and no attempt was made to put the French navy on an immediate war footing.[3] In-

1. Jonathan R. Dull, *The French Navy and American Independence: A Study of Arms and Diplomacy, 1774–1787* (Princeton, N.J.: Princeton University Press, 1975), 30–36.

2. Henri Doniol, ed., *Histoire de la participation de la France à l'établissement des Etats-Unis d'Amérique: Correspondance diplomatique et documents*, 5 vols. and supplement (Paris: Imprimerie Nationale, 1886–99), 1: 273–78; Benjamin Franklin Stevens, ed., *Facsimiles of Manuscripts in European Archives Relating to America, 1773–1783*, 25 vols. (London: privately printed, 1889–98), vol. 13, no. 1316.

3. Dull, *French Navy and American Independence*, 33–35, 56–58.

stead, the arguments put forward in the "Considerations" appear to have been designed to make the proposed arms aid appear defensive in nature to the king.

King Louis XVI responded by asking his chief minister, Maurepas, and other advisers for position papers. Vergennes's paper was drafted by the younger of two brothers who served as his undersecretaries of state, Joseph-Mathias Gérard (1736–1812).[4]

The elder brother, Conrad-Alexandre Gérard (1729–90), is better known to Americans, as he helped negotiate the treaties of 1778 and then served as the first French minister to the United States.[5] (A minister is a diplomatic representative at a post of lesser importance than one served by an ambassador.) Joseph-Mathias, however, played an equally important diplomatic role. In 1778 he was ennobled, and henceforth was known as Joseph-Mathias Gérard de Rayneval; four years later he was sent on several secret missions to England in the course of the peace negotiations. (I shall discuss these later activities in chapter 19.) The younger Gérard's background, like that of Vergennes, was predominantly in dealing with the affairs of eastern Europe. Moreover, both he and his friend Pierre-Michel Hennin (who succeeded Conrad-Alexandre Gérard as undersecretary of state in 1778) had been in Poland during its great diplomatic crisis. Gérard was even suspected by King Frederick II of Prussia of having translated a satire against Poland's occupiers.[6]

The memoir he prepared in March 1776 for Vergennes was labled "Reflections."[7] It was considerably more frank about the

4. For J.-M. Gérard, see Jonathan R. Dull, "Vergennes, Rayneval, and the Diplomacy of Trust," in Ronald Hoffman and Peter J. Albert, eds., *Peace and the Peacemakers: The Treaty of 1783* (Charlottesville: University Press of Virginia, forthcoming).

5. For C.-A. Gérard, see John J. Meng, ed., *Despatches and Instructions of Conrad Alexandre Gérard, 1778–1780* (Baltimore: Johns Hopkins Press, 1939), 33–122.

6. David Bayne Horn, *British Public Opinion and the First Partition of Poland* (Edinburgh and London: Oliver and Boyd, 1945), 29. Hennin's service in Poland is one of the topics of a 1973 University of Wisconsin dissertation, Michael Leigh Berkvam, "Pierre-Michel Hennin: Ses voyages, sa correspondance, 1757–1765."

7. Doniol, *Participation de la France* 1:243–49; Gérard's draft is reproduced in Stevens, *Facsimiles of Manuscripts*, vol. 13, no. 1310, where it is misdated (by

foreign ministry's aims that the "Considerations" had been. It discussed the advantages France would gain from American independence, including the trade she would take from Britain and the bases for the Newfoundland fishery she would acquire (although it specifically excluded the recapture of Canada). It placed first, however, the weakening of Britain's position in the balance of power. Gérard argued, as did most Britons, that it was a monopoly of American trade that formed the basis for Britain's wealth and naval power.[8] Although he did not discuss the recent events in eastern Europe, the implications of his argument were clear to anyone familiar with the friendship between Britain and Russia.

Although it cannot be proven, it seems likely that the appeal of American independence to Vergennes lay chiefly in its probable effect on the European balance of power. If Britain were sufficiently weakened by her loss of American trade, she, at the very least, could no longer provide subsidies to eastern powers like Russia; at best, a chastened Britain might become more cooperative with French desires in eastern Europe. For a brief period in late 1782 and early 1783 France was offered such cooperation (as we shall see); Vergennes's undersecretary, Hennin, later claimed that this accorded with Vergennes's earnest desires.[9] Such immediate cooperation with a recent enemy was not unprecedented in European diplomacy; in 1735, for example, Cardinal Fleury used the French defeat of Austria as a tool for rapprochement (diplomatic reconciliation) between the two countries.[10]

---

a later clerk) as 1775. See John J. Meng, "A Footnote to Secret Aid in the American Revolution," *American Historical Review* 43 (1937–38): 791–95.

8. Dull, *French Navy and American Independence*, 36–44, discusses in detail the supposed British dependence on an American trade monopoly.

9. Henri Doniol, *Politiques d'autrefois: Le Cte. de Vergennes et P. M. Hennin, 1749–1787* (Paris: Armand Colin, 1898), 103–04; see also Jonathan R. Dull, "France and the American Revolution Seen as Tragedy," in Ronald Hoffman and Peter J. Albert, eds., *Diplomacy and Revolution: The Franco-American Alliance of 1778* (Charlottesville: University Press of Virginia, 1981), 83–89.

10. Derek McKay and H. M. Scott, *The Rise of the Great Powers, 1648–1815* (London and New York: Longman, 1983), 150–51; Arthur McCandless Wilson, *French Foreign Policy during the Administration of Cardinal Fleury, 1726–1743: A Study in Diplomacy and Commercial Development* (Cambridge, Mass.: Harvard University Press, 1936), 264.

The plan of using the American war to resolve France's problems was triply flawed, however. First, the British economy did not suffer from the loss of the American colonies—America long continued to be an economic satellite of Britain. Second, Parliament, angered at the French intervention, proved all the more suspicious of French intentions, even in eastern Europe. Finally, the greatest threat to the French monarchy came, not from Russia or the other eastern powers, but from the social and political injustices in France associated with the monarchy and which it failed to address. It was these injustices which destroyed King Louis XVI and the world Vergennes sought to preserve. I shall return to these points in chapter 20. Suffice it for now to say that Vergennes's intervention in Britain's problems in America was a response to what he appears to have perceived as the pressing problem of French foreign policy, the deterioration of France's position in the European balance of power. Interestingly, despite his personal dislike of Choiseul, Vergennes's diplomatic goals greatly resembled those of his more flamboyant predecessor: opposing Russia, attempting to balance between Prussia and Austria (while maintaining the Austrian alliance to forestall the possibility of an Austro-British alliance), and now seeking through America a way of weakening Britain.

Gérard's "Considerations" argued for secretly providing arms to the American rebels. This policy met with little resistance in the royal council of state. Only the finance minister, Controller General Turgot, expressed reservations, arguing that the need for fiscal reform made foreign policy risks unacceptable and that rather than being harmed Britain would benefit from American independence.[11] Turgot's arguments were valid: participation in the American war brought France no real long-term diplomatic benefits, cut short one of the last attempts at internal reform before the French Revolution, and added enough to the government's debts to drive it into virtual bankruptcy. Nevertheless, Turgot lost the argument and soon thereafter was forced into re-

11. Gustave Schelle, ed., Œuvres de Turgot et documents le concernant, 5 vols. (Paris: Félix Alcan, 1913–23), 5:384–420; for a summary, see Dull, French Navy and American Independence, 44–49.

tirement by King Louis XVI, whose admirable intentions were not backed by strength of character or intellect. In early May 1776, the king approved an appropriation of one million livres tournois (very roughly equivalent in purchasing power to several million of today's dollars) to provide arms for the Americans; he already had ordered the navy to place two squadrons in readiness in case Britain tried to blockade French ports.[12]

The problem now was how to minimize the danger of Britain's using the French aid to the American rebels as an excuse for declaring war, since the French navy was completely unprepared for hostilities. The solution was to set up a commercial company to handle the transaction, so the French government's role could be hidden. This company, christened Roderique Hortalez and Company, was loaned the one million livres tournois in order to purchase obsolete arms at low prices from government arsenals. It then sold weapons, powder, and other military supplies to Congress on credit, anticipating repayment in American tobacco to be shipped to Europe. As head of the company, Vergennes selected Pierre-Augustin Caron de Beaumarchais (1732–99), author of *The Barber of Seville*, who recently had been successfully employed to recover secret papers that had been in the hands of a disgruntled former French diplomat in London.[13] While in England he had met Arthur Lee and had written memoirs on behalf of the Americans, which Vergennes used with the king.[14] Beaumarchais probably was of only minor importance in the French decision to aid the Americans, but as head of Roderigue

12. Ibid., 48, 52–53.

13. For Beaumarchais's activities as head of Roderigue Hortalez and Company, see Roger Lafon, *Beaumarchais, le brillant armateur* (Paris: Société d'éditions géographiques, maritimes et coloniales, 1928); its establishment is briefly described in Leonard W. Labaree, William B. Willcox et al., eds., *The Papers of Benjamin Franklin*, 24 vols. to date (New Haven and London: Yale University Press, 1959–), 22:454. His secret mission to England is discussed in Albert, duc de Broglie, *The King's Secret: Being the Secret Correspondence of Louis XV with His Diplomatic Agents from 1752 to 1774*, trans. unidentified, 2 vols. (London, Paris, and New York: Cassell, Pelter and Galpin, 1879), 2:489–516.

14. Brian N. Morton and Donald C. Spinelli, eds., *Beaumarchais Correspondance*, 4 vols. to date (Paris: A.-G. Nizet, 1969–), 2:150–55, 171–76; Dull, *French Navy and American Independence*, 31.

Hortalez and Company (whose name he devised) he rendered important service indeed. By March 1777 he had chartered a fleet of nine merchantmen, only one of which the British were able to intercept on its way to America. Their cargoes of military supplies were of considerable value to the Continental Army (although by the time they arrived the powder shortage in the army had already been much alleviated).[15] Beaumarchais continued his efforts through the remainder of the war, in spite of ship captures, the difficulty of obtaining tobacco in payment for his cargoes, and the campaign conducted against him by Arthur Lee, who unjustly claimed that his former friend was asking payment for what was actually a gift of the French government.[16]

It took several months to assemble the necessary war supplies, a task made somewhat easier by the arrival of Pierre Penet, a merchant from St. Domingue who had met with Congress and who brought a list of the items most needed.[17] Meanwhile Gabriel de Sartine (1729–1801), the French naval minister, used the orders he had received to prepare two small squadrons as an excuse to overspend the government's naval budget. He then asked for supplemental appropriations. The king was committed to economy in government, but again his good intentions were easy prey for the cunning of his advisers. Once Sartine had overcome resistance to his spending, he began the restocking of the navy's dockyards and the reconditioning of its warships.[18] The process of preparing for war had begun, although the king probably was too naïve to realize it. One doubts that Vergennes, Maurepas, and Sartine, the dominant members of his chief advisory body (the royal council of state), were so innocent of the probable outcome of the decision to intervene in Britain's war.

15. Stevens, *Facsimiles of Manuscripts*, vol. 3, nos. 240 and 241, and vol. 14, no. 1445; Orlando W. Stephenson, "The Supply of Gunpowder in 1776," *American Historical Review* 30 (1924–25): 271–81.

16. Stevens, *Facsimiles of Manuscripts*, vol. 3, no. 271.

17. Robert Rhodes Crout, "The Diplomacy of Trade: The Influence of Commercial Considerations on French Involvement in the Angloamerican War of Independence, 1775–78" (Ph.D. diss., University of Georgia, 1977), 117–19; Labaree, Willcox et al., *Papers of Benjamin Franklin*, 22:311–12, 332–33, 454.

18. Dull, *French Navy and American Independence*, 49–56.

In selecting Beaumarchais to handle the arms shipments, the French government bypassed another candidate, a friend of Franklin's named Jacques Barbeu-Dubourg. It was a letter from Dubourg written in June, however, which prompted Congress to send Franklin and Arthur Lee to Paris to join Silas Deane.[19] Deane, as already mentioned, arrived there in July 1776. He was introduced to Beaumarchais and soon became involved in the operations of Roderigue Hortalez and Company, much to the chagrin of a jealous Arthur Lee.[20] Deane (1737–89) was the first example in American history of a species of diplomat indigenous to this country, the defeated politician given a diplomatic post to soothe his wounds. He was all too typical of what we have come to expect from political appointees: pompous, convivial, somewhat less than honest (although careful to hide it), braggingly patriotic, and rather unintelligent.[21] During the five months before he was joined by Franklin and Lee he exceeded his instructions from the Committee of Secret Correspondence in numerous ways—by badgering the French government, hiring four French army officers as major generals for the Continental Army (as well as a number of lesser officers), becoming involved in a scheme to replace George Washington as army commander with the count de Broglie (Aiguillon's rival), and even paying a pyromaniac to burn British dockyards.[22]

The most costly of Deane's indiscretions was his hiring of generals for the Continental Army. Although two of them, de Kalb and Lafayette, proved very useful, Deane's action caused enormous disruption to the army and eventually forced Congress to recall him. He was probably innocent, however, of the charge

19. Labaree, Willcox et al., *Papers of Benjamin Franklin*, 22:453–71; Crout, "Diplomacy of Trade," 124–33.

20. Ibid., 126–28; Charles Isham, ed., *The Deane Papers*, 5 vols. (New York: New-York Historical Society, 1887–91 [*Collections*, vols. 19–23]), 1:177–84, 195–218, 221–22.

21. There is no adequate biography of Deane, but for his early life and career, see Kalman Goldstein, "Silas Deane: Preparation for Rascality," *Historian* 43 (1980–81): 75–97.

22. Jonathan R. Dull, *Franklin the Diplomat: the French Mission* (Philadelphia: American Philosophical Society, 1982 [*Transactions* 72, pt. 1]), 36.

historians subsequently have brought against him—that of being a British double agent.[23] The charge is based on guilt by association. Deane had been instructed by the Committee of Secret Correspondence to contact upon his arrival in Paris an American in London named Edward Bancroft.[24] Bancroft (1744–1821), a fellow scientist and friend of Franklin, once had been tutored by Deane. In July 1776 he met with Deane in Paris and soon after returning to London offered the British government his services as a spy. The genial Bancroft had his own motives; his great goal was to make a fortune playing the British stock market, and his spying was strictly a sideline to make extra money. King George III was astute enough to comprehend Bancroft's motives and to complain he was a waste of money.[25] First news of the American treaties with France in 1778 was provided to King George not by "Edwards," Bancroft's alias as a spy, but by "Benson," Bancroft's alias for playing the stock market—luckily for the British they were intercepting "Benson's" mail.[26] Deane, meanwhile, had become a partner in Bancroft's stockjobbing;[27] it seems likely that the gullible Deane was unaware of his friend's other career as a halfhearted spy. Franklin, who was even more easily taken advantage of by his friends than was Deane, was involved in neither activity and almost certainly unaware of them.[28]

23. For example, Julian P. Boyd, "Silas Deane: Death by a Kindly Teacher of Treason?" *William and Mary Quarterly*, 3rd series, 16 (1959): 187. Deane in 1781, however, did sell his services to the British: see below, chapter 14.

24. Labaree, Willcox et al., *Papers of Benjamin Franklin*, 22:373.

25. Sir John Fortescue, *The Correspondence of King George the Third from 1760 to December 1783*, 6 vols. (London: Macmillan and Co., 1927–28), 3:481–82, 532; for acounts of Bancroft's spying, see Boyd, "Silas Deane," 165–87, 319–42, 515–50, and Samuel Flagg Bemis, "British Secret Service and the French-American Alliance," *American Historical Review* 29 (1923–24): 474–95. Lord North defended Bancroft: Samuel Flagg Bemis, "British Intelligence, 1777: Two Documents," *Huntington Library Quarterly* 24 (1960–61): 237n.

26. Fortescue, *Correspondence of King George the Third* 4:34; see also Stevens, *Facsimiles*, vol. 5, no. 492; Dull, *Franklin the Diplomat*, 33–35; Labaree, Willcox et al., *Papers of Benjamin Franklin*, 23: 202–05.

27. Dull, *Franklin the Diplomat*, 35–36.

28. See below, chapter 9, for a further discussion of Franklin's character.

Just before Christmas of 1776, Deane was joined by Arthur Lee from London and by Franklin, who had landed on December 3 at a Breton fishing port. In later chapters I shall examine the operations of America's first overseas diplomatic mission, with its three ill-matched commissioners. They attempted to establish contacts not only with the French government but also with those of other European powers. In order to understand the reception they received, let us look at the impact of the American Revolution elsewhere in Europe.

CHAPTER 8

The Revolution's Impact
on Europe

Until the conclusion of the 1778 Franco-American alliance, the impact of the American Revolution on continental Europe was slight. This is true of its political, cultural, and economic impact, as well as of its diplomatic impact.

Knowledge of the Revolution was largely limited to the minority of Europeans who could read; probably only in France, where Franklin's presence publicized it, and perhaps in the Netherlands, did interest in it spread beyond a small number of intellectuals, noblemen, bourgeois, and clerics. Even in France support for the Revolution was based more on hatred of Britain than on any real understanding of the issues for which it was fought. This is apparent in the letters of the hundreds of Frenchmen, Germans, Swiss, and other Europeans, predominantly unemployed army officers, who applied for commissions in the Continental army. Their announced motive for applying generally related to self-advancement, although a minority did profess to idealistic concerns, almost always expressing them in the vaguest of generalizations.[1]

---

1. See Leonard W. Labaree, William B. Willcox et al., eds., *The Papers of Benjamin Franklin*, 24 vols. to date (New Haven and London: Yale University Press, 1959–) 23:167–72; 24:25–37; 25:forthcoming (see under October 2, 1777); Catherine M. Prelinger, "Less Lucky then Lafayette: A Note on the French Applicants to Benjamin Franklin for Commisions in the American Army, 1776–1785," *Proceedings of the Fourth Annual Meeting of the Western Society for French History* (Santa Barbara, Calif., 1977), 263–71; Stanley Idzerda,

Outside of France news of the Revolution was spread chiefly by newspaper accounts. To measure public response by these articles (or by mentions in personal correspondence) is risky, however, because of the danger of overestimating their significance.[2] It appears, though, that the American Revolution made a significant impact on the political life of only one continental country, the Netherlands. In that country the unpopular stadholder helped popularize the American cause by his support for Britain. Among the "patriots" who opposed him support for America eventually coalesced with the desire for domestic political reform, the wish to weaken the stadholder's power, and the hope of reasserting the Netherlands' place in the world (particularly relative to Britain).[3] These issues were just beginning to surface in the States General in 1777 and centered around resistance to the bullying tactics of British Ambassador Yorke.[4] Opposition to the stadholder would be fueled by Britain's humiliation of the Netherlands, particularly after the outbreak of war between the two countries in 1780.

The American Revolution also had a significant impact on British political life, but initially it was, from an American standpoint, a negative one. Both before and after the outbreak of hostilities the Continental Congress appealed for popular support in Britain.[5] The British merchant community earlier had helped win repeal of the Stamp Act and the Townshend Duties, but by

---

"When and Why Lafayette Became a Revolutionary," *Consortium on Revolutionary Europe, 1750–1850 Proceedings* (1977), 34–50.

2. A common failing of even the best research, such as Horst Dippel, *Germany and the American Revolution, 1770–1800: A Sociohistorical Investigation of Late Eighteenth-Century Political Thinking,* trans. Bernard A. Uhlendorf (Chapel Hill: University of North Carolina Press, 1977). See Bibliography, below, for listing of other books on the cultural and political impact of the Revolution.

3. See Simon Schama, *Patriots and Liberators: Revolution in the Netherlands, 1780–1813* (New York: Alfred A. Knopf, 1977).

4. Daniel A. Miller, *Sir Joseph Yorke and Anglo-Dutch Relations, 1774–1780* (The Hague and Paris: Mouton, 1970), 30–59.

5. Worthington Chauncey Ford et al., eds., *Journals of the Continental Congress,* 35 vols. (Washington, D.C.: Government Printing Office, 1904–76) 1:82–90 and 2:163–71.

1774 its influence had greatly declined.[6] The outbreak of war gravely weakened the already poor position of America's friends. Divided and hopelessly outnumbered, the parliamentary opposition had no chance of reversing a war policy that was broadly popular and grounded in national pride and fear. They would have to wait until war weariness undermined British optimism and bellicosity (a process also at work in the United States).

Congress also issued an appeal to the inhabitants of Ireland, theoretically an independent kingdom ruled by George III but in practice a British colony. There, as in Canada, a predominantly Catholic population distrusted the Americans. An internal Irish reform movement eventually did arise, but for it the American Revolution was chiefly a tool to extract concessions from the British. Parliament finally did concede an increased measure of self-government to the Irish in 1782, defusing the possibility of an Irish rebellion (for which Americans had hoped). Throughout the war the Irish provided help to the British war effort in America, including much of the food shipped to British garrisons there.[7]

Economically, the consequences of the American Revolution, not surprisingly, seem to have been felt chiefly by America. The British economy appears to have suffered some damage from the loss of markets, although there is no evidence that the American privateering effort against British trade did anything to shorten the conflict.[8] (British exports averaged about 15 percent less from 1776 through 1782 than from 1772 through 1775, though it is unclear precisely to what extent this was related to the war.)[9]

6. Jack M. Sosin, *Agents and Merchants: British Colonial Policy and the Origins of the American Revolution, 1763–1775* (Lincoln: University of Nebraska Press, 1965), 196–99, 218–21.

7. Owen Dudley Edwards, "The Impact of the American Revolution on Ireland," in *The Impact of the American Revolution Abroad* (Washington, D.C.: Library of Congress, 1976), 127–59; Ford et al., *Journals of the Continental Congress*, 2:212–18.

8. American privateering activity is discussed in Gardner Weld Allen, *A Naval History of the American Revolution*, 2 vols. (Boston and New York: Houghton Mifflin Co., 1913).

9. Computed from B. R. Mitchell, *Abstract of British Historical Statistics* (Cambridge: Cambridge University Press, 1962), 281. These figures do not take account of smuggling.

The cost of the war also was not a decisive factor. It was not the heaviness of taxes which undermined the British taxpayer's support for the war, but the lack of results. Other economic consequences are difficult to measure. The war did serve as a great inducement to smuggling. A large traffic in gunpowder proceeded from Europe to the West Indies and America, but this traffic, like that of alcoholic beverages in the 1920s or drugs in recent times, is not easy to document. The expansion of the British navy and the interruption of naval supplies from America profited Baltic suppliers (like Russia and Sweden) of masts and naval stores.[10] Similarly, the rebuilding of the French navy in 1776–77 forced a European-wide search for naval matériel.[11] Once France entered the war she was enormously aided by the neutrality of the Austrian Netherlands. This neutrality facilitated the importation of naval stores, particularly masts, which were transshipped from Amsterdam to France through the inland canals of the Austrian possession.[12] Similarly, Italian neutrality was of great assistance to the French navy. Its great Mediterranean base of Toulon was supplied with timber from Italy and the Balkans; moreover, Italian sailors helped man the crews of its warships.[13]

The major impact of the war upon European trade came after 1778. The entrance of France into the war, followed by Spain (1779), and then the Netherlands (1780), favored the growth of neutral shippers like Prussia and Russia.[14]

Diplomatically, the American Revolution varied greatly in its impact. As we have seen, France sought to use it to improve her position in the European balance of power. The Netherlands also saw opportunities. The Dutch sought to expand their trade as a result of the war while maintaining their neutrality, as they had

10. Robert Greenhalgh Albion, *Forests and Sea Power: The Timber Problem of the Royal Navy, 1652–1862* (Hamden, Conn.: Archon Books, 1965), 281–315.

11. Jonathan R. Dull, *The French Navy and American Independence: A Study of Arms and Diplomacy, 1774–1787* (Princeton, N.J.: Princeton University Press, 1975), 23–24, 66–68. See also Paul Walden Bamford, *Forests and French Sea Power, 1660–1789* (Toronto: University of Toronto Press, 1956).

12. Dull, *French Navy and American Independence*, 208n.

13. Ibid., 144–45.

14. See below, chapter 15.

during the Seven Years' War.[15] The other European powers
most interested in the American conflict were Spain and Portugal. The Portuguese controlled most of the eastern half of South
America, the Spaniards the west and south. Since 1774 they had
been embroiled in a boundary dispute along the borders of what
today are Brazil and Uruguay. As the situation worsened, Spain
sought assistance from the French, Portugal from the British.[16]
Spain even agreed to match the one million livres tournois
France had decided to give the American rebels, so as to prolong
the American war and prevent the British from helping Portugal.
The Spanish governor of Louisiana, Bernardo de Gálvez, was
particularly helpful in supplying munitions to the Americans.[17]
Portugal, in contrast, took a particularly hostile attitude toward
the Revolution, expelling American ships from her ports. Silas
Deane urged America to curry favor with Spain and France by attacking Portuguese shipping; in 1777 he and his colleagues offered, under congressional orders, to help Spain in exchange for
an alliance and sent a protest to the Portuguese government.[18]
During the spring of that year, however, the Portuguese–
Spanish crisis dissipated. A Spanish expeditionary force captured
a key Portuguese island base off southern Brazil, and the death in
February of the Portuguese king led to the dismissal of the belli-
cose chief minister, Pombal, and the signing of an armistice.
Queen Maria I quickly sought a reconciliation with Spain, and
Britain lost its only remaining friend in Europe.[19]

15. Alice Clare Carter, *The Dutch Republic in Europe in the Seven Years' War*
(London: Macmillan, 1971).

16. Orville T. Murphy, *Charles Gravier, Comte de Vergennes: French Diplomacy in the Age of Revolution, 1719–1787* (Albany: State University of New York
Press, 1982), 222–31, 237–41; Dull, *French Navy and American Independence*,
61–63.

17. John Walton Caughey, *Bernardo de Gálvez in Louisiana, 1776–1783*
(Berkeley: University of California Press, 1934).

18. Charles Isham, ed., *The Deane Papers*, 5 vols. (New York: New-York Historical Society, 1887–1891 [*Collections*, vols. 19–23]), 1:247, 290–91, 311; Labaree, Willcox et al., *Papers of Benjamin Franklin*, 23:57, 97, 504, 509, 562,
611–13; 24:321–22; 25: forthcoming (see under December 2, 1777).

19. W. N. Hargreaves-Mawdsley, *Eighteenth-Century Spain, 1700–1788: A
Political, Diplomatic and Institutional History* (London and elsewhere: Macmillan, 1979), 126–27.

Other European rulers expressed an interest in the American Revolution, but it is difficult to see any concrete changes in their diplomatic policy as a result. Empress Catherine II of Russia, echoing the comments of the British parliamentary Opposition, expressed her contempt for the policies of Lord North's government. Russian policy, however, was governed chiefly by the need to recuperate from internal problems and from the recently concluded war against the Turks and Poles. Catherine maintained Russian neutrality, refusing an alliance with Britain (although she was no friend of revolutionaries). In time she would attempt to exploit the war in order to expand Russian trade and, eventually, Russian boundaries.[20]

King Frederick II of Prussia's contempt for the British government surpassed even that of Catherine. He was delighted to inflict discomfort on it, for example by hindering the passage of Hessian auxiliaries through his territory. Nonetheless, his overall policy was to maintain tolerable relations with Britain, and hence American attempts to woo him had little success.[21]

Perhaps the European ruler most hostile to the Revolution was King Gustavus III of Sweden, by no coincidence the monarch with the most bitter experience of parliamentary bodies. Again, it is difficult to see how his feelings on this subject influenced Swedish diplomacy, which remained oriented chiefly toward potential expansion at the expense of Denmark.[22]

Emperor Joseph of the Holy Roman Empire and coregent of Austria visited his brother-in-law King Louis XVI in 1777 and

20. David M. Griffiths, "Catherine the Great, the British Opposition and the American Revolution," in Lawrence S. Kaplan, ed., *The American Revolution and "A Candid World"* (Kent, Ohio: Kent State University Press, 1977), 85–110; Nikolaï N. Bolkhovtinov, *Russia and the American Revolution*, trans. C. Jay Smith (Tallahassee, Fla.: Diplomatic Press, 1976), 10–11. Later developments are discussed below, chapter 16.

21. Horst Dippel, "Prussia's English Policy after the Seven Years' War," *Central European History* 4 (1971): 195–214.

22. H. A. Barton, "Sweden and the War of American Independence," *William and Mary Quarterly*, 3rd ser., 23 (1966): 408–30; Stewart Oakley, "Gustavus III's Plans for War with Denmark in 1783–84," in Ragnhild Hatton and M. S. Anderson, eds., *Studies in Diplomatic History: Essays in Memory of David Bayne Horn* (London: Longman, 1970), 268–86.

avoided a meeting with Benjamin Franklin;[23] Austria, which had little maritime trade and no colonies, showed little interest in the American war, particularly since Frederick and Joseph had already agreed to remain neutral in case of a Franco-British war.[24] Except for the few German rulers who provided troops to the British, the smaller European states also had little diplomatic interest in the war. At the end of 1777, however, Austrian ambitions and Russo-Turkish suspicions suddenly presented obstacles to the French signing of an alliance with the United States. How the French and Americans reached that point will be the subject of the next three chapters.

23. Labaree, Willcox et al., *Papers of Benjamin Franklin*, 24:85n.

24. Albert Sorel, *The Eastern Question in the Eighteenth Century: The Partition of Poland and the Treaty of Kainardji*, trans. F. C. Bramwell (London: Methuen and Co., 1898), 64, 123–24.

PART THREE
The Franco-American Alliance

CHAPTER 9

America's First
Diplomatic Mission

On December 21, 1776, Benjamin Franklin arrived in Paris
with two of his grandsons, seven-year-old Benjamin Franklin
Bache and sixteen-year-old William Temple Franklin. The next
day Arthur Lee, summoned from London by Silas Deane, joined
his fellow commissioners.[1]

Lee and Franklin were old acquaintances, if somewhat less
than friends. When Franklin returned to America in March 1775,
Lee remained in London to represent the interests of the Massachusetts and New Jersey assemblies. The young Lee (1740–92)
had tried a variety of careers—physician, lawyer, author on political subjects, colonial agent, and intelligence source for the
Committee of Secret Correspondence—before becoming a diplomat. Upright, intelligent, learned, articulate, fiercely patriotic,
he unfortunately also had many of the faults of a zealot. His arrogance and suspiciousness made him a difficult colleague; gradually he came to believe that the more convivial Deane and Franklin, already acquainted from their service in Congress, were
plotting against him.[2]

1. Leonard W. Labaree, William B. Willcox et al., *The Papers of Benjamin
Franklin*, 24 vols. to date (New Haven and London: Yale University Press,
1959–), 1:lxii–lxiii; 22:67n; 23:23n, 47,82n.

2. Best biography of him is Louis W. Potts, *Arthur Lee: A Virtuous Revolutionary* (Baton Rouge and London: Louisiana State University Press, 1981). Part
of his correspondence and journals are printed in Richard Henry Lee, *Life of Arthur Lee, LL.D., Joint Commissioner of the United States to the Court of France,
and Sole Commissioner to the Courts of Spain and Prussia during the Revolution-*

Franklin (1706–90) was, in his own way, as zealous a patriot as was Lee. Reserved and cautious in his public life, in private Franklin was a man of considerable emotion. He had spent fifteen years in England (1757–62, 1764–75) as a colonial agent. His mission ended in humiliation and rejection. The British government spurned his advice, thereafter hired Indians and Hessians to kill his fellow Americans, and alienated from him his only surviving son, William Franklin, ex-governor of New Jersey and now a prisoner of the Americans. George III commented, "The many instances of the inimical conduct of Franklin towards this country, make me aware that hatred to this Country is the constant object of his mind"; for many other Britons as well he was the arch-conspirator.[3] In one sense they were wrong—Franklin's anger was directed at the British government, not the country. They were right, however, to see that his loyalty to America was unshakable; he donated his salary as America's first postmaster general to disabled war veterans and used his personal savings to purchase loan-office certificates, the equivalent of war bonds. When in 1781 Deane sold his services to the British, a shocked Franklin broke contact with his former friend. Unlike Arthur Lee, however, Franklin combined his patriotism with the virtues of cosmopolitanism, toleration, and intellectual openness. His reputation as a writer and scientist preceded him to France; his gift for public relations and obvious appreciation for the culture and pleasures of France reassured French noblemen and wealthy bourgeois that American revolutionaries posed no threat to them. He did possess drawbacks as a diplomat, though. His age and frail health restricted his activities, sometimes severely. (He suffered from psoriasis and sporadic gout and kidney stone.)

---

ary War, 2 vols. (Boston: Wells & Lilly, 1829). Most of his correspondence is available on microfilm: Paul P. Hoffman, ed., The Lee Family Papers, 1742–1795, 8 reels (Charlottesville: University of Virginia Library, 1966). His journal for December 1776 to September 1777 is at the Library of Congress.

3. Sir John Fortescue, The Correspondence of King George the Third from 1760 to December 1783, 6 vols. (London: Macmillan and Co., 1927–28), 4:80; Pauline Maier, The Old Revolutionaries: Political Lives in the Age of Samuel Adams (New York: Alfred A. Knopf, 1980), 8–9.

Worse still, his trusting nature and susceptibility to flattery made him an easy mark for spies as well as swindlers.[4]

For two months the American mission was housed in the commissioners' hotel rooms. At the end of February 1777, however, Franklin moved to a wing of a mansion in the Parisian suburb of Passy provided by Jacques-Donatien Le Ray de Chaumont, a government contractor and friend of Sartine who became Vergennes's liaison with the commissioners.[5] (Franklin's elder grandson accompanied him as his personal secretary; the younger was placed in a boarding school.) Chaumont's residence eventually became not only home to Deane (Lee lived separately) but also an unsanctioned headquarters for the British secret service. In addition to the commissioners' secretary, Bancroft, the mission was penetrated by Isaac Van Zandt, the son of a New York patriot leader, hanger-on at the mission, and British spy.[6] John Thornton (perhaps an alias), Lee's secretary, became a British agent while in England on a mission to examine the condition of American prisoners of war;[7] and Deane's secretary William Carmichael met separately with British ambassador Stormont's secretary and chaplain and may have agreed to provide intelligence as did the others.[8] Only Franklin's secretary,

4. Jonathan R. Dull, *Franklin the Diplomat: the French Mission* (Philadelphia: American Philosophical Society, 1982 [*Transactions* 72, pt. 1]); Jonathan R. Dull, "Benjamin Franklin and the Nature of American Diplomacy," *International History Review* 5 (1983): 346–63.

5. Labaree, Willcox et al., *Papers of Benjamin Franklin*, 23:85n, 244–46.

6. Matthew Ridley's Journal, Dec. 22, 1777 (Massachusetts Historical Society) provides his first name and other data. I am indebted for this citation to Robert H. Elias and Eugene D. Finch, editors of the papers of Thomas Digges (see Bibliography under Clark, William Bell). For further information on Van Zandt, who as a spy used the alias George Lupton, see Lewis Einstein, *Divided Loyalties: Americans in England during the War of Independence* (London: Cobden-Sanderson, 1933), 55, 421–23, and Benjamin Franklin Stevens, ed., *Facsimiles of Manuscripts in European Archives Relating to America*, 1773–83, 25 vols. (London: privately printed, 1889–98) 25:254, under "Lupton."

7. Labaree, Willcox et al., *Papers of Benjamin Franklin*, 25: forthcoming (see under October 4, 1777).

8. Ibid., 23:621–22n. The anonymous letter there cited is in the hand of Horace St. Paul, Stormont's secretary.

William Temple Franklin, was beyond suspicion. Franklin laughed off the danger of spies,[9] but they did much harm to the American mission. The French took care not to entrust the Americans with secrets, thereby impeding good relations. Moreover, the commissioners' communications with Congress were broken off when several months' of dispatches were stolen by yet another British agent, ship captain Joseph Hynson.[10]

The commissioners' first experiences in France, though, were encouraging. Their initial meetings with Vergennes and the count de Aranda, now serving as Spanish ambassador to France, were cordial. Their requests for a treaty of amity and commerce and for military supplies and the loan of French ships of the line were refused, but the blow was softened by a grant of two million livres tournois, to be paid in four quarterly installments.[11] In addition, Vergennes put the commissioners in contact with the Farmers General, a consortium of French bankers and businessmen who collected much of the French government's taxes. The Farmers General, who ran the government's tobacco monopoly, signed a contract with the commissioners for two million livres-worth of American tobacco, with half the money paid in advance—an indirect subsidy, since there was little hope of getting the tobacco through the British blockade of the American coast.[12]

The commissioners quickly became overconfident. In February 1777 Arthur Lee traveled to Spain, where he created much embarrassment for the Spanish government but received promises of aid in money and supplies.[13] The commissioners began massive purchases, ordering the tens of thousands of uniforms wished by Congress, frigates (20- to 40-gun warships) of a new design to be built in Amsterdam, reconditioned muskets, and

9. Ibid., 23:211.

10. Ibid., 25: forthcoming (see under October 7, 1777).

11. Ibid., 23:90n, 113–14, 120–24, 126–27, 164–66, 173–82, 198–99.

12. Ibid., 23:129–40, 328–29, 373–75, 383–84, 493–95, 514–17.

13. Mario Rodríguez, *La revolución americana de 1776 y el mundo hispanico: ensayos y documentos* (Madrid: Editorial Tecnos, 1976), 77–115; Potts, *Arthur Lee*, 167–72.

other military supplies.[14] Franklin, provided contacts by his Masonic and scientific connections, was well received by Parisian society (though he was cautioned against appearing at the French court at nearby Versailles). His campaign of reassuring the rich and influential about the American Revolution was conducted with care to avoid bruising the sensibilities of the French government; in contrast to his days in London, he avoided writing for the press. He restricted himself to donating pieces to the *Affaires de l'Angleterre et de l'Amérique,* a journal secretly run by the French foreign ministry. Of these pieces probably only one, praising America as a good credit risk, was original.[15]

Franklin and his fellow commissioners showed considerably less tact in their direct dealings with the French foreign ministry. Before leaving Philadelphia, Franklin had composed a fictitious set of peace proposals to the British for use in frightening the French (or in case he was captured at sea).[16] Luckily he had second thoughts about using so crude a tactic, but the commissioners' initial appeals were scarcely more subtle. Lacking anything substantive to offer in return for France's risking war by signing a commercial treaty with America, they issued thinly veiled threats that the American cause risked collapse if France remained aloof. These bullying tactics had some success in January, as we have seen, but they lost their effectiveness when they were repeated in February and March. The commissioners then received congressional authorization to offer the promise of American military assistance in exchange for France's signing the commercial treaty. Vergennes's rejection of the offer seems finally to have led them to reconsider their approach.[17] According to Deane's later recollections, Franklin had had reservations from the beginning about pressuring the French government. Begging for help and warning of the danger of American failure

14. Labaree, Willcox et al., *Papers of Benjamin Franklin,* 23:306–08; 24:100–01, 122–26.

15. Ibid., 22:112–14; 23:214, 480–84; 24:177–91, 508–14. See also below, chapter 11.

16. Labaree, Willcox et al., *Papers of Benjamin Franklin,* 22:630–33.

17. Ibid., 23:96–100, 120–24, 260–62, 409–12, 502–05.

merely discredited their cause, he believed; by May he was able to convince his colleagues that they should wait for further negotiations until events made the French more receptive.[18]

Unfortunately, the events of the summer of 1777 made the French even less receptive and badly discredited the American mission to France. The cause was a basic misunderstanding between the commissioners and the French government about the use of French ports by American warships. Congress had instructed the commissioners to obtain whatever privileges they could, including if possible the right of selling prizes—that is, captured British merchant ships.[19] The American brig *Reprisal*, which brought Franklin and his grandsons to France, captured two British merchant ships en route; by falsifying their papers, Captain Lambert Wickes of the *Reprisal* was quickly able to dispose of them to a French purchaser.[20] Vergennes warned the commissioners that the use of French ports to prepare for cruises or to sell prizes was forbidden by treaties with Britain,[21] but the commissioners did not take him seriously. In February, Wickes took and sold five more prizes. Far worse were the actions of the *Surprize*, a small American warship that sailed from Dunkirk on May 1 and within a few days returned with two prizes, including a packetboat.[22] The use of Dunkirk was a particular embarrassment to France, since by treaty it was a demilitarized port with a resident British commissioner. Vergennes was not unduly concerned in general by the commissioners' evading French neutrality,[23] but this flagrant violation provoked British protests he

18. Ibid., 23:510–11; 24:76; Charles Isham, ed., *The Deane Papers*, 5 vols. (New York: New-York Historical Society, 1887–1891 [*Collections*, vols. 19–23]), 5:438.

19. Labaree, Willcox et al., *Papers of Benjamin Franklin*, 22:667–69.

20. Ibid., 23:31–33; William Bell Clark, *Lambert Wickes, Sea Raider and Diplomat: The Story of a Naval Captain of the Revolution* (New Haven: Yale University Press, 1932), 98–99, 104–09.

21. Labaree, Willcox et al., *Papers of Benjamin Franklin*, 24:323.

22. Clark, *Lambert Wickes*, 126–57; Robert Wilden Neeser, ed., *Letters and Papers Relating to the Cruises of Gustavus Conyngham, a Captain of the Continental Navy, 1777–1779* (New York: Naval History Society, 1915), xxx–xxxi.

23. Stevens, *Facsimiles of Manuscripts*, vol. 15, no. 1488; see also below, chapter 10.

could not ignore. Consequently, he threw Captain Gustavus Conyngham and the entire crew of the *Surprize* into jail at Dunkirk for several weeks.[24] The commissioners, however, still did not grasp the potential diplomatic consequences of their mounting naval operations in French ports. At the end of May a squadron of three American warships under Wickes's overall command sailed from French ports. Their cruise was highly successful; they took eighteen prizes in the waters between Britain and Ireland.[25] When they had the audacity to return on June 27 to French ports, closely pursued by the British navy, the ground was laid for a major crisis.

---

24. Neeser, *Gustavus Conyngham*, xxxi–xxxii, 16–31, 36–46.
25. Clark, *Lambert Wickes*, 194–206, 220–39. Clark claims (pp. 189–193) that the cruise was a deliberate provocation, but this appears to be a misreading of the evidence—see Dull, *Franklin the Diplomat*, 40n; Labaree, Willcox et al., *Papers of Benjamin Franklin*, 24:327n.

CHAPTER 10

The Commissioners Discredited

The use of French ports by warships of the Continental navy and by American privateers (privately owned warships sanctioned by Congress) posed more than an annoyance to the French government. Once King Louis XVI's opposition had been overcome, Naval Minister Sartine's rearmament program proceeded briskly, but not until 1778 were the navy's dockyards filled with supplies and its ships in condition to fight.[1] Had a war broken out before then, the navy would easily have been crushed by the British or blockaded in port. While in the long run tension with Britain helped Vergennes prepare the king and country for war, for now it had to be kept within manageable proportions. For this reason France refrained from sending a squadron to the Caribbean and was willing to discuss with Spain a British proposal that all three countries decommission some of their ships. The growth of tension proved hard to control, however, as both Britain and France responded to real and imagined provocations; by the spring of 1777 increasingly larger patrols of British and French warships were coming into contact in the Bay of Biscay.[2]

Given the increasing danger of premature hostilities, Vergennes simply could not tolerate the American use of French ports to prepare cruises and sell prizes. Wickes's cruise, which outraged British public opinion, was particularly provocative. On the

1. Jonathan R. Dull, *The French Navy and American Independence: A Study of Arms and Diplomacy, 1774–1787* (Princeton, N.J.: Princeton University Press, 1975), 66–68.
2. Ibid., 63–65, 68–75.

other hand, Vergennes and Sartine had no desire to alienate the United States. They quickly reversed their initial decision to expel Wickes's ships, which probably would have resulted in their capture. Instead they decided to sequester the squadron, in other words to detain it in port under French supervision.[3] Within a few weeks, however, an even more serious incident occurred. Captain Gustavus Conyngham at Dunkirk was given a new ship purchased for him by William Hodge, a representative of the commissioners. On July 17 his cutter, the *Revenge*, sailed from Dunkirk with orders to return directly to America without taking any hostile action except in self-defense. Instead, he immediately began capturing British merchant ships, one of which was promptly recaptured—with a prize crew from the *Revenge* comprised chiefly of Frenchmen![4] What had happened to cause this terrible provocation?

It seems clear that Conyngham had been delivered a secret set of verbal orders countermanding his written ones.[5] The commissioners' written orders were carried to Dunkirk by Deane's secretary, William Carmichael. Carmichael is a puzzling character. As a young and wealthy student living a dissipated life in London in 1776, he had been recruited by Arthur Lee to carry to America an intelligence dispatch (hidden inside the cover of a dictionary). Passing through Paris on his circuitous way home, he instead switched his allegiance to Silas Deane and agreed to go on his behalf to the Netherlands and Prussia, partly on public business, but chiefly to help organize a business consortium to handle American trade. When this grandiose scheme fell through, Carmichael returned to France, where he periodically was used by the commissioners to carry messages to French ports. The vain

3. Leonard W. Labaree, William B. Willcox et al., eds., *Papers of Benjamin Franklin*, 24 vols. to date (New Haven and London: Yale University Press, 1959–), 24:287–88, 322–25.

4. Robert Wilden Neeser, ed., *Letters and Papers Relating to the Cruises of Gustavus Conyngham, a Captain of the Continental Navy, 1777–1779* (New York: Naval History Society, 1915), xxxiii–xxxv, 68–79.

5. The following paragraph is based on Jonathan R. Dull, *Franklin the Diplomat: the French Mission* (Philadelphia: American Philosophical Society, 1982 [*Transactions* 72, pt. 1]), 37–40.

and arrogant Carmichael developed a passionate contempt for the French, who, he believed, were not doing enough to help the United States; at some time in early 1777 he conceived the idea that America and Britain could be reconciled if a war were provoked between Britain and France. We cannot be sure if his hatred of France led him to become a British agent, but we do know that he suggested to William Bingham, American commercial agent at Martinique, that he encourage American privateers to provoke such a war. He also told Bingham that he, Carmichael, was sending Conyngham to cruise against the British.[6]

Was Carmichael acting alone when he countermanded Conyngham's orders to return directly to America? In the case of Silas Deane we cannot be certain. Deane later confessed that, in frustration at the commissioners' lack of progress, he had done everything in his power to bring the French court "into other measures, such as should beyond a question commit them in the dispute," and Arthur Lee, who blamed Deane for the fiasco, claimed that his colleague had felt compelled to write and privately circulate an apology.[7] There is little reason, however, to suspect Franklin, who had left the drafting of Conyngham's written orders to Deane[8] and who had argued for patience with the French.

The use of French crewmen on the *Revenge* and the cruising for prizes from Dunkirk were blatant contradictions of French assurances to Britain. The French government attempted to mollify Britain by sending William Hodge to the Bastille for purchasing the *Revenge* and falsifying its papers.[9] This was not enough.

6. See the sources listed in ibid., 39n, especially Carmichael to William Bingham, June 25-July 6, 1777, Francis P. Wharton, ed., *The Revolutionary Diplomatic Correspondence of the United States*, 6 vols. (Washington, D.C.: Government Printing Office, 1889), 2:346–49.

7. Charles Isham, ed., *The Deane Papers*, 5 vols. (New York: New-York Historical Society, 1887–91 [*Collections*, vols. 19–23]), 5:447; Benjamin Franklin Stevens, ed., *Facsimiles of Manuscripts in European Archives Relating to America, 1773–1783*, 25 vols. (London: privately printed, 1889–98), vol. 3, no. 269.

8. Ibid., vol. 3, no. 269; vol. 19, no. 1714; Labaree, Willcox et al., *Papers of Benjamin Franklin*, 24:344–45.

9. William Bell Clark, *Lambert Wickes, Sea Raider and Diplomat: The Story of a Naval Captain of the Revolution* (New Haven: Yale University Press, 1932), 303; Stevens, *Facsimiles of Manuscripts*, vol. 18, no. 1651.

On August 19 Stormont demanded that Wickes's squadron be expelled, and three days later a personal representative from Lord North appeared at Versailles to threaten war if a favorable response were not immediately forthcoming. (King George III had approved this mission in the belief that the French were more likely to accede to the demands of a special envoy than to those of the regular ambassador.)[10] This threat produced something close to panic—the council of state recalled both the fishing fleet from Newfoundland and warship patrols from the Bay of Biscay and ordered shipping to be held in port in France and the French West Indies. Vergennes told his ambassador in London that he expected war to break out before his letter arrived.[11] The crisis, however, passed as quickly as it had begun. To the amazement of Vergennes, Maurepas, and the remainder of the council of state, the British were willing to accept French promises to expel Wickes's ships. A few weeks later the American squadron sailed for home; one of the ships was soon captured and another, Wickes's own *Reprisal*, sank in a storm off Newfoundland.[12] The British perhaps were bluffing—North was as fearful of war as was Vergennes—but they accomplished all that could have been wished. Wickes's squadron was gone and an angry Vergennes temporarily broke contact with the American commissioners.[13]

Meanwhile the internal unity of the American mission was cracking. From mid-May to mid-July Arthur Lee was absent. His success in Spain encouraged him to travel to Berlin in hope of obtaining permission for American ships to use Prussian ports. His mission proved to be a fiasco, capped by the theft of his personal papers by a servant of the British ambassador.[14] Frederick II had

10. Ibid., nos. 1652–1656; Dull, *French Navy and American Independence*, 79; Sir John Fortescue, *The Correspondence of King George the Third from 1760 to December 1783*, 6 vols. (London: Macmillan and Co., 1927–28), 3:467; Samuel Flagg Bemis, "British Intelligence, 1777: Two Documents," *Huntington Library Quarterly* 24 (1960–61): 233–49.

11. Dull, *French Navy and American Independence*, 79–80.

12. Clark, *Lambert Wickes*, 339–53, 359–61.

13. Fortescue, *Correspondence of King George the Third*, 3:470; Edward D. Ingraham, ed., *Papers in Relation to the Case of Silas Deane* (Philadelphia: Seventy-Six Society, 1855), 156. Much work remains to be done on British diplomacy during 1777.

14. Louis W. Potts, *Arthur Lee, a Virtuous Revolutionary* (Baton Rouge and

no desire to risk alienating the British, and a disappointed Lee returned to France to discover that Silas Deane had moved into the suite at Passy he had been expecting to inhabit himself. Furthermore, as Lee complained, his fellow commissioners had disregarded his letters from Germany.[15] An even greater irritant in the commissioners' relationship, however, seems to have been a dispute involving Arthur Lee's brother, William.

William Lee (1739–95), a London merchant of no greater charm and considerably less honesty than his younger brother, arrived in Paris in June after learning of his appointment by Congress as joint commercial agent in France.[16] Initially the position of commercial agent, involving control over shipping and prizes, had been the responsibility of Thomas Morris, the alcoholic half-brother of the powerful congressional delegate Robert Morris. Rumors of his misconduct caused the Secret Committee (which oversaw commercial matters) to add William Lee as co-agent.[17] It took several months for Lee to learn of his appointment and wind up his affairs in England. Meanwhile, the commissioners, finding Morris uncooperative, had appointed their own agent, Franklin's grand-nephew Jonathan Williams, Jr., to handle commercial affairs in Nantes, the French port most used by Americans. Although Williams was honest and diligent, his appointment created a fierce conflict with Morris, who claimed sole authority over the disposition of prizes (a major responsibility of the commercial agent) by virtue of his powers from the Secret Committee.[18]

Upon his arrival in Paris, William Lee was detained by Franklin and Deane in the hope that Morris could be talked into resigning, and also because Lee had not yet received his official instructions from Congress. (They had been intercepted and were being hidden by Morris.)[19] Soon after Arthur Lee's return from

---

London: Louisiana State University Press, 1981), 173–78; "Private Journal of Arthur Lee, 1776–1777" (Library of Congress), 60–82.

15. Ibid., 83.

16. Isham, *Deane Papers*, 2:102.

17. Ibid., 1:476.

18. Labaree, Willcox et al., *Papers of Benjamin Franklin* 24:3–4, 246, 263–64, 305–06, 313.

19. Ibid., 24:377n; Worthington Chauncey Ford, ed., *Letters of William Lee,*

Germany, his brother did proceed to Nantes, but Arthur vetoed Deane's and Franklin's suggestion for resolving the dispute—to strip both Williams and Morris of their authority and leave William Lee in sole charge. (His motives are unclear, but it is possible the Lee brothers did not wish to concede that the commissioners had any authority over commercial agents in France.)[20] At the end of September the commissioners learned that Congress had elected William Lee commissioner to the Holy Roman Empire and Prussia; Arthur Lee commissioner to Spain; and Ralph Izard, a South Carolina merchant in London, commissioner to Tuscany (an Italian principality ruled by a brother of Emperor Joseph II and Queen Marie Antionette).[21] William Lee now came to Paris to ask the commissioners to France to affirm his continuing powers as commercial agent; Deane and Franklin refused on the grounds that his new appointment superseded the old.[22] The question of authority at Nantes remained in confusion until Morris's death from alcoholism on January 31, 1778, and William Lee's departure for Germany at the end of March. Luckily, however, no new prize dispute arose, and Williams continued his work at Nantes of assembling supplies and repairing muskets to ship to America.

The commissioners, already suffering from the displeasure of the French government and the growing animosity between Arthur Lee and his colleagues, soon faced a new and terrifying problem, the threat of bankruptcy. They had ordered a large frigate (another was canceled), thirty thousand uniforms, and a huge quantity of other military stores; moreover, they had rashly suggested that they could obtain from the French government the money to pay interest on American loan-office certificates. By

Sheriff and Alderman of London; Commerical Agent of the Continental Congress in France; and Minister to the Courts of Vienna and Berlin, 1776–1783, 3 vols. (Brooklyn, N.Y.: Historical Printing Club, 1891), 1:199–203; "Private Journal of Arthur Lee," 83.

20. See Labaree, Willcox et al., *Papers of Benjamin Franklin*, 24:451–53 for an alternative explanation.

21. Richard Henry Lee, *Life of Arthur Lee, LL.D., Joint Commissioner of the United States to the Court of France, and Sole Commissioner to the Courts of Spain and Prussia during the Revolutionary War*, 2 vols. (Boston: Wells and Lilly, 1829), 1:335: Labaree, Willcox et al., *Papers of Benjamin Franklin*, 24:253.

22. Ford, *Letters of William Lee*, 1:255–63.

late September their financial situation was so dire that they were forced to ask the French and Spanish governments for a subsidy of fourteen million livres tournois or a loan of £2 million (forty-seven million livres tournois). American prospects looked virtually hopeless. With the news of the British capture of Fort Ticonderoga, abandoned without a fight to General John Burgoyne, it was commonly assumed in France that the American cause was doomed.[23]

In spite of his anger, Vergennes was not prepared to let the commissioners go bankrupt. He released William Hodge from the Bastille as a sign of his good intentions and promised to consult Spain about the money they had requested. To help with their financial burden, the French government took over the frigate building in Amsterdam and Vergennes told them not to worry about paying for the supplies they had received from Roderigue Hortalez and Company.[24] (This convinced Lee that Beaumarchais had been defrauding Congress; he soon made similar accusations against Deane.)[25] Finally, in early November, the commissioners were informed that France would provide them another three million livres.[26]

Although the commissioners' financial status was improved, they were no closer to concluding a commercial treaty. On November 27, Deane proposed to his colleagues giving France an ultimatum: if she would not sign the treaty America would settle with Britain. Franklin and Lee rejected the idea.[27] Their patience was justified. A week later Jonathan Loring Austin, the young messenger of the Massachusetts Board of War, arrived with the news that General Burgoyne had surrendered to an American army at Saratoga.[28]

23. Labaree, Willcox et al., *Papers of Benjamin Franklin*, 23:470–71; 24:75, 555–63; Lee, *Life of Arthur Lee*, 1:335; Isham, *Deane Papers*, 5:446.

24. Lee, *Life of Arthur Lee*, 1:336–38; Stevens, *Facsimiles of Manuscripts*, vol. 3, no. 271; Labaree, Willcox et al., *Papers of Benjamin Franklin*, 25: forthcoming (see under November 30, 1777).

25. Lee, *Life of Arthur Lee*, 2:124–25, 126–27.

26. Ibid., 1:347.

27. Ibid., 1:354–55.

28. Edward E. Hale and Edward E. Hale, Jr., *Franklin in France*, 2 vols. (Boston: Roberts Brothers, 1888), 1:154–61.

CHAPTER 11
The Making of
the Alliance

According to popular belief, the American victory at Saratoga was responsible for the French decision to enter the war. Supposedly, the victory convinced them that the United States would be a reliable ally while simultaneously prompting them quickly to conclude an alliance before the Americans could reach a compromise peace with Britain and perhaps attack the French West Indies.[1]

This explanation presents some logical contradictions. If the Americans were militarily successful on their own, why would either France or the United States want an alliance? How could the Americans be such desirable allies if they were contemplating a reconciliation with Britain? Moreover, if the American victory prompted a British peace initiative one of two things must happen: either the British would offer independence, thereby accomplishing French policy aims without France having to enter the war; or they would offer something short of independence, which the Americans after their greatest triumph hardly would accept. The possibility that an independent America would consent to continued British trade privileges had effectively disappeared. Even the supposed threat to the French West Indies seems exaggerated—a second wave of reinforcements had just been dispatched to the islands, which in any case were not

---

1. See, for example, Claude H. Van Tyne, "Influences Which Determined the French Government to Make the Treaty with America, 1778," *American Historical Review* 21 (1915–16): 528–41.

greatly endangered by the battered British army in North America, even with American help.[2]

The standard interpretation of Saratoga's diplomatic consequences looks even less probable in light of a body of evidence that France for many months had considered the beginning of 1778 as the logical time to enter the war. We already have seen that the program of naval rearmament was to be completed in time for the 1778 campaigning season. In the spring of 1777, Joseph-Mathias Gérard drew up a policy analysis, proposing that France plan as if hostilities were going to commence in March 1778 and that she send a squadron to attack Admiral Howe in North America.[3] (In fact, France did break off diplomatic relations with Britain in March 1778 and shortly thereafter sent a squadron to attack Howe.) Serious discussion of going beyond limited aid to America did not begin, however, until July 1777. In that month the *Affaires de l'Angleterre et de l'Amérique*, the government's secretly-run journal on the war, published two strange articles entitled "Memoir" and "Supplemental Observations." Written apparently by an American, probably Edward Bancroft, they argued that a French war with Britain was inevitable and that it had best be fought with the Americans as allies rather than enemies.[4] The threatening tone of the articles presents a puzzling contradiction to the commissioners' recently announced program of patience and restraint;[5] even more curiously, the French foreign ministry chose to publicize the threat by publishing it in its own journal. Rather than an unwanted American attempt to apply pressure, it seems likely that the articles were tacitly encouraged, if not directly commissioned, by the French foreign ministry. Within weeks Vergennes used vir-

---

2. Jonathan R. Dull, *The French Navy and American Independence: A Study of Arms and Diplomacy, 1774–1787* (Princeton, N.J.: Princeton University Press, 1975), 81, 377. See also Leonard W. Labaree, William B. Willcox et al., eds., *The Papers of Benjamin Franklin*, 24 vols. to date (New Haven and London: Yale University Press, 1959–), 25: forthcoming (see under January 5, 1778).

3. Dull, *French Navy and American Independence*, 84–85.

4. Labaree, Willcox et al., *Papers of Benjamin Franklin*, 24:177–91, I differ slightly with the conclusions there expressed.

5. See above, chapter 9, note 18.

tually identical arguments as the opening volley of a battle to win
Spain's cooperation in a joint war against Britain.[6] To this end he
argued that the decision on peace or war must be made by January or February 1778. Spain was not convinced. Having resolved
her difficulties with Portugal, she no longer had reason to desire
British misfortune in America, particularly at the hands of revolutionaries who might set a bad example for Spain's own colonists. She was even reluctant to grant more financial aid to the
Americans, thereby leaving France to act alone.[7]

The news of Saratoga therefore arrived at an opportune time
for France. It seems likely, though ultimately unprovable, that
Vergennes's purported concern about the prospect of an American-British agreement was deliberately exaggerated. It probably
served two purposes. One was to overcome King Louis XVI's
scruples about subjecting France to war; Vergennes therefore argued that if America and Britain were reconciled they would attack the French West Indies, and thus a Franco-American alliance would be basically defensive.[8] The other purpose was to
convince Spain also to ally with the United States. Lord North's
government played into Vergennes's hands by sending Paul
Wentworth, one of the chief operatives of the secret service,
to negotiate with the commissioners; they, in turn, helped
Vergennes by notifying the French government of the meetings.[9] In addition, Franklin took no pains to hide his discussions
in early January with James Hutton, a religious leader and old
friend, and Sir Philip Gibbes, a member of Parliament, both of
whom carried back to London Franklin's warnings that Britain

6. Dull, *French Navy and American Independence*, 86; Henri Doniol, ed.,
*Histoire de la participation de la France à l'établissement des Etats-Unis d'Améri-
que: Correspondance diplomatique et documents*, 5 vols. and supplement (Paris:
Imprimerie Nationale, 1886–99), 2:460–69.

7. Ibid., 2:580. For the French aid, see above, chapter 10, note 26. For the
eventual resumption of Spanish financial aid, see Francis P. Wharton, ed., *The
Revolutionary Diplomatic Correspondence of the United States*, 6 vols. (Washington, D.C.: Government Printing Office, 1889), 3:15.

8. See, for example, Doniol, *Participation de la France*, 2:722–34.

9. Charles R. Ritcheson, *British Politics and the American Revolution* (Norman: University of Oklahoma Press, 1954), 234–39.

must quickly grant independence if she did not want a general war.[10] (The same message was given the parliamentary Opposition by a secret messenger, Jonathan Loring Austin.)[11]

As the British were not ready to consider granting independence, the meetings with Franklin and his fellow commissioners served only to assist Vergennes, who finally was able in early January to win royal approval for offering an alliance to the Americans.[12] He was less successful with the shrewd Spanish foreign minister, José Moñino y Redondo, count de Floridablanca (1728–1808), who pointed out the illogic of Vergennes's fears and rejected his proposal.[13] Although the commissioners had held a preliminary meeting with Vergennes in mid-December, serious negotiations began only on January 8.[14] Vergennes's representative, Conrad-Alexandre Gérard, asked the commissioners what France could do to prevent them from listening to any British proposal short of independence and also what would prevent Congress and the American people from considering such proposals. After an hour's discussion among themselves, the commissioners replied that the French acceptance of a treaty of amity and commerce would cause them to reject any such British offers. To their delight, Gérard agreed in principle and proposed that their countries conclude not only a commercial treaty but also a treaty of military alliance, leaving France to decide when to go to war. The commissioners' only objection was that they wanted France to enter the war immediately. (Three days later they responded to Gérard's second question; they believed that Congress and the American people would expect either an immediate French entry into the war or financial aid until France was ready.) They also expressed disappointment that the Frenchman could not speak for Spain. According to Gérard's report to Vergennes, he also hinted that France might help the Americans

10. Labaree, Willcox et al., *Papers of Benjamin Franklin*, 25: forthcoming (see under January 3 and 5, 1778).

11. Edward E. Hale and Edward E. Hale, Jr., *Franklin in France*, 2 vols. (Boston: Roberts Brothers, 1887–88), 1:163–64.

12. Doniol, *Participation de la France*, 2:722–34.

13. Dull, *French Navy and American Independence*, 94, 104.

14. For Gérard's account of the meeting, see Labaree, Willcox et al., *Papers of Benjamin Franklin*, 25: forthcoming (see under January 8, 1778).

capture Canada; Arthur Lee's journal, however, indicates that
the French representative told the commissioners his country
did not expect a French army to be welcome in America and
would hence provide only naval support.[15]

The fact that Gérard and the commissioners were in fundamental agreement promised that the negotiation of the treaty of
amity and commerce and the treaty of alliance would be relatively easy. The former treaty, based on commercial reciprocity,
met only one major obstacle, Arthur Lee's objection to two articles in which the United States promised to forego any export
duties on goods shipped to the French West Indies if France in
return promised to forego any export duties on molasses shipped
from the West Indies to America. Franklin favored the two articles because of his belief in free trade, Deane because he realized
the importance of molasses to the economy of his native New
England. (It was used primarily for the making of rum.) Nevertheless, to placate Lee they agreed that these two articles should
be left to the discretion of Congress, and Gérard went along.
(The two articles eventually were deleted.)[16] The treaty of alliance was drafted by the French government and was adopted virtually intact, in spite of the commissioners' misplaced fears that
France would delay her entry into the war. To the dismay of
Ralph Izard, the commissioner-designate to Tuscany who observed the negotiations, Franklin and Deane failed to press for
specific geographical definition of the areas of North America reserved for American conquest. This left France free to claim exclusive fishing rights off a portion of Newfoundland and Spain
free to attempt the reconquest of Florida.[17] It is just as well,

15. Richard Henry Lee, *Life of Arthur Lee, LL.D., Joint Commissioner of the
United States to the Court of France, and Sole Commissioner to the Courts of
Spain and Prussia during the Revolutionary War*, 2 vols. (Boston: Wells and
Lilly, 1829), 1:377.

16. Ibid., 1:383–84; Wharton, *Revolutionary Diplomatic Correspondence*,
2:657–58; Labaree, Willcox et al., *Papers of Benjamin Franklin*, 25: forthcoming
(see under February 1, 2 and 6, 1778); Robert J. Taylor, ed., *Papers of John
Adams*, 6 vols. to date (Cambridge, Mass.: Belknap Press of Harvard University
Press, 1977–), 6:119–20.

17. Wharton, *Revolutionary Diplomatic Correspondence*, 2:497–501, 586–88
629–32, 710–14, 740–42.

however, that the Americans did not attempt to resist these points: exclusive fishing rights off a portion of Newfoundland were critical to France and Florida was a potential lure to bring Spain into the war. On the fundamental point of the alliance—that France and the United States each refrain from making a separate peace with Britain and continue the war until America was fully independent—there was no dispute. On February 4, 1778, Vergennes learned that Spain had again refused to join the alliance. Two days later Gérard and the commissioners signed the two treaties. A separate article in the treaty of alliance left Spain free to join at a future date.[18]

In signing the treaties France took a calculated risk that a major war would not occur in Europe while she was involved in a predominantly naval war against Britain. There were two danger spots where war might break out. One was the Crimea, where a revolt of the Moslem inhabitants against their ruler, the pro-Russian khan, threatened to expand into a general war between Russia and the Ottoman Empire. The French ambassador in Constantinople labored to keep the hostilities from spreading, and eventually it proved that neither the Russians nor the Turks were ready for war.[19] The second danger did not pass so easily. On December 30, 1777, the ruler of Bavaria died; his successor soon was bribed by Austria into giving her a third of his new territories, with the possibility of more to follow. This threatened the balance of power in Germany, and Prussia quickly responded by threatening action if Austria did not renounce the agreement. Austria soon called on France for military assistance and Prussia offered her an alliance; in going to war against Britain, Vergennes gambled that France could maintain her neutrality between the two great German powers, one of them her ostensible ally.[20]

18. Dull, *French Navy and American Independence*, 100–01. A copy of the treaty of alliance is given in Appendix 1, below.

19. M. S. Anderson, "The Great Powers and the Russian Annexation of the Crimea, 1783–84," *Slavonic and East European Review* 37 (1958–59): 17; Alan W. Fisher, *The Russian Annexation of the Crimea, 1772–1783* (Cambridge: Cambridge University Press, 1970), 73–81, 108.

20. John G. Gagliardo, *Reich and Nation: The Holy Roman Empire as Idea and Reality, 1763–1806* (Bloomington and London: Indiana University Press, 1980),

The American commissioners had now achieved their chief goal. Their success was not primarily of their own making. The French policy of limited arms aid had so raised tension with Britain that eventual war had become very likely. Only a king as naïve as Louis XVI could have failed to see the implications of the arms aid and the French naval rearmament program. For the moment France could proceed without Spain to enter the war directly. Her rearmament was almost complete, and she could quickly man her fleet with fishermen and sailors from her coastal shipping. Britain, more dependent on such local shipping, had to go through the time-consuming process of taking sailors from returning overseas shipping and hence could man only part of her fleet.[21] It therefore was to France's advantage to seize the opportunity. Moreover, there was abundant evidence that the Americans still needed help. General Howe had twice defeated Washington and had captured Philadelphia. The commissioners were optimistic that he would be trapped there as Burgoyne had been at Saratoga; one cannot be sure about Vergennes's claims to share that mistaken belief.[22] Thus, the major causes of the French entry into the war in 1778 seem to have been the completion of their rearmament and the deterioration of their relations with Britain rather than the sudden news of Saratoga.

The commissioners do deserve credit for not retarding the progress of events. They succeeded in avoiding a number of traps—frightening French public opinion by being too radical, harming relations with the French government by issuing ultimata or breaking off diplomatic contact, precipitating a premature war that would have endangered the French navy, or dis-

---

67–71; Paul P. Bernard, *Joseph II and Bavaria: Two Eighteenth-Century Attempts at German Unification* (The Hague: Martinus Nijhoff, 1965), 35–57; Harold William Vazeille Temperley, *Frederic the Great and Kaiser Joseph: An Episode of War and Diplomacy in the Eighteenth Century*, 2nd ed. (London: Frank Cass and Co., 1968), 87; Samuel Flagg Bemis, *The Diplomacy of the American Revolution*, rev. ed. (Bloomington: Indiana University Press, 1957), 70–74.

21. Dull, *French Navy and American Independence*, 97–99.

22. For the view that Vergennes was sincere, see Orville T. Murphy, "The Battle of Germantown and the Franco-American Alliance of 1778," *Pennsylvania Magazine of History and Biography* 82 (1958): 55–64.

crediting themselves by offering the British government terms short of independence. They had to overcome discouraging news from America and the apparent coldness of the French government, which dared not entrust them with the secret of France's unpreparedness for war in 1777. Even Franklin's courage was severely tested;[23] but the commissioners endured and, in spite of the Conyngham fiasco, avoided making any fatal mistake. Their rewards were the treaty of amity and commerce and the French alliance.

The commissioners' triumph demonstrated how shrewd the leaders of the Continental Congress were in assuming that ultimately France would come to America's assistance. The fact that French policy was more complex and devious (and also misguided) than they imagined was irrelevant. What mattered now was that a second assumption also be proven correct—their assumption that France and the United States in combination could overcome the enormous military and naval power of Great Britain.

23. See Benjamin Franklin Stevens, ed., *Facsimiles of Manuscripts in European Archives Relating to America, 1773–1783*, 25 vols. (London: privately printed, 1889–98), vol. 18, no. 1691.

CHAPTER 12
The Outbreak
of Hostilities

The French had good diplomatic and military reasons for insisting that they preserve their option when to enter the war. They hoped they could maneuver the British into declaring war on them, or at least into appearing to have started the war. This would assist the Dutch in evading compliance with their treaty of defensive alliance with Britain, which only applied if one of the parties was attacked. More importantly, if it could be made to appear that France was being attacked, she could call for assistance under the terms of her own defensive alliance with Austria. Doubtless Austria would refuse, giving France an excuse to remain neutral in case the Bavarian crisis led to an Austro-Prussian war. Militarily, delaying the beginning of war would buy a little extra time to finish ship repairs and dockyard replenishment. Even more importantly, it would help France make best use of the advantage of surprise. Even with the slow British war mobilization, the French navy would be outnumbered in the coming campaign. (When hostilities did begin in late June, the French had in service only fifty-two ships of the line to fight sixty-six British.)[1] France, however, did have a great advantage in possessing the Mediterranean naval base of Toulon, whose fleet could be sent either against Britain and Ireland or against British forces in North America. Exactly as Joseph-Mathias Gérard had recom-

1. Jonathan R. Dull, *The French Navy and American Independence: A Study of Arms and Diplomacy, 1774–1787* (Princeton, N.J.: Princeton University Press, 1975), 359–60.

mended a year earlier,[2] the council of state decided to send a dozen ships of the line from Toulon to attack Admiral Howe at New York.[3] Howe had a similar number of ships, but they were scattered along the Atlantic seaboard. The French fleet, to be commanded by Vice-Admiral count d'Estaing, would attempt to attack him before he could concentrate his forces; if successful, it could then blockade New York until the huge British garrison was starved into surrender. Meanwhile, French army units would converge on Brittany, Picardy, and Normandy in order to threaten an invasion of England, thereby frightening the British into delaying naval reinforcements for New York.

A month after signing the treaties with the Americans, Vergennes decided to announce publicly to the British the existence of the treaty of amity and commerce (though not the treaty of alliance).[4] Although the British secret service had already provided evidence of the treaties (thanks to intercepting Bancroft's mail), this public notification was a calculated insult that forced the government to order Ambassador Stormont home from Paris. The French responded by withdrawing their ambassador from London. Although the French insult failed to draw a British declaration of war, it did accomplish several things. It gave publicity to the treaty of commerce and, by recognizing the United States, gave King Louis XVI the opportunity of publicly receiving the American commissioners. This furthered good will—Arthur Lee had suggested the idea[5]—and hindered the possibility of any reconciliation between Britain and America. The breaking of relations also freed the French from having to deal with the persistent protests of Stormont, an able ambassador who later became a secretary of state.[6] Finally, it helped prepare French public opinion for war.

2. See above, chapter 11, note 3.

3. Dull, *French Navy and American Independence*, 107–11.

4. Ibid., 102–05.

5. Richard Henry Lee, *Life of Arthur Lee, LL.D., Joint Commissioner of the United States to the Court of France, and Sole Commissioner to the Courts of Spain and Prussia during the Revolutionary War*, 2 vols. (Boston: Wells and Lilly, 1829), 1:398–99.

6. See below, chapter 15.

A month after the breaking of diplomatic relations d'Estaing's fleet sailed for America.[7] Aboard his flagship the *Languedoc* was Conrad-Alexandre Gérard, France's first minister plenipotentiary to the United States. As France had hoped, the earl of Sandwich, paralyzed by the fear of invasion, delayed sending reinforcements to New York until he felt sure d'Estaing was not headed for a rendezvous with the main French fleet stationed at the Atlantic port of Brest.[8] Vergennes expected news of Franco-British hostilities in America to reach Europe by July. How could France provoke an attack by Britain before then?

She was rescued by the courage, if not lunacy, of the captain of a French frigate.[9] As part of a patrol of three small ships, on June 16 he refused to salute an entire British fleet, instead daring to engage in combat. His ship was mauled and the two other French ships captured, but the captain became a national hero, and both France and Britain could claim that the other had begun hostilities. Both countries ordered reprisals on the other's shipping, and by mid-July they were, for all practical purposes, at war.[10]

The months between the signing of the Franco-American alliance and the outbreak of hostilities had been difficult ones for Lord North's government. After the secret service learned of the impending signing of the alliance, North rushed through Parliament two bills to end the American war before France could join it.[11] The first of these offered the Americans repeal of the Coercive Acts of 1774 and freedom from parliamentary taxation. The second established a commission to negotiate peace with America. The commission nominally was headed by the young and rather empty-headed earl of Carlisle; its brains were provided by

7. Dull, *French Navy and American Independence*, 112.

8. Ibid., 115.

9. Ibid., 118–19; for details, see Georges Lacour-Gayet, *La Marine militaire de la France sous la règne de Louis XVI* (Paris: H. Champion, 1905), 112–13.

10. Dull, *French Navy and American Independence*, 120.

11. Charles R. Ritcheson, *British Politics and the American Revolution* (Norman: University of Oklahoma Press, 1954), 258–71; see also Jonathan R. Dull, *Franklin the Diplomat: The French Mission* (Philadelphia: American Philosophical Society, 1982 [*Transactions* 72: part 1]), 33–34.

Suffolk's undersecretary of state, William Eden. Eden (1744–1814) had previously commanded the secret service's penetration of the American mission in Paris[12] and had helped draft North's new proposals. In mid-April Carlisle, Eden, and George Johnstone, a commodore and member of Parliament, embarked for America, carrying a list of other concessions they were empowered to offer, including making the Continental Congress a permanent body (subject, however, to Parliament).

Their mission was doomed. News of North's proposals barely outraced to America the copies of the commissioners' treaties with France; the proposals met a cold reception, and when the Franco-American treaties arrived Congress immediately ratified them. When the British peace commissioners reached Philadelphia they learned that General Howe was about to evacuate the city (so as to concentrate his forces at New York and send troops to attack the French Caribbean island of St. Lucia). The peace commissioners offered their terms to Congress and sailed for New York; their proposals were treated with contempt.[13]

Within weeks French minister Gérard arrived in a newly liberated Philadelphia to a far warmer reception.[14] Diplomatic etiquette required that America have a diplomatic agent of equal rank at the French court. In September 1778 Congress therefore dissolved the commission which had heretofore represented the United States and elected Franklin as American minister plenipotentiary to the court of France.[15] Franklin and his present col-

12. Lewis Einstein, *Divided Loyalties: Americans in England during the War of Independence* (London: Cobden-Sanderson, 1933), 59.

13. Weldon A. Brown, *Empire or Independence: A Study in the Failure of Reconciliation, 1774–1783* (University, La.: Louisiana State University Press, 1941), 244–92; Ritcheson, *British Politics and the American Revolution*, 272–83; Nathan R. Einhorn, "The Reception of the British Peace Offer of 1778," *Pennsylvania History* 16 (1949): 153–78. Technically, the commission included Admiral Richard and General William Howe, but they refused to serve.

14. William C. Stinchcombe, *The American Revolution and the French Alliance* (Syracuse, N.Y.: Syracuse University Press, 1969), 32–33; Worthington Chauncey Ford et al., eds., *Journals of the Continental Congress, 1774–1789*, 35 vols. (Washington, D.C.: Government Printing Office, 1904–76), vol. 11, passim.

15. Ibid., 12:908; 1035–42. Elimination of the commission in the interest of economy had already been recommended by Adams: Lyman H. Butterfield, ed.,

leagues did not learn officially of the change, however, until February 1779.

During the months following the signing of the treaties with France, the American commissioners functioned as accredited diplomats—or at least Franklin and Arthur Lee did. Silas Deane learned in early March 1778 that he had been recalled by Congress, although he was not told that the recall was motivated by his wholesale granting of commissions in the Continental Army.[16] Deane did have the twin honors of being received by King Louis XVI and of traveling to America with Gérard aboard the *Languedoc*. His replacement was John Adams, for whom lay ahead ten frustrating months of attempting to straighten out the commission's records and to remain neutral in the continual disputes between the now bitter enemies Lee and Franklin. (Their feud was exacerbated by Lee's friend Izard, awaiting vainly a call to assume his duties in Florence as American commissioner to Tuscany.)[17]

Luckily for the commissioners' fragile unity, authority over the ports was no longer an issue. The commissioners accepted the choices of port officials made by William Lee before he left for Germany. (Jonathan Williams, Jr., was considered for Nantes, but, on the basis of the now wary Franklin's objections, the position was given to another merchant).[18] The troublesome William

Diary and Autobiography of John Adams, 4 vols. (Cambridge, Mass.: Belknap Press of Harvard University Press, 1961), 4:107–08.

16. Francis P. Wharton, ed., *The Revolutionary Diplomatic Correspondence of the United States*, 6 vols. (Washington, D.C.: Government Printing Office, 1889), 2:424, 444; Jack N. Rakove, *The Beginnings of National Politics: An Interpretive History of the Continental Congress* (New York: Alfred A. Knopf, 1979), 250–51.

17. James H. Hutson, *John Adams and the Diplomacy of the American Revolution* (Lexington: University Press of Kentucky, 1980), 37–41; Butterfield, *Diary and Autobiography of John Adams*, 4:41–172.

18. Worthington Chauncey Ford, ed., *Letters of William Lee, Sheriff and Alderman of London; Commercial Agent of the Continental Congress in France; and Minister to the Courts of Vienna and Berlin, 1766–1783*, 3 vols. (Brooklyn, N.Y.: Historical Printing Club, 1891), 2:387–98, 401–08; Leonard W. Labaree, William B. Willcox et al., eds., *The Papers of Benjamin Franklin*, 24 vols. to date (New Haven and London: Yale University Press, 1959–), 25: forthcoming (see under February 28, 1778); Butterfield, *Diary and Autobiography of John Adams*, 4: 51–53, 114–17.

Carmichael also left France, sailing to America aboard the *Deane*, one of two small frigates purchased at Nantes by the commissioners. These frigates were supposed to escort a convoy of merchant ships, but only one merchantman reached the rendezvous in time (and it became separated at sea and was captured). The frigates safely reached America, though, as did three tardy merchantmen that sailed without escort. Thus, largely by good fortune, arrived the uniforms and military supplies purchased at such expense by the commissioners and collected with such effort by Jonathan Williams, Jr.[19]

In general, the work of the commissioners was routine after the signing of the treaties, although the British did make several futile attempts to undertake negotiations with Franklin.[20] A more momentous event took place in Germany without their knowledge. There, in the city of Aix-la-Chapelle (Aachen), William Lee, rebuffed at Vienna, agreed to a draft commercial treaty with a representative of the city fathers of Amsterdam. Although neither negotiator had any diplomatic authority for his actions, the draft treaty eventually provided Britain a pretext for declaring war on the Netherlands.[21]

Other, more immediate diplomatic developments also were taking place in Germany, where Prussia mobilized its army for a war against Austria. As already mentioned, both parties had called on France for aid. Vergennes managed to elude both, and Britain also maintained neutrality. Hostilities between the two German powers began in July 1778. The vain Emperor Joseph commanded the Austrian army in person, but, probably luckily, did not have the opportunity of testing himself in battle against King Frederick of Prussia. Both armies chose to take the defensive, and the conflict played itself out as farce rather than trag-

19. Labaree, Willcox, et al., *Papers of Benajmin Franklin*, 25: forthcoming (see under January 19, 1778).

20. See below, chapter 15, note 7.

21. Samuel Flagg Bemis, *The Diplomacy of the American Revolution*, rev. ed. (Bloomington: Indiana University Press, 1957), 157–61; see below, chapter 15, for the British declaration of war. Lee's brief stay in Vienna is discussed in Karl A. Roider, Jr., "William Lee, our First Envoy in Vienna," *Virginia Magazine of History and Biography* 86 (1978): 163–68.

edy. This is epitomized by the name commonly given to this war in which the armies struggled harder to find food than to kill each other—the "potato war." When the campaigning season ended with the onset of winter, the contest shifted to the conference table. Russia threatened to mobilize her army on behalf of her ally Prussia if the war continued, thereby forcing Austria to back down. In March 1779 an armistice was signed at the Silesian town of Teschen. By the subsequent peace, named after the same town, Austria agreed to evacuate virtually all of Bavaria.[22]

The war between Britain and France was not to be resolved so quickly. The following chapters discuss the diplomacy that accompanied their war, beginning with the momentous diplomatic consequences of the initial campaign of 1778.

22. Paul P. Bernard, *Joseph II and Bavaria: Two Eighteenth-Century Attempts at German Unification* (The Hague: Martinus Nijhoff, 1965), 51–133; Orville T. Murphy, *Charles Gravier, Comte de Vergennes: French Diplomacy in the Age of Revolution, 1719–1787* (Albany: State University of New York Press, 1982), 291–311.

PART FOUR
The Coalition against Britain

CHAPTER 13

The Franco-Spanish Alliance

The French hoped to win the war in a single campaign by capturing or destroying Admiral Howe's fleet and blockading New York into surrender. Admiral d'Estaing failed to do either. Frustrated by Howe's skillful defense of New York harbor, the French admiral switched his attack to Newport, Rhode Island, where a smaller British garrison was besieged by an American army commanded by Generals Sullivan, Greene, and Lafayette. Again, d'Estaing failed and was forced to flee to Boston when naval reinforcements finally began reaching Howe. Finally, in November he sailed for the Caribbean, having failed to capture or destroy a single British ship of the line.[1]

His failure had major diplomatic consequences. In the next chapter I shall discuss its implications for American diplomacy. To Vergennes and the council of state it meant that they could no longer continue the war with only American help. For the next campaign Britain would be able to man 90 ships of the line instead of 66, while France could add only a dozen to her 52.[2] America had no ships of the line. Unless France could enlist the help of the Spanish navy the struggle against Britain was likely to be hopeless. Unfortunately, the price for obtaining that help would be high. Spain had no interest in American independence

---

1. Jonathan R. Dull, *The French Navy and American Independence: A Study of Arms and Diplomacy, 1774–1787* (Princeton, N.J.: Princeton University Press, 1975), 122–24; Douglas Southall Freeman et al., *George Washington: A Biography,* 7 vols. (New York: Charles Scribner's Sons, 1948–57), 5:47–86.

2. Dull, *French Navy and American Independence,* 361–64.

and, given her secure borders, little interest in the European balance of power. Instead she wished to regain Gibraltar and Minorca, taken from her by Britain at the beginning of the eighteenth century. She also wished to protect her colonial empire in America from British penetration. To do so she hoped to drive British timber cutters from Central America, recapture Florida (particularly the great port of Pensacola), and, at best, retake Jamaica, lost to Britain one hundred and twenty years before. She would accomplish these goals by whatever means were at hand—by striking a bargain with Britain or, should that fail, concluding a military alliance with France to conquer what she wanted. Spain opened the bidding for her services by offering to mediate the conflict between Britain and France, prudently waiting to make any decisions herself until her annual treasure ships had arrived with silver and gold from her Mexican and Peruvian mines.[3] Neither Britain nor France could refuse the offer of mediation, but the Spanish move was basically a device to discover what each of the rivals was willing to give for her assistance. All Britain needed was the indirect assistance of Spanish neutrality, which she could have procured by offering to return Gibraltar and Minorca. Contemptuous of the Spanish navy and confident of her own ability to withstand even a coalition of Spain, France, and the United States, she refused.[4] Even had the British government wished to oblige Spain, Parliament hardly would have agreed to the transfer of Gibraltar; as had been the case with the secret French negotiations of 1773, public opinion circumscribed Britain's diplomatic options.

Spain now named her price for entering the war as France's ally: not only help in obtaining her objectives, but also agreement to a joint invasion of England so as to end the war before Spain's overextended and vulnerable colonial empire could be attacked.[5]

3. Ibid., 126–31.

4. Piers Mackesy, *The War for America, 1775–1783* (Cambridge, Mass.: Harvard University Press, 1965), 249–50; Stetson Conn, *Gibraltar in British Diplomacy in the Eighteenth Century* (New Haven: Yale University Press, 1942), 181–88.

5. Dull, *French Navy and American Independence*, 128–35.

Vergennes was appalled by the price Spain was asking, but, as he advised King Louis XVI, France had no choice but to pay it.[6] The alliance negotiations were one-sided: an almost total capitulation to the Spanish demands. The Franco-Spanish alliance was signed on April 12, 1779, at King Charles III's summer palace of Aranjuez. Spain promised not to make peace with Britain without French consent and recognized that France could not make peace until American independence was secured; this was the closest Spain would come to an alliance with the United States herself. France promised not to make peace until Spain had obtained Gibraltar. (To save French face, Spain agreed not to make peace until Britain promised to remove its commissioner from Dunkirk, a trivial objective compared to Gibraltar.) The two countries agreed to attempt the invasion of England and to help each other achieve their other war objectives, which were specified in the treaty: for Spain, Minorca, West and East Florida, and expulsion of the British from Central America; for France, the Newfoundland fisheries, the African colony of Senegal, the Caribbean island of Dominica, a better position in India, and a rectification of the Anglo-French commercial treaty of 1713 (with which Britain had not complied). Jamaica was not mentioned.[7]

Was the alliance with Spain a violation of France's earlier alliance with the United States? It is true that without consulting the United States France in effect committed them both to continuing the war until Spain captured Gibraltar. On the other hand, it is almost inconceivable that France and the United States could have defeated Britain without Spanish help. Had the French navy been crushed, Britain could have tightly blockaded the American coast and would have made New York impregnable. Without money and supplies from France the survival of the United States would have been unlikely, and without French military and naval help the expulsion of the British from all their

6. See the quotation given in ibid., 133.

7. Henri Doniol, ed., *Histoire de la participation de la France à l'établissement des Etats-Unis d'Amérique: Correspondance diplomatique et documents*, 5 vols. and supplement (Paris: Imprimerie Nationale, 1886–99), 3:803–10.

8. For a picture of one state's economic collapse by the end of the war, see

American positions would have been almost impossible.[8] It was only with the help of the Spanish navy (and to a lesser extent the Dutch navy) that France in 1781 established a temporary naval superiority over Britain and won the decisive battle of Yorktown. This can be illustrated graphically by the number of ships of the line provided by each of the war's combatants:[9]

Year	French	Spanish	Dutch	American	Total Allied	British
1778	52	—	—	0	52	66
1779	63	58	—	0	121	90
1780	69	48	—	0	117	95
1781	70	54	13	0	137	94
1782	73	54	19	0	146	94

Precisely how did the Spaniards and Dutch contribute to the winning of the war? The contributions of the Spanish army are easiest to see. The Spanish governor of Louisiana, Bernardo de Gálvez (1746–86; the city of Galveston is named after him) proved to be one of the war's most successful generals. In a series of brilliant campaigns from 1779 to 1781, he cleared the lower Mississippi valley and Gulf coast of British troops, winning his greatest victory at the successful siege of Pensacola.[10] These victories not only diverted British resources from other parts of

Richard Buel, Jr., *Dear Liberty: Connecticut's Mobilization for the Revolutionary War* (Middletown, Conn.: Wesleyan University Press, 1980), 188–281.

9. Jonathan R. Dull, "France and the American Revolution Seen as Tragedy," in Ronald Hoffman and Peter J. Albert, eds., *Diplomacy and Revolution: The Franco-American Alliance of 1778* (Charlottesville: University Press of Virginia, 1981), 97; Jonathan R. Dull, "France and the American Revolution: Questioning the Myths," *Proceedings of the First Annual Meeting of the Western Society for French History* (1974), 115. Figures for 1778–80 are as of July 1; figures for 1781–82 are as of April 1. All figures include 50-gun ships. For their names and locations, see Dull, *French Navy and American Independence*, 359–76.

10. John Walton Caughey, *Bernardo de Gálvez in Louisiana, 1776–1783* (Berkeley: University of California Press, 1934); N. Orwin Rush, *Spain's Final Triumph over Great Britain in the Gulf of Mexico: The Battle of Pensacola, March 9 to May 8, 1781* (Tallahassee: Florida State University Press, 1966).

America but also restricted British supplies to the Indian tribes besieging the borders of the southern states. Gálvez's final triumph was his capture of the Bahamas in 1782.

The Spaniards also provided assistance to the French fleet that participated in the 1781 Yorktown campaign; an aide of Gálvez helped draft the campaign plans and the citizens of Havana raised by subscription money carried by the fleet to pay the French troops in Virginia.[11] The main help provided by Spain, however, was indirect. The attempted invasion of England in 1779 miscarried, although a gigantic Franco-Spanish fleet of sixty-six ships of the line created considerable panic when it appeared off Plymouth. Disease and bad weather prevented the allies from exploiting their temporary superiority at sea, but the invasion scare greatly increased Sandwich's preoccupation with the security of the British Isles. A smaller Franco-Spanish fleet reappeared off the English coast in 1781, while a Dutch fleet appeared in the North Sea. Because of them British forces in North America received virtually no naval reinforcements during the critical campaign that ended with the surrender of Cornwallis's army at Yorktown. The Spaniards also captured Minorca in early 1781 and maintained a blockade of Gibraltar throughout the war, forcing the British to send several replenishment convoys escorted by detachments from the fleet. This further complicated British strategic planning and drained naval forces needed elsewhere. Although the Spanish navy captured not a single British ship of the line, it nevertheless was vital to the allied war effort.[12]

The British wasted major opportunities, both military and diplomatic, to remove Spain from the war. The British navy won a major victory during the first replenishment of Gibraltar (January 1780), capturing or destroying six Spanish ships of the line.[13] It

11. Dull, *French Navy and American Independence*, 243–45.

12. Mackesy, *War for America*, 391–97, gives a good illustration of the strategic interaction between Gibraltar, the North Sea, and America. For the participation of the Spanish navy in the war, see Dull, *French Navy and American Independence*, passim.

13. Mackesy, *War for America*, 312–23; Dull, *French Navy and American Independence*, 173–86.

failed to follow up the victory, however, and the Spanish navy gradually recovered some of its confidence. Moreover, the British government failed to exploit the Spaniards' eagerness to escape what by 1780 appeared would be a long and dangerous war. Several months' negotiations were carried on that year at the Spanish court by Richard Cumberland, a British envoy. There was less to the negotiations than met the eye, however. The British, more overconfident than ever, were still unwilling to buy the Spaniards out of the war by offering them Gibraltar; the Spaniards publicized the negotiations to frighten the French into accepting Spanish wishes on such questions as military strategy.[14]

The Cumberland negotiations helped contribute to American distrust of Spain. As part of their mediation efforts in 1778–79, Spain had offered a compromise peace plan that would have left the British in control of New York; by rejecting discussion of the plan the British government lost the opportunity of totally destroying American trust of Spain.[15] Nevertheless, Americans were alienated by Spanish reluctance to become direct allies of the United States or even to grant America major financial aid. This was particularly the case with John Jay, former president of Congress, who was sent as minister plenipotentiary to the Spanish court at the end of 1779. Jay's unfriendly reception by Floridablanca and the rest of the court bitterly alienated him and, as we shall see, this may have affected his conduct during the 1782 peace negotiations.[16] James Madison appears to have been the only major congressional figure to have recognized the Spanish

---

14. Unfortunately, the fullest account of the negotiations overestimates their importance: Samuel Flagg Bemis, *The Hussey-Cumberland Mission and American Independence* (Princeton, N.J.: Princeton University Press, 1931). See also Dull, *French Navy and American Independence*, 194–95; Conn, *Gibraltar in British Diplomacy*, 190–97.

15. Dull, *French Navy and American Independence*, 141.

16. For Jay's mission, see Richard B. Morris, *The Peacemakers: The Great Powers and American Independence* (New York, Evanston and London: Harper & Row, 1970), 43–66, 218–47; Richard B. Morris, ed., *John Jay, the Winning of the Peace: Unpublished Papers, 1780–1784* (New York, Evanston and London: Harper & Row, 1980), 1–234. For his role in the peace negotiations, see below, chapter 18.

contribution to American victory.[17] That contribution, nonetheless, was critical and, in spite of the price paid for it, the Spanish alliance was the greatest accomplishment of French diplomacy during the war.

17. Irving Brant, *James Madison: The Nationalist, 1780–7* (Indianapolis and New York: Bobbs-Merrill, 1948), 278–79.

CHAPTER 14

The American Consensus
Disintegrates

Admiral d'Estaing's abrupt departure from Newport in August 1778 greatly disturbed the commanders of the Continental army units there, who had to abandon their siege and flee for safety. None was more distressed than the marquis de Lafayette. D'Estaing was not only a fellow Frenchman but also a distant relative. Rather than sharing in his glory, Lafayette now had to defend him from American criticism. Lafayette soon wrote the admiral to suggest ways of erasing the memory of the defeat. Among his ideas was that a corps of six to ten thousand French troops might permit a joint Franco-American attack on Canada.[1]

Apparently Lafayette was told subsequently by French minister Gérard not to encourage such ideas—France had no desire to help the United States capture Canada. A congressional committee was already discussing the idea of a joint attack on Halifax, Newfoundland, and Quebec.

Shortly thereafter, Lafayette, anxious to serve again in the French army now that France was at war, was given leave from the Continental army to return home. Congress asked him to carry its instructions to Franklin, newly named minister plenipotentiary. Among these instructions were that Franklin should solicit a French attack on Halifax and Quebec for America's bene-

---

1. Stanley J. Idzerda, Robert R. Crout et al., eds., *Lafayette in the Age of the American Revolution: Selected Letters and Papers, 1776–1790*, 5 vols. to date (Ithaca, N.Y. and London: Cornell University Press, 1977–), 2:102, 142–47.

fit.[2] After Lafayette left for Boston to take passage for France, Congress changed its mind. General Washington feared that the French might keep Canada for themselves; on his advice Congress attempted to rescind the orders to Franklin. Its messenger arrived in Boston too late; Lafayette had already sailed.[3]

The young Frenchman had not forgotten the humiliation at Newport. After reporting to the French court, he met with Franklin and John Adams on the evening of February 20, 1779. It seems likely he proposed a new attack on the British-held city. On the next day Adams wrote Lafayette to discuss possible operations for a French fleet and expeditionary force of five thousand soldiers in America; a few days later Franklin wrote Vergennes on the same subject. Both Americans specifically mentioned an attack on Rhode Island, even though Franklin's orders had said nothing about French troops being sent to the United States. This departure from orders was much out of character for the cautious Franklin, who subsequently told Congress only that he had asked for French help against Halifax and Quebec. Thereafter Franklin retreated, telling Lafayette he had no orders to ask for troops to be sent to the United States. The proposal soon was shelved, as France prepared for the invasion of England demanded by Spain.[4]

Congress's reversal of policy on French troops was a sign that the consensus on foreign policy issues had begun to crack. Another sign of the fragility of that consensus was the refusal of Congress to approve Silas Deane's financial accounts brought from France. The former commissioner's hopes of quickly resolving his affairs and returning to Europe were frustrated by the accusations sent by Arthur Lee and by the testimony of Deane's former friend William Carmichael, who had turned against him because

2. Ibid., 2: 192–93n; Worthington Chauncey Ford et al., eds., *Journals of the Continental Congress, 1774–1789*, 35 vols. (Washington, D.C.: Government Printing Office, 1904–76), 12:1041, 1042–48.

3. Idzerda, Crout et al., *Lafayette in the Age of the American Revolution*, 2:207n, 217, 219n.

4. Ibid., 2:234–36; Jonathan R. Dull, *Franklin the Diplomat: The French Mission* (Philadelphia: American Philosophical Society, 1982 [*Transactions* 72, part 1]), 50–51.

of a perceived insult. Deane probably was innocent of most of the
charges of financial mismanagement but his combative style did
him little good. His case brought to the surface the mutual antip-
athy of "radicals" like Samuel Adams, who were concerned about
the moral integrity of America and who distrusted wealth and
commerce, and "moderates" like Deane's friend Robert Morris,
who called for political "realism" and favored wealth and commerce. This ideological dispute, foreshadowing the later split between Republicans and Federalists, was aggravated by French
minister Gérard, who saw the radicals as anti-French. Deane's
accounts were not approved and his ordeal so embittered him
that after his return to Europe in 1780 he accepted a British bribe
to propagandize on their behalf.[5]

Another divisive issue arose in early 1779 as a result of the impending Spanish entry into the war. Because of French insistence, Congress had to face the need to engage eventually in
peace negotiations with Britain. It attempted both to agree on a
set of war objectives (as France and Spain secretly were doing)
and to elect a peace commissioner to negotiate with Britain once
the latter was ready to accept American independence. The ensuing debates revealed deep sectional differences within the
United States as New Englanders insisted on fishing rights off
Newfoundland as a precondition for negotiations, while southerners and westerners were concerned about extensive western
boundaries and navigation rights on the Mississippi River.
Gérard was able to play off section against section and finally to
obtain a more moderate set of demands, which would not inhibit
future negotiations.[6] A combination of sectional animosities and
ideological disputes (similar to those in the Deane case) also em-

5. Edmund S. Morgan, "The Puritan Ethic and the American Revolution,"
William and Mary Quarterly, 3rd ser., 24 (1967): 3–43; Jack N. Rakove, *The Beginnings of National Politics: An Interpretive History of the Continental Congress*
(New York: Alfred A. Knopf, 1979), 246–55; Charles Isham, ed., *The Deane Papers*, 5 vols. (New York: New-York Historical Society, 1887–91 [*Collections*, vols.
19–23]), 2:491–99; 3:passim; 4:1–170; H. James Henderson, *Party Politics in the
Continental Congress* (New York: McGraw-Hill, 1974), 187–96; Julian Boyd,
"Silas Deane: Death by a Kindly Teacher of Treason?" *William and Mary Quarterly*, 3rd ser., 16 (1959): 336.
6. William C. Stinchcombe, *The American Revolution and the French Alliance* (Syracuse, N.Y.: Syracuse University Press, 1969), 62–76; Rakove, *Begin-*

bittered the choice of America's new diplomatic representatives. After a series of votes Congress kept Franklin as minister to France and elected the "radical" John Adams as peace commissioner, the "moderate" John Jay as minister to Spain, and the unaffiliated South Carolinian Henry Laurens as minister to the Netherlands. Ralph Izard, Arthur Lee, and William Lee lost their diplomatic posts.[7]

Gérard's hard-fought victories in Congress were aided by the deteriorating American military situation. British troops opened a second front in late 1778 and 1779 by capturing Savannah and threatening Charleston. The governor of South Carolina wrote for help to Admiral d'Estaing, who in the autumn of 1779 brought his fleet back from the West Indies. Unfortunately, the admiral was unsuccessful in his attempt to recapture Savannah. He was wounded when, after coming ashore, he attacked the city with French troops and volunteers, both black and white, from the French colony of Saint Domingue. Ironically, though his attack failed, the surprise return of the French fleet to America so frightened the British that they evacuated their exposed garrison at Newport.[8] The changed military situation in the south also appears to have overcome Washington's scruples about French troops. In the autumn of 1779 he wrote to encourage Lafayette to return to America and to inform him that a French expeditionary force would be welcome. Washington's aide Alexander Hamilton also wrote to suggest that two thousand French regular troops be sent.[9]

nings of National Politics, 255–74; Henderson, Party Politics in the Continental Congress, 196–99, 206–10.

7. H. James Henderson, "Congressional Factionalism and the Attempt to Recall Benjamin Franklin," William and Mary Quarterly, 3rd ser., 27 (1970), 246–67; Rakove, Beginnings of National Politics, 255–74; Henderson, Party Politics in the Continental Congress, 196–217.

8. Jonathan R. Dull, The French Navy and American Independence: A Study of Arms and Diplomacy, 1774–1787 (Princeton, N.J.: Princeton University Press, 1975), 159–62; Alexander A. Lawrence, Storm over Savannah: The Story of Count d'Estaing and the Siege of the Town in 1779 (Athens, Ga.: University of Georgia Press, 1951); Piers Mackesy, The War for America, 1775–1783 (Cambridge, Mass.: Harvard University Press, 1965), 276–77.

9. Idzerda, Crout et al., Lafayette in the Age of the American Revolution, 2:313–19, 344–49.

This news that America would happily receive French troops came at an opportune time for France. The failure of the 1779 attempt to invade England convinced Vergennes that a war of attrition against Britain would be necessary. She would still be threatened with invasion but the main French effort would be made elsewhere. Within weeks of Lafayette's reception of Washington's letter, the royal council of state decided to send an expeditionary corps to America. (Both France and Spain also decided to send major reinforcements to the Caribbean.) Lafayette was sent to carry the news to General Washington, and in August 1780 a naval squadron and 5,500 French troops arrived at Newport, happily now in American hands.[10] France also sent a new minister to Philadelphia. Gérard resigned for reasons of health; his replacement, the ingratiating young chevalier de la Luzerne (1741–91), proved far more subtle in influencing Congress than had the rather tactless Gérard.[11]

John Adams, who returned to Europe in 1780, had an effect the opposite of Luzerne's. Upon arriving in Paris, he suggested to Vergennes that the British be notified of his arrival. Vergennes was shocked, and Adams's subsequent rudeness over this and other issues raised serious questions for Vergennes about the American's professional competence and loyalty to the alliance. Vergennes ordered that Luzerne attempt to have Congress recall Adams; meanwhile, the peace commissioner, having no business in Paris, left for the Netherlands to attempt to raise a loan for the United States.[12]

Adams's conduct and the resultant French protests threatened a renewal of the bitter congressional debates of 1779. Instead,

10. Dull, *French Navy and American Independence*, 163–69, 187–92; Lee Kennett, *The French Forces in America, 1780–1783* (Westport, Conn. and London: Greenwood Press, 1977), 3–63.

11. Stinchcombe, *American Revolution and the French Alliance*, 77–90; William Emmett O'Donnell, *The Chevalier de la Luzerne, French Minister to the United States, 1779–1784* (Louvain: Bibliothèque de l'Université, 1938).

12. James H. Hutson, *John Adams and the Diplomacy of the American Revolution* (Lexington: University Press of Kentucky, 1980), 55–74; Henri Doniol, ed., *Histoire de la participation de la France à l'établissement des Etats-Unis d'Amérique: Correspondance diplomatique et documents*, 5 vols. (Paris: Imprimerie Nationale, 1886–99), 4:423–24.

during 1781 Congress tamely acquiesed to Luzerne's wishes, electing a commission of five members to conduct future peace negotiations (Adams, Jay, Franklin, Laurens, and Thomas Jefferson). It established the position of secretary for foreign affairs and selected for the post Robert R. Livingston (1746–1813), who was regarded as sympathetic to France. Furthermore, it ordered the commissioners to do nothing without consulting the French government.[13]

The orders to the commissioners, although disregarded in practice, have been subject to almost universal condemnation by historians. They have regarded the subjecting of American diplomats to the advice of a foreign court as both a threat to American interests and a surrender of sovereignty. Although neither criticism is invalid, the congressional actions should be understood in context. Vergennes's motives were not as dark as has often been portrayed; he appears to have been genuinely concerned by Adams's erratic behavior and, as I shall discuss later, was still dedicated to the winning of American independence (although indifferent to such issues as America's boundaries and fishing rights).[14] Moreover, Congress's supineness before Luzerne's demands was less a result of its own failings than a symptom of underlying American weakness and dependence on France. The early months of 1781 were a low point in the American war effort; revolts broke out in the Continental army and the American currency system collapsed.[15] Government finances were restored only through massive infusions of French money, obtained chiefly by Franklin (rather than by the blustering amateur diplomat Colonel John Laurens, sent to France to obtain supplies for the Continental army).[16] Furthermore, the French expedition-

13. Stinchcombe, *American Revolution and the French Alliance*, 153–169; Henderson, *Party Politics in the Continental Congress*, 298–304.

14. See below, chapter 18.

15. Douglas Southall Freeman et al., *George Washington: A Biography*, 7 vols. (New York: Charles Scribner's Sons, 1948–57), 5:223–51; E. James Ferguson, *The Power of the Purse: A History of American Public Finance, 1776–1790* (Chapel Hill: University of North Carolina Press, 1961), 25–69.

16. Ibid., 126–28; Dull, *Franklin the Diplomat*, 48–49; D. E. Huger Smith, ed., "The Mission of Col. John Laurens in Europe in 1781," *South Carolina His-*

ary corps at Newport was needed to drive the British from
America.

By the end of the year the military situation in America was
transformed. The French and Continental armies were shifted to
Virginia, a French fleet arrived in Chesapeake Bay and the entire
army of General Cornwallis was captured at Yorktown in October. The campaign was an unparalleled example of cooperation
among Americans, French, and Spaniards (who released French
troops under their command to come to Virginia, aided in drafting campaign plans, and provided financial help).[17] The victory
at Yorktown probably saved the allied war effort from collapse. It
also undermined the support of British public opinion for continuing the effort to force a return of American obedience to the
crown. The main British army at New York was still intact, the
British held bases at Charleston and Savannah, and the navy was
anxious for revenge—in theory there was no reason for despair.
The most important result of Yorktown was its effect on British
morale. Every moment of British optimism had been followed
by defeat—Concord, Bunker Hill (in effect a defeat), Trenton
and Princeton, Saratoga, and now Yorktown. The revolt of Parliament (and its taxpaying constituents) against the war in America
doomed the government of Lord North. The North government's
failure, however, was not only military. The British war effort
was seriously, if not fatally, harmed by the failures of British
diplomacy.

torical and Genealogical Magazine 1 (1900): 13–41, 136–51, 213–22, 311–22; 2
(1901): 27–43, 108–25.

17. Dull, French Navy and American Independence, 238–49; Kennett, French
Forces in America, 112–53; Charles Lee Lewis, Admiral de Grasse and American
Independence (Annapolis: United States Naval Institute Press, 1945).

CHAPTER 15

British Wartime Diplomacy

The states of Europe being indifferent or hostile, British diplomats faced problems that proved beyond their ability to solve. Even new leadership was insufficient to devise ways of ending Britain's isolation. Two-thirds of the initial secretarial trio of Suffolk, Weymouth, and Germain were replaced in 1779. Suffolk, now deceased, was succeeded at the northern department by Viscount Stormont, while the inept Weymouth resigned and was replaced at the southern department by the earl of Hillsborough (1718–93).[1] The new secretaries of state were experienced enough; Stormont had been ambassador to Saxony-Poland, Austria, and France, while Hillsborough had served as secretary of state for the American colonies from 1768 to 1772 (where he aroused considerable American hatred). They and Germain proved unable, though, to overcome the central challenges facing British diplomacy, those of breaking the coalition of France, Spain, and the United States and of finding diplomatic support for Britain elsewhere in Europe. Instead, problems worsened during their tenure: the neutral states of Europe combined to enforce their right to carry supplies to Britain's enemies, and to the coalition of those enemies were added the small but significant forces of the Netherlands.

Adding to her enemies was a serious mistake; it is somewhat

1. Herbert Butterfield, *George III, Lord North and the People, 1779–80* (New York: Russell & Russell, 1949), 26–41, 69–70, 117–38; Piers Mackesy, *The War for America, 1775–1783* (Cambridge, Mass.: Harvard University Press, 1965), 246, 301–03.

easier to excuse Britain's failure to divide her prior enemies or to find an ally. The greatest of these failures was Britain's inability to remove Spain from the war by either diplomacy or force. Spain was the weakest link in the chain of Britain's enemies and, as we have seen, in Gibraltar Britain possessed a way of snapping that link.[2] Her failure to offer Gibraltar to Spain was motivated both by overconfidence in her own navy and by fear of public opinion and parliamentary opposition. As perceptive British statesmen had realized for the last sixty years, possession of Gibraltar was a dubious blessing.[3] It threw Spain into France's arms; it served little strategic function unless Britain intended to establish a permanent fleet in the Mediterranean (particularly after Minorca was lost in 1781); and its replenishment was a recurring drain on British naval resources. Nevertheless, the British public demanded its retention. As Britain had not given it to Spain to prevent war, it could hardly offer it to terminate a war in which, seemingly, the Spanish navy was being humiliated.[4] More promising was the hope of driving Spain from the war, but, as already mentioned, Britain failed to follow up its one successful battle against the navy of Spain.[5]

A similar caution inhibited the British from attacking the French expeditionary corps at Newport or Washington's army in New Jersey and along the Hudson. Instead, Britain in 1780 and 1781 concentrated her attention on the American South, attempting to reestablish control over North and South Carolina with the use of Loyalists, as she had done with some success in Georgia.[6] The British strategy was disastrous; with the defeat of Cornwallis, Britain was thrown on the defensive, as her presence in North America gradually shrank to Canada, East Florida, and

2. See above, chapter 13, note 4.

3. Derek McKay and H. M. Scott, *The Rise of the Great Powers, 1648–1815* (London and New York: Longman, 1983), 116; Paul Langford, *The Eighteenth Century, 1688–1815* (London: Adam and Charles Black, 1976), 142–43.

4. Stetson Conn, *Gibraltar in British Diplomacy in the Eighteenth Century* (New Haven: Yale University Press, 1942), 196.

5. See above, chapter 13, note 13.

6. Paul H. Smith, *Loyalists and Redcoats: A Study in British Revolutionary Policy* (New York: W. W. Norton & Co., 1964), 79–174.

the cities and environs of Charleston, Savannah, and New York. Britain had long since given up attempts to find a diplomatic solution to the war. After the failure of the Carlisle commission, no serious attempt was made to negotiate with Congress, and negotiations with Franklin and his fellow commissioners gradually were abandoned as well.[7]

Despite increasing French war weariness, little effort was made to detach France from the allied coalition. The North government rejected peace feelers from French Finance Minister Jacques Necker, Vergennes's political rival.[8] In mid-1781 Necker was driven from office as Turgot had been; moreover, after Maurepas's death later that year, Vergennes effectively became chief minister as well as foreign minister. (His was not undisputed power, though; his ally Sartine had been sacrificed in late 1780 to appease Spanish criticism of the French war effort, and the marquis de Castries, the new naval minister, was a political enemy.)[9] A major British victory in 1780 or 1781 or even the continuation of the military stalemate into 1782 might nevertheless have driven the French out of the war, in spite of Vergennes's desire for American independence. By the autumn of 1780 the French government's financial situation had become so serious that the council of state was forced to contemplate the possibility of a truce which would leave the British in occupation of part of the United States. In early 1781 Joseph-Mathias Gérard, now Gérard de Rayneval, drafted for Vergennes a memorandum on what concessions France should make if she were no longer able to continue the war. In this dire case France still hoped for an independent United States; Rayneval advised that the Ameri-

7. See Frederick B. Tolles, "Franklin and the Pulteney Mission: An Episode in the Secret History of the American Revolution," *Huntington Library Quarterly* 17 (1953–54): 37–58, and George Herbert Guttridge, *David Hartley, M.P., an Advocate of Conciliation, 1774–1783* (Berkeley: University of California Press, 1926 [*University of California Publications in History* 14, no. 3]), 281–87, for two attempts in the spring of 1778 to conduct negotiations with Franklin.

8. Richard B. Morris, *The Peacemakers: The Great Powers and American Independence* (New York, Evanston and London: Harper & Row, 1965), 88–111.

9. Jonathan R. Dull, *The French Navy and American Independence: A Study of Arms and Diplomacy, 1774–1787* (Princeton, N.J.: Princeton University Press, 1975), 194–202, 255–56.

cans could better survive the loss of the Carolinas than the loss of New York. Fortunately, the victory at Yorktown rejuvenated the French war effort and rendered unnecessary further consideration of French acquiesence in a partition of the United States.[10]

Britain had no better luck finding an ally than she did eliminating an enemy. As we shall see, Russia and Austria were reconciled, leaving Prussia without an ally. King Frederick II sought closer ties with France, leaving Britain little hope of a Prussian alliance.[11] Austria had no interest in helping Britain, which had remained neutral during the Bavarian succession crisis.[12] North's government therefore returned to the pursuit of a Russian alliance. Empress Catherine II rejected the increasingly desperate British appeals, which culminated in the offer of Minorca shortly before its capture by Spain in early 1781.[13] The British were not well served by their ambassador in St. Petersburg, Sir James Harris, whose sense of British superiority and male arrogance combined to make him seriously underestimate the Russian empress.[14] As I shall discuss in the next chapter, Russia not only refused help but indirectly opposed Britain by sponsoring a league of neutrals to protect their shipping rights against British (or other) interference.

Perhaps the chief folly of the Germain-Stormont-Hillsborough foreign ministry was its Dutch policy. As in the Seven Years' War, the Netherlands wished to remain neutral and profit by trading with all the belligerents. The British government was outraged both at the clandestine trade of the United States with the Dutch Caribbean colony of St. Eustatius and at the Dutch wish to provide France and Spain with naval supplies like timber and masts, which the British considered contraband. It is easy to understand British anger at seeing a nominal ally supplying her

10. Ibid., 213–14.

11. See M. S. Anderson, "The Great Powers and the Russian Annexation of the Crimea, 1783–4," *Slavonic and East European Review* 37 (1958–59): 34.

12. Isabel de Madariaga, *Britain, Russia and the Armed Neutrality of 1780: Sir James Harris's Mission to St. Petersburg during the American Revolution* (New Haven: Yale University Press, 1962), 287.

13. Ibid., 121–39, 239–312.

14. Ibid., 448–54 and passim.

enemies. On the other hand, the British overestimated the importance of this trade. France had stockpiled large quantities of naval matériel before the war and had secure sources of supply from Italy and from the Dutch (through the inland canals of the Austrian Netherlands). The Dutch seaborne trade hence was not as critical to the French war effort as the British believed.

This can be seen by comparing French naval shipbuilding in the American war with that during the French Revolution, when her sources of supply were disrupted. In spite of a partial blockade of her coast by the British navy during the American conflict, France launched 29 ships of the line during five years of war (while losing nineteen, all but four of them during 1782).[15] During her own revolution she launched only 26 ships of the line in nine years of war (while losing 52).[16] Indeed, the earlier French navy, though suffering occasional shortages, created a problem for itself by building more warships than it could man with its available officers and sailors.[17] The British navy did little more than overextend itself by intercepting Dutch and other neutral commerce. More wisely, France accepted the Dutch desire to trade with belligerents and used selective economic pressure against Dutch provinces and towns which favored the British. Gradually, relations between Britain and the Netherlands deteriorated. The Dutch rejected a renewed British demand for assistance under their treaty of alliance, gave refuge to an American squadron under the command of John Paul Jones, and began convoying their merchant ships.[18] Most menacing of all from a Brit-

15. Dull, *French Navy and American Independence*, 352–55.

16. There is no survey of French naval construction comparable to the recent work on British construction and repair, Roger Morriss, *The Royal Dockyards during the Revolutionary and Napoleonic Wars* (Leicester, Eng.: Leicester University Press, 1983). See, however, Norman Hampson, *La Marine de l'an II: Mobilisation de la flotte de l'Océan, 1793–1794* (Paris: Marcel Rivière, 1959), 241–44, and Pierre Le Conte, *Répertoire des navires de guerre français* (Cherbourg: La Villarion, 1932). For French losses, see William Laird Clowes, *The Royal Navy: A History from the Earliest Times to the Present*, 7 vols. (Boston: Little, Brown & Co., 1897–1903), 4: 552–58.

17. Dull, *French Navy and American Independence*, 278–79.

18. Samuel Flagg Bemis, *The Diplomacy of the American Revolution*, rev. ed. (Bloomington: Indiana University Press, 1957), 130–48.

ish standpoint, they undertook negotiations with Russia to join the latter's league of neutral shippers. Panic-stricken at the possibility of Russia's providing military support to the Dutch, the British in December 1780 declared war on the Netherlands so as to preclude a Russo-Dutch treaty. (In fact, the treaty was signed shortly thereafter in St. Petersburg, but Empress Catherine II disavowed it when she learned that the Netherlands was already at war.) Britain used as her excuse the draft treaty of commerce between William Lee and the representative from Amsterdam; she had procured a copy when the British navy captured Henry Laurens on his way to the Netherlands.[19]

The war with Britain was a disaster for the Dutch. The British captured St. Eustatius with its huge accumulation of war supplies, took Trincomali, the great Dutch port on the island of Ceylon (off southern India), and were barely outraced by the French to the Cape colony at the southwest tip of Africa.[20] The Dutch defeats were due to lack of ships rather than lack of courage; the results, nevertheless, were humiliating. Key parts of the Dutch colonial empire were either in British hands or in the hands of the French, who thereby gained ascendancy over their ally. The British gains, however, were not worth the price the North government paid for them. The French eventually recaptured St. Eustatius and Trincomali. The flow of war matériel soon resumed under Russian and Prussian flags. (Some of the ships were actually Dutch merchantmen under false colors.)[21] Perhaps most important, the diversions caused by the British plundering of St. Eustatius and the need to counter a Dutch fleet in the North Sea disrupted British strategy during the Yorktown campaign and may have cost the few ships' difference between defeat and victory. For this reason the Dutch, like the Spaniards, deserve a share of the credit for the Allied victory.

The results of Yorktown doomed the government of Lord North. As the Opposition in the House of Commons grew to a majority, the North government launched a desperate series of

19. Madariaga, *Britain, Russia and the Armed Neutrality*, 216–38.
20. Mackesy, *War for America*, 380–90, 416–18, 494–500.
21. Madariaga, *Britain, Russia and the Armed Neutrality*, 361–82.

attempts to initiate negotiations with Vergennes, with Franklin, or with John Adams, whose stay in the Netherlands was finally rewarded by his public recognition by the States General.[22] The British government's attempt was as hopeless as was its effort to stave off defeat in Parliament. On March 20, 1782, North abandoned the attempts and resigned from office.[23] A new government in Britain would bear the responsibility for ending the war in America and choosing between peace and continued war with France, Spain, and the Netherlands. The negotiations it began were influenced greatly, however, by the drastic changes that had occurred recently in the European diplomatic situation. The guiding force behind those changes was Russia; before we can understand fully the negotiations of 1782–83, we must know something of Russian diplomacy and its consequences.

22. Morris, *The Peacemakers*, 253–57; James H. Hutson, *John Adams and the Diplomacy of the American Revolution* (Lexington: University Press of Kentucky, 1980), 75–116.

23. See Ian R. Christie, *The End of North's Ministry, 1780–1782* (London: Macmillan and Co.; New York: St. Martin's Press, 1958).

CHAPTER 16

Russian Diplomacy during
the American Revolution

In spite of the Turkish war and the partition of Poland, Russian foreign policy during the first eighteen years of Catherine's reign (1763–81) generally was defensive rather than aggressive. During this period Count Nikita Ivanovich Panin (1718–83) served as Russia's foreign minister.[1] Panin's diplomacy, often referred to as the "Northern system," considered France and her ally Austria as potential threats to Russian security. Panin sought to protect Russia by linking the powers of northern Europe. He hoped to make alliances with Prussia, Denmark, and Britain and to maintain Sweden and Poland as Russian "client states" (that is, states under Russian influence or domination).[2] He looked with disfavor on territorial expansion and opposed the partition of Poland, which he would have preferred left intact under Russian protection.[3] Panin's system was less than fully successful: Poland was

1. Panin did not hold the title of foreign minister but exercised those responsibilities. For a brief sketch of him, see Isabel de Madariaga, *Britain, Russia and the Armed Neutrality of 1780: Sir James Harris's Mission to St. Petersburg during the American Revolution* (New Haven: Yale University Press, 1962), 17–19. For a full account of his political career, see David L. Ransel, *The Politics of Catherinian Russia: The Panin Party* (New Haven and London: Yale University Press, 1975).

2. For the "Northern system," see David M. Griffiths, "The Rise and Fall of the Northern System: Court Politics and Foreign Policy during the First Half of Catherine II's Reign," *Canadian Slavic Studies* 4 (1970): 547–69, and Michael Roberts, *British Diplomacy and Swedish Politics, 1758–1773* (Minneapolis: University of Minnesota Press, 1980), passim.

3. Isabel de Madariaga, *Russia in the Age of Catherine the Great* (New Haven and London: Yale University Press, 1981), 235.

divided between Austria and Prussia, an alliance was not concluded with Britain, and Sweden achieved an unwelcome degree of independence. Nevertheless, Panin achieved some of his greatest triumphs in the years following the end of the Turkish and Polish troubles. The 1779 Peace of Teschen was a great triumph for the Russo-Prussian alliance. The aggressive Austrians were forced to return almost all the territory they had taken from Bavaria, and this restoration of the status quo was achieved without Russia's having to go to war. This boost to the empress's reputation was followed in 1780 by another diplomatic coup. To the surprise of Europe (and the shock of the British), Catherine announced the formation of a League of Armed Neutrality to enforce her interpretation of the rights of neutral shippers. This interpretation included the following points:

1. Neutrals had the right to sail between the ports and along the coasts of nations at war;
2. Neutrals had the right to carry without interference goods belonging to belligerents, except for contraband (prohibited goods of war);
3. Only a limited number of goods should be considered contraband and naval matériel should not be considered as such;
4. Neutral shipping could not enter a blockaded port, but this prohibition was defined very narrowly.[4]

Catherine announced the arming of a fleet to enforce the terms of the league and invited the other powers of Europe to participate. Gradually, most of the major neutral powers of Europe did join: Sweden and Denmark in 1780, Prussia, Portugal, and Austria in 1781, the Kingdom of Naples in 1783. As we have seen, the Netherlands tried unsuccessfully to join, and the United States was so enthusiastic about Catherine's ideas that it too tried to join, even though it was a belligerent![5] (The United States, mistakenly believing Catherine to be sympathetic, also

4. Madariaga, *Britain, Russia and the Armed Neutrality*, 172–73; Sir Francis Piggot and G. W. T. Omond, eds., *Documentary History of the Armed Neutralities, 1780 and 1800* (London: University of London Press, 1919), 198–206; James Brown Scott, ed., *The Armed Neutralities of 1780 and 1800* (New York: Oxford University Press, 1918), 273–76.

5. Madariaga, *Britain, Russia and the Armed Neutrality*, 172–94, 361–86;

sent a diplomatic representative, John Adams's secretary, Francis Dana, on a fruitless mission to St. Petersburg, against the advice of Vergennes and Franklin.)[6]

Although Catherine herself was responsible for establishing the league, Panin soon realized that it would favor the goals of his Northern system by linking the states surrounding the Baltic Sea under Russian sponsorship. Moreover, it served to increase Russian prestige and to favor the growth of the Russian merchant marine.[7]

Panin himself was behind Catherine's next move, the informal offer of her services to mediate between Britain and her enemies.[8] This "insinuation verbale" of December 1780 was not unwelcome to Vergennes. As mentioned above, the French war effort was at a critical stage and Vergennes hoped the Russians might force an acceptable peace on the British or, if worse came to worst, provide France a graceful exit from the American alliance.[9] British Secretary of State Stormont, who had come to distrust the Russians, was less enthusiastic. He sought to deflect what he regarded as a threat by instead accepting the joint mediation of Russia and Austria. The Austrians were pleased, and

---

Samuel Flagg Bemis, *The Diplomacy of the American Revolution*, rev. ed. (Bloomington: Indiana University Press, 1957), 164–71.

6. David M. Griffiths, "American Commercial Diplomacy in Russia, 1780 to 1783," *William and Mary Quarterly*, 3rd ser., 27 (1970): 379–410; Nikolaĭ N. Bokhovitinov, *Russia and the American Revolution*, trans. C. Jay Smith (Tallahassee, Fla.: Diplomatic Press, 1976), 62–74; William Penn Cresson, *Francis Dana, A Puritan Diplomat at the Court of Catherine the Great* (New York: Dial Press, 1930); David Grayson Allen et al., eds., *Diary of John Quincy Adams*, 2 vols. to date (Cambridge, Mass. and London: Belknap Press of Harvard University Press, 1981–), 1:102–53.

7. Madariaga, *Britain, Russia and the Armed Neutrality*, 140–71; David M. Griffiths, "Nikita Panin, Russian Diplomacy and the American Revolution," *Slavic Review* 28 (1969): 1–24.

8. Ibid.; Madariaga, *Britain, Russia and the Armed Neutrality*, 245–46.

9. Ibid., 245–46, 273–74; Henri Doniol, ed., *Histoire de la participation de la France á l'établissement des Etats-Unis d'Amérique: Correspondance diplomatique et documents*, 5 vols. and supplement (Paris: Imprimerie Nationale, 1886–99), 4:485–530; Jonathan R. Dull, *The French Navy and American Independence: A Study of Arms and Diplomacy, 1774–1787* (Princeton, N.J.: Princeton University Press, 1975), 204, 206–07. See also above, chapter 15, note 10.

France and Spain had little choice but to accept (even though Vergennes had little love for Austria and no hope for the success of the joint mediation).[10] Catherine evaded Dutch appeals for military assistance by adding their case against Britain to the items to be mediated.[11]

Vergennes summoned John Adams from the Netherlands to Paris to ascertain his response as peace commissioner to the subsequent Austro-Russian peace proposals. Adams posed strict conditions for American acceptance of the mediation.[12] Some historians have believed he thereby foiled a European plot to partition America.[13] The truth is more prosaic: by the time of Adams's visit to Paris in the summer of 1781 all the belligerents were seeking ways to escape the mediation and Catherine herself was rapidly losing interest in it.[14]

Her interest was being diverted by what proved to be the major diplomatic development in eastern Europe between the Polish partition and the Turkish war of 1787. The humiliating Peace of Teschen probably helped convince Emperor Joseph II that it was necessary for Austria to seek an alliance with Russia. The death of his mother, Maria Theresa, in December 1780 made Joseph sole ruler of Austria and the other Habsburg possessions, as well as Holy Roman Emperor. He was now free to seek an alliance with Catherine of Russia. By an exchange of letters in May and June of 1781, Joseph and Catherine secretly became allies.[15]

10. Madariaga, *Britain, Russia and the Armed Neutrality*, 264–70, 275–78, 323.

11. Ibid., 310–12.

12. James H. Hutson, *John Adams and the Diplomacy of the American Revolution* (Lexington: University Press of Kentucky, 1980), 96–97.

13. E.g., Richard B. Morris, *The Peacemakers: The Great Powers and American Independence* (New York, Evanston and London: Harper & Row, 1965), 173–217.

14. Madariaga, *Britain, Russia and the Armed Neutrality*, 325–30; Dull, *French Navy and American Independence*, 214–15.

15. Isabel de Madariaga, "The Secret Austro-Russian Treaty of 1781," *Slavonic and East European Review* 38 (1959): 114–45; Robert Salomon, *La Politique orientale de Vergennes (1780–1784)* (Paris: Les Presses modernes, 1935), 287–309. For other reasons for Austria's approach to Russia, see Harvey L. Dyck, "Pondering the Russian Fact: Kaunitz and the Catherinian Empire in the 1770s," *Canadian Slavonic Papers* 22 (1980): 451–69.

The Austro-Russian agreement left Prussia without a major ally. As already mentioned, Prussia sought closer ties with France[16] and joined the League of Armed Neutrality, but for several years she still had little diplomatic influence. Austria ended her own diplomatic isolation, but at the price of having to support Empress Catherine's projects. Panin's career ended with the breaking of the Prussian alliance that was the centerpiece of the Northern system; he left on a vacation which became permanent. Catherine now totally reoriented Russian diplomacy. She had made an ally of the power that was the greatest obstacle to her dreams of driving the Turks from Europe, capturing Constantinople, and establishing a Russian client state in the Balkans.[17] Vergennes, who guessed the existence of the Russo-Austrian alliance, feared as much and warned his ambassador in Spain that the Turks were in danger.[18]

The French foreign minister did not have long to wait before his fears were realized. In May 1782 the pro-Russian khan was driven from the Crimea.[19] The French ambassador in St. Petersburg soon warned of Russian preparations for war, and that autumn Russian troops captured the Crimea.[20] Catherine offered Emperor Joseph a share in the spoils if he would support her plans for wider acquisitions. Joseph, frightened by his new ally's ambitions, demanded that France (his other ally) also be included and offered her Egypt—an offer probably designed to be refused so that Austria would have an excuse not to support Russia.[21] In spite of Joseph's caution, there was a clear threat of a major war in eastern Europe that might destroy or seriously dam-

16. See above, chapter 15, note 11.

17. Madariaga, *Russia in the Age of Catherine the Great*, 383–88.

18. Dull, *French Navy and American Independence*, 216.

19. Alan W. Fisher, *The Russian Annexation of the Crimea, 1772–1783* (Cambridge: Cambridge University Press, 1970), 125–27.

20. Salomon, *La Politique orientale de Vergennes*, 106–52; Fisher, *Russian Annexation of the Crimea*, 128–30.

21. Madariaga, *Russia in the Age of Catherine the Great*, 387–88; Karl A. Roider, Jr., *Austria's Eastern Question, 1700–1790* (Princeton, N.J.: Princeton University Press, 1982), 162–64; Orville T. Murphy, *Charles Gravier, Comte de Vergennes: French Diplomacy in the Age of Revolution, 1719–1787* (Albany: State University of New York Press, 1982), 318–20.

age the Ottoman Empire, one of France's oldest friends. The terrible dangers posed by the Crimean crisis form the background to the 1782 negotiations which ended the American war. The frenzied French search for peace cannot be understood in isolation from that crisis, although, as we shall see, France had other pressing reasons to desire a quick end to the war with Britain. Vergennes had gambled that such a war would improve France's position in continental diplomacy before the danger from Russia revived. The gamble had failed.

PART FIVE
The Making of Peace

CHAPTER 17

The Opening of Negotiations

In March 1782 Lord North's government was replaced by a government headed by the former Opposition leader, the marquis of Rockingham (1730–82).[1] Rockingham had had previous experience in pacifying the Americans; he had headed the cabinet of 1765–66 that repealed the Stamp Act. He was no more forceful a chief minister, however, than North had been; like his predecessor, he left foreign affairs to the secretaries of state. Theoretically it should have been easier to achieve a unified foreign policy than had previously been the case. The old northern and southern departments were combined, so that Britain finally had a single secretary of state for foreign affairs. In practice, however, the situation became worse. The office of secretary of state for American affairs, formerly held by Germain, retained its independence under the amended title "secretary of state for home and colonial affairs." Rockingham's two secretaries of state soon began a fierce struggle for control of the peace negotiations with America, a struggle embittered by deep philosophical, political, and personal differences.

The secretary of state for foreign affairs was the great orator Charles James Fox (1749–1806). Young Fox, totally inexperienced in conducting foreign affairs, was vehemently anti-French and favored a quick grant of independence to the United States, so Britain could better fight France, Spain, and the Netherlands.

1. See Ross J. S. Hoffman, *The Marquis: A Study of Lord Rockingham, 1730–1782* (New York: Fordham University Press, 1973).

With an amazing lack of realism he attempted to procure alliances with both Prussia and Russia.[2] The secretary of state for home and colonial affairs was the earl of Shelburne (1737–1805), political heir to William Pitt, earl of Chatham, and a former secretary of state for the southern department (1766–68).[3] He hoped, as Pitt had hoped, that Britain could preserve some link with America; in terms of jurisdiction, this would place the American negotiations under his control rather than Fox's. He might have been expected to share his colleague's anti-French feelings, since as secretary of state he formerly had taken a hard line against the French annexation of Corsica.[4] In actuality he proved to be less prejudiced against France than any British statesman in decades. Partly this was due to his friendship with French intellectuals like the abbé Morellet; in greater part, perhaps, it reflected his desire for a stable peace in which to realize his goals of domestic political reform and the restoration of British trade, particularly with America.[5]

Opinion in Parliament and among its constituents reflected the confusion in Rockingham's cabinet. There was a general desire to end the war with America but considerable reluctance to recognize American independence, a desire to reduce taxes but a strong desire for revenge on France and Spain, despair about military possibilities in America but growing optimism that Brit-

2. Isabel de Madariaga, *Britain, Russia and the Armed Neutrality of 1780: Sir James Harris's Mission to St. Petersburg during the American Revolution* (New Haven: Yale University Press, 1962), 387–412.

3. The fullest biography of him, although it is very flawed, is Lord Edmond Fitzmaurice, *Life of William, Earl of Shelburne, Afterwards First Marquis of Landsdowne with Extracts from His Papers and Correspondence*, rev. ed., 2 vols. (London: Macmillan and Co., 1912). For his role in the peace negotiations, see Vincent T. Harlow, *The Founding of the Second British Empire, 1763–1793*, vol. 1: *Discovery and Revolution* (London: Longmans, Green and Co., 1952), 223–447, and Charles R. Ritcheson, "The Earl of Shelburne and Peace with America, 1782–1783: Vision and Reality," *International History Review* 5 (1983): 322–45.

4. Nicholas Tracy, "The Administration of the Duke of Grafton and the French Invasion of Corsica," *Eighteenth-Century Studies* 8 (1974–75): 169–82.

5. Ritcheson, "Earl of Shelburne and Peace with America," 329–30; John Norris, *Shelburne and Reform* (London: Macmillan and Co.; New York: St. Martin's Press, 1963).

ain could take from her other enemies recompense for her lost colonies. Without American insistence on a general peace, it can be doubted that Fox would have bothered to negotiate with Britain's European enemies.

In the struggle to control the American negotiations Shelburne had the initial advantage. Even before news of North's fall reached Paris, Franklin wrote his old acquaintance Shelburne to thank him for giving some gooseberry bushes to one of Franklin's neighbors in Passy and to express his pleasure at the changed political disposition of Britain.[6] This, of course, was a hint too broad for Shelburne to miss. As soon as he joined the cabinet, the new secretary of state responded by sending to talk with Franklin an elderly amateur diplomat, Richard Oswald (1705–84).[7] Oswald, a Scot, combined a philosophical liberalism designed to appeal to Franklin with the astuteness for which his countrymen are renowned. Franklin welcomed Shelburne's call for negotiations, expressed his approval of Oswald, and took his visitor to meet Vergennes. Fox was not willing to surrender; quickly he sent his own representative to initiate discussions with both the Americans and the French. His selection was Thomas Grenville (1755–1846), son of the former chief minister George Grenville, whose superb political connections were recompense for his lack of experience.[8]

For several months the British negotiators had only Benjamin Franklin with whom to deal. John Adams, summoned by Franklin to assume his duties on the peace commission, decided to remain in the Netherlands to complete negotiations for a treaty of amity and commerce.[9] John Jay arrived from Spain in late June

6. Albert Henry Smyth, ed., *The Writings of Benjamin Franklin*, 10 vols. (New York: Macmillan Co., 1907), 8:460–61.

7. Ibid., 461–63. For Oswald's role in the negotiations, see Charles R. Ritcheson, "Britain's Peacemakers, 1782–1783: 'To an Astonishing Degree Unfit for the Task'?," in Ronald Hoffman and Peter J. Albert, eds., *Peace and the Peacemakers: The Treaty of 1783* (Charlottesville: University Press of Virginia, forthcoming).

8. For Grenville's role in the negotiations, see Lord John Russell, ed., *Memorials and Correspondence of Charles James Fox*, 4 vols. (London: Richard Bentley, 1853–57), 4:174–279.

9. Smyth, *Writings of Benjamin Franklin*, 8:480–81. James H. Hutson, *John Adams and the Diplomacy of the American Revolution* (Lexington: University

1782 but soon was bedridden with influenza,[10] while Henry
Laurens, now released from captivity in Britain, declined to
serve.[11] The last commissioner, Thomas Jefferson, had not yet
left the United States. Franklin hoped, like Shelburne, for a gen-
uine reconciliation between Britain and the United States, but
he was adamant in his refusal to compromise on the issue of
American independence.[12] He argued that a liberal peace settlement by Britain would assist Anglo-American friendship and
even suggested, rather imprudently, that Britain cede Canada to
the United States in the interest of good relations.[13] Fortunately
Shelburne, who rejected the proposal, complied with Franklin's
request for secrecy rather than using it to foster suspicion between France and the United States. Franklin's attitude, however, indicated the improbability of preserving America as part of
the British Empire. Within Rockingham's cabinet the main issue
in the American negotiation became the terms on which independence would be granted. Fox favored an immediate grant in
the expectation that the United States then would promptly drop
out of the war. Shelburne, more cautious, was willing to recognize American independence only as part of a comprehensive
peace settlement with the United States.[14] Until King George
III and the cabinet as a whole resolved the conflict, the American
negotiations could not proceed.

Franklin, who does not seem to have realized the nature of the
dispute between Fox and Shelburne, had chosen to negotiate

Press of Kentucky, 1980), 102–16, describes Adams's negotiations with the
Dutch.

10. Richard B. Morris, *The Peacemakers: The Great Powers and American Independence* (New York, Evanston and London: Harper & Row, 1965), 282–87.

11. Smyth, *Writings of Benjamin Franklin*, 8:481–82, 503–05; David Duncan
Wallace, *The Life of Henry Laurens with a Sketch of the Life of Lieutenant-
Colonel John Laurens* (New York and London: G. P. Putnam's Sons, 1915),
394–402.

12. Gerald Stourzh, *Benjamin Franklin and American Foreign Policy*, rev. ed.
(Chicago and London: University of Chicago Press, 1969), 186–213.

13. Smyth, *Writings of Benjamin Franklin*, 8:469–73.

14. Ritcheson, "Earl of Shelburne and Peace with America," 331–38; Harlow,
Founding of the Second British Empire, 1:247–57.

through Oswald with the latter.[15] He eventually managed to convince Shelburne that if Britain offered sufficiently generous peace terms America would help Britain to reach agreement with France and Spain by threatening to make a separate peace. (Such a threat would force France and Spain to be reasonable in their demands, enabling Britain to make peace with all her enemies.) At the same time Franklin took care not to make any direct statement that might compromise relations with France, on whom the United States was still economically dependent. Franklin played this delicate double game with great subtlety.

Meanwhile, Grenville's negotiations with Vergennes also were stalemated. From early May to mid-June negotiations were delayed until Grenville received authorization to deal also with Spain and the Netherlands (to whom Vergennes would transmit the British proposals).[16] A second obstacle was Grenville's insistence on using the hated Treaty of Paris of 1763 as a basis for negotiations. Vergennes finally reluctantly accepted in order to speed the discussions. While these obstacles were being removed, news reached Europe of a major war development in the Caribbean. Admiral de Grasse, the victor at Yorktown, had suffered a major defeat near a small group of islands south of Guadeloupe called the Saintes. Seven ships of the line had been lost, de Grasse captured, and plans disrupted for a joint Franco-Spanish attack on Jamaica.[17] Soon increasingly ominous news also began arriving from the French ambassador at St. Petersburg, warning of the impending crisis in the Crimea. There was little Vergennes could do, however, to speed the negotiations. Given the huge differences to be resolved, for the time being he could hope for little more than to keep the negotiations alive. To do so

15. William Temple Franklin, ed., *Memoirs of the Life and Writings of Benjamin Franklin, LL.D.*, 3 vols. (London: Henry Colburn, 1818), 2:389–90; Russell, *Memorials and Correspondence of Charles James Fox*, 4:253–55; Smyth, *Writings of Benjamin Franklin*, 8:528–29.

16. Jonathan R. Dull, *The French Navy and American Independence: A Study of Arms and Diplomacy, 1774–1787* (Princeton, N.J.: Princeton University Press, 1975), 282, 288–89.

17. Ibid., 283–84.

he began by concentrating on the relatively simple issue of the boundary between the French and British fishing zones off Newfoundland.[18]

Vergennes's difficulties were compounded by the necessity of seeing that France's allies were also satisfied. With his blessings the Americans undertook separate negotiations with Britain.[19] The Netherlands was in such a weak position that France, occupying key Dutch colonies like the Cape colony of Africa, eventually could bargain on their behalf. Spain, however, was such an important ally that France could not hope to reach an agreement with Britain without her concurrence. Thus far the Spaniards had been surprisingly successful in the war, capturing Minorca and West Florida in 1781, as well as repulsing a British attack on Central America. Nonetheless, Spain had not achieved her major objective, the capture of Gibraltar, although she had blockaded the fortress by land and sea since her entry into the war. She was now preparing an assault on it, in which newly designed floating gun batteries would be used to silence the British cannon and prepare the way for the final attack by Spanish troops.[20] Spanish ambassador Aranda, responsible for conducting discussions with Grenville, was ordered to do nothing substantive until the attack.[21]

Although the Dutch negotiations were less critical, they were no further advanced. Attempts to reach a separate agreement with Britain had broken down in March. Fox's willingness to compromise on the issue of neutral trade regulations if Russia would ally with Britain gave promise of removing a major source of dispute with the Netherlands, but this too failed.[22] The Dutch terms for making peace were wildly unrealistic, and it was August 1782 before they named a peace commissioner, Gerard

18. Jonathan R. Dull, "Vergennes, Rayneval and the Diplomacy of Trust," in Hoffman and Albert, *Peace and the Peacemakers*, forthcoming.

19. Smyth, *Writings of Benjamin Franklin*, 8:513.

20. Dull, *French Navy and American Independence*, 270, 278, 307.

21. Ibid., 292.

22. Hutson, *John Adams and the Diplomacy of the American Revolution*, 105–08; Madariaga, *Britain, Russia and the Armed Neutrality*, 337–52, 387–412.

Brantsen (1734-1809), to join their aged ambassador at the French court, Mattheus Lestevenon van Berkenrode (1719–97).[23] The first break in the various impasses came at the end of June. Fox had overreached himself and incurred King George III's distrust. In a climactic battle in the British cabinet, Shelburne finally defeated him on the issue of the American negotiations.[24] On the following day Shelburne's position was even more drastically altered. On that day, July 1, 1782, Rockingham died of influenza. The king immediately asked Shelburne to form a new government.[25] Henceforth the negotiations would be Shelburne's, not as secretary of state, but as George III's chief minister and head of the cabinet.

23. Dull, *French Navy and American Independence*, 292; F. J. L. Krämer, *Archives ou correspondance inédite de la maison d'Orange-Nassau. Cinquième série (1766–1789)*, 3 vols. (Leyden: A. J. Sijthoff, 1910–15), 3:130–31; Orville T. Murphy, *Charles Gravier, Comte de Vergennes: French Diplomacy in the Age of Revolution, 1719–1787* (Albany: State University of New York Press, 1982), 326–27; Jan Willem Schulte Nordholt, *The Dutch Republic and American Independence*, trans. Herbert H. Rowen (Chapel Hill: University of North Carolina Press, 1982), 198–200.

24. Harlow, *Founding of the Second British Empire*, 1:258–63.

25. Sir John Fortescue, ed., *The Correspondence of King George the Third from 1760 to December 1783*, 6 vols. (London: Macmillan and Co., 1927–28), 6:71.

CHAPTER 18

The Americans
Reach Agreement

Shelburne as chief minister exercised direct personal control of the negotiations with both France and the United States. His secretary of state for home and colonial affairs, Thomas Townshend (1733–1800), played a relatively minor role in the American negotiations. To deal with France Shelburne chose two professional diplomats, Baron Grantham (1738–86) as his secretary of state for foreign affairs and Alleyne Fitzherbert (1753–1839) as his representative at the French court; but here as well the chief minister himself guided policy.[1] He retained Oswald as his representative with the Americans, although he also sent a mutual friend, Franklin's editor Benjamin Vaughan, to reassure the American peace commissioner of his good intentions.[2]

Franklin now moved to conclude the negotiations. On July 10 he read for Oswald his list of "necessary" and "advisable" articles for a peace treaty and implied that acceptance of at least the former was an ultimatum. The "necessary" articles were full and complete American independence, acceptable American bound-

1. For Fitzherbert's mission, see L. G. Wickham Legg, *British Diplomatic Instructions, 1689–1789*, vol. 7: *France, part IV, 1745–1798* (London: Royal Society, 1934 [Camden third series, vol. 49]), 179–247.
2. Vincent T. Harlow, *The Founding of the Second British Empire, 1763–1793*, vol. 1: *Discovery and Revolution* (London: Longmans, Green and Co., 1952), 271–72. Page 264n gives a reasonable appraisal of Vaughan's limited role in the negotiations; for his correspondence, see Charles C. Smith, ed., "Letters of Benjamin Vaughan to the Earl of Shelburne," *Massachusetts Historical Society Proceedings*, 2nd ser., 17 (1903): 406–38.

aries and fishing rights off Newfoundland and elsewhere; "advisable" articles were an acknowledgment by Britain of her war guilt, compensation for damages, the transfer to the United States of all of Canada, and freedom from British customs duties for American goods and shipping.[3]

At the end of July Shelburne finally capitulated to the necessity of accepting American independence. Oswald was given new instructions authorizing the British acknowledgment provided that America became fully independent of France as well; moreover, Shelburne wrote to Oswald privately that he was prepared to make a peace on the basis of Franklin's "necessary" articles.[4] It is important to realize that Franklin won this victory not because America's bargaining position was so strong, but rather because Shelburne was so anxious for peace. Indeed, he might even have surrendered what is today southern Ontario had Franklin pushed for it.[5] By showering the Americans with concessions he hoped to cause France, Spain, and the Netherlands to face the necessity of concluding peace on reasonable terms lest the Americans make a separate peace, thereby freeing tens of thousands of British troops for military operations against the West Indies. Shelburne's generous treatment of America may also have been partly conditioned by the expectation that America would continue to be economically dependent on Great Britain, in which case the granting of generous boundaries to her would do Britain no economic harm.[6]

3. Samuel Flagg Bemis, *The Diplomacy of the American Revolution*, rev. ed. (Bloomington: Indiana University Press, 1957), 207–08; Harlow, *Founding of the Second British Empire*, 1:269.

4. Ibid., 1:273–76; Lord John Russell, ed., *Memorials and Correspondence of Charles James Fox*, 4 vols. (London: Richard Bentley, 1853–57), 4:262–65, 267–73; Lord Edmond Fitzmaurice, *Life of William, Earl of Shelburne, Afterwards First Marquis of Lansdowne, with Extracts from His Papers and Correspondence*, rev. ed. (London: Macmillan and Co., 1912), 2: 167–69.

5. Bradford Perkins, "The Peace of Paris: Patterns and Legacies," in Ronald Hoffman and Peter J. Albert, eds., *Peace and the Peacemakers: The Treaty of 1783* (Charlottesville: University Press of Virginia, forthcoming); see also Harlow, *Founding of the Second British Empire*, 1: 275.

6. For conflicting interpretations of Shelburne's motivation, compare ibid., 1:146–447, to Charles R. Ritcheson, "The Earl of Shelburne and Peace with

A few issues remained to be negotiated, particularly American compensation for Loyalists, which Shelburne needed for his political survival. (Unfortunately, this was an issue on which Franklin, the father of a Loyalist, was too embittered to reciprocate Shelburne's generosity, even had he had the authority to do so.) In spite of the potential difficulties, a quick agreement might have been reached had not John Jay, recovered from his influenza, rejoined the negotiations.[7] Jay balked at negotiating with Oswald because the latter's commission to deal with the Americans did not acknowledge the United States as an independent country. Jay feared a British trick, and Franklin, hating to argue with his friends, agreed to suspend the talks. Franklin then fell so ill with kidney stone that he feared for his life, leaving the negotiations entirely in Jay's hands. The younger American became consumed with the suspicion that France and Britain were preparing to strike a bargain at America's expense. Jay was already mistrustful of France because of Joseph-Mathias Gérard de Rayneval's attempts to mediate conflicting American and Spanish claims to the lands between the Appalachians and the Mississippi.[8]

The issue of these western lands was among the most important topics in the peace talks. The area in question now forms all or part of eleven states (Minnesota, Wisconsin, Michigan, Illinois, Indiana, Ohio, Kentucky, Tennessee, Mississippi, Alabama, and Georgia). Franklin was no less insistent than Jay that

America, 1782–1783: Vision and Reality," *International History Review* 5 (1983): 322–45.

7. The following account of Jay's role in the negotiations follows the same arguments as Jonathan R. Dull, *Franklin the Diplomat: The French Mission* (Philadelphia: American Philosophical Society, 1982 [*Transactions* 72: part 1]), 53–64. A vastly most positive appraisal of Jay's performance and a detailed day-by-day account of the American-British negotiations is given by Richard B. Morris, *The Peacemakers: The Great Powers and American Independence* (New York, Evanston and London: Harper & Row, 1965), 248–385.

8. A full, although hardly unbiased, treatment of Rayneval's attempt to mediate the Jay-Aranda negotiations can be found in Samuel Flagg Bemis, "The Rayneval Memoranda of 1782 on Western Boundaries and Some Comments on the French Historian Doniol," *Proceedings of the American Antiquarian Society* 47 (1937): 15–92.

the United States extended to the Mississippi and, indeed, was entitled to Britain's right of navigation there (under the terms of the 1763 Treaty of Paris), even though Spain controlled both banks of the lower river. About giving up such a right he wrote, "A Neighbor might as well ask me to sell my Street Door."[9] No other country had so strong a commitment to acquiring the area. Spain possessed an adjacent post at St. Louis and had sent an expedition to establish a claim by capturing Fort St. Joseph (now St. Joseph, Michigan), but the area was less important to her than was Gibraltar, West Florida, or Minorca. Britain herself held the most important posts in the area, particularly Detroit; but without an assured access to the sea she too was uninterested. Had Spain been willing to part with New Orleans, Shelburne might have been willing to give Spain something in exchange and keep the area; when Spain declined, Shelburne was willing to give up British claims to the American West in hopes of reciprocal American concessions (such as on the Loyalist issue).[10] France had no direct interest in the area, although one suspects that, given her choice, she would have preferred to have the West left, like Canada, in British hands so as to increase American dependence on the French alliance.[11] France's main concern, however, was a quick peace so she could devote full attention to the impending crisis in eastern Europe. Rayneval, hence, was honestly attempting to find a compromise solution for who should exercise sovereignty over an area in which the strongest military presence was that of the native Indian tribes.

9. Albert Henry Smyth, ed., *The Writings of Benjamin Franklin*, 10 vols. (New York: Macmillan Co., 1907), 8:144. During the war Spain had permitted Americans access to the lower river.

10. For the proposed exchange of New Orleans, see Jonathan R. Dull, *The French Navy and American Independence: A Study of Arms and Diplomacy, 1774–1787* (Princeton, N.J.: Princeton University Press, 1975), 328. For opposition in Britain and Canada to the surrender of the area, see Charles R. Ritcheson, *Aftermath of Revolution: British Policy toward the United States, 1783–1795* (Dallas: Southern Methodist University Press, 1969), 75. Shelburne's belief that the area would remain economically dependent on Britain is discussed above.

11. For further discussion, see Jonathan R. Dull, "Vergennes, Rayneval and the Diplomacy of Trust," in Hoffman and Albert, *Peace and the Peacemakers*, forthcoming.

The French had little respect for the United States' legal claim to the area; Rayneval later hinted to the British France's willingness to support British claims in the region, although Shelburne wisely refrained from accepting the help.[12]

In mid-August Rayneval suddenly left for London. As we shall see in the next chapter, his mission to England basically was unrelated to America, but to Jay it seemed a clear confirmation of his suspicions about an impending Franco-British separate agreement. Simultaneously, the British leaked to him an intercepted letter from Luzerne's secretary in Philadelphia, which indicated, in a rather exaggerated manner, that France was hostile to American claims of Newfoundland fishing rights.[13] Without consulting Franklin, Jay now sent Benjamin Vaughan to inform Shelburne that the United States was prepared to abandon the French alliance. Soon thereafter the impasse in the Anglo-American negotiations was broken. Jay, a former lawyer, won his point; Oswald received a new commission mentioning by name the United States. In real terms, however, the victory was illusory, since Britain remained free to disclaim that Oswald's commission constituted formal British recognition of American independence.[14] Moreover, Jay's nominal triumph was won at a substantial cost. During the seven-week break in negotiations the Spaniards had attacked Gibraltar and failed. The war party in Parliament had been so strengthened that Shelburne's freedom to offer diplomatic concessions was circumscribed. Furthermore, when formal negotiations with Oswald resumed in October, Jay began by making his own damaging concessions on boundaries and fishing rights.[15] Soon Oswald was reinforced by a seasoned undersecretary of state, Henry Strachey, while Jay was joined by Franklin, now sufficiently healthy to resume public affairs, and by Adams,

---

12. Harlow, *Founding of the Second British Empire*, 1:284, 301.

13. Orville T. Murphy, *Charles Gravier, Comte de Vergennes: French Diplomacy in the Age of Revolution, 1719–1787* (Albany: State University of New York Press, 1982), 379–81.

14. Jay's part in this stage of the negotiations is treated by Harlow, *Founding of the Second British Empire*, 1:276–87.

15. James H. Hutson, *John Adams and the Diplomacy of the American Revolution* (Lexington: University Press of Kentucky, 1980), 124–25.

who arrived from the Netherlands after concluding the Dutch-American Treaty of Amity and Commerce.[16]

Before being joined by his colleagues, Jay had the opportunity to avenge himself on the Spaniards. He encouraged the British to recapture Pensacola from Spain. Luckily the British did not take up his suggestion, in part because Adams and Franklin later refused to promise safe passage from New York for British troops.[17] Jay's proposal was extraordinarily shortsighted. Once recaptured, Florida likely would have remained British, with enormous future consequences to the United States. (Among other things, it would have made the suppression of the Confederacy much more difficult.) It is also an example of the all-too-common American self-righteous contempt for other nations. Spain had made an indispensable contribution to American independence, but even had this not been the case Jay's solicitation of an attack on her would have been an act of bad faith. Although the British made no move to capture West Florida, a secret article in the preliminary peace agreement with Britain promised more extensive boundaries to the area if it were British than if it remained Spanish.[18] This part of the agreement caused great concern in the Continental Congress, which feared the alliance with France would be endangered if the French learned of it. As it happened, when Britain made peace with Spain all of Florida was assigned to the Spaniards. Their agreement did not discuss Florida's northern boundary and thus implicitly confirmed Spain's right to the existing, more extensive borders and thereby contradicted Britain's agreement with the United States;[19] the

16. For which see ibid., 108–16, and Friedrich Edler, *The Dutch Republic and the American Revolution* (Baltimore: Johns Hopkins Press, 1911 [*Johns Hopkins University Studies in Historical and Political Science*, ser. 29, no. 2]), 222–32.

17. Dull, *Franklin the Diplomat*, 59. For evidence of British interest in Jay's proposal, see Godfrey Davies and Marion Tinling, "The Independence of America: Six Unpublished Items on the Treaty in 1782–1783," *Huntington Library Quarterly* 12 (1948–49): 219 and J. Leitch Wright, Jr., *Britain and the American Frontier, 1783–1818* (Athens, Ga. University of Georgia Press, 1975), 9–10.

18. See Appendix 2 for the text of the preliminary agreement.

19. Irving Brant, *James Madison: The Nationalist, 1780–1787* (New York and Indianapolis: Bobbs-Merrill Co., 1948), 269–79; Lawrence S. Kaplan, *Colonies into Nation: American Diplomacy, 1763–1801* (New York and London: Macmil-

dispute was left for the United States and Spain to settle. (With poetic justice, the agonizing discussions had to be conducted by the then American secretary for foreign affairs, John Jay.)

The final British-American discussions of October-November 1782 gave abundant opportunities to such skilled lawyers as Adams and Jay and such a skilled negotiator as Franklin. (Henry Laurens also finally joined his fellow peace commissioners for the final negotiating session.) Agreement at last was reached on November 30. The United States received boundaries to her liking, fishing rights with some right to dry fish on shore, and a share in the British right to navigation of the Mississippi (although Spain's consent to the arrangement had not been asked). Above all, the British acknowledged American independence and promised to withdraw their troops. They received little in exchange except the American agreement to honor their debts and a vague promise that Congress would recommend to the states fair treatment for the Loyalists.

The terms represented a considerable triumph for the American commissioners, but their victory was partly illusory. As we have seen, it was based less on American strength than on Shelburne's desire to pressure Britain's other enemies into making peace and his wish for close ties between Britain and the United States. As such, it was affected by Shelburne's fall from office in early 1783, caused largely by the perception that he had been too generous to Britain's enemies. His successors could not repudiate the agreement or refuse to evacuate New York. On the other hand, they were hardly willing to interpret the agreement in America's favor. Ambiguities such as the precise location of the northeast border of the United States or the exact nature of American fishing rights remained for decades to bedevil American-British relations.[20] Furthermore, America's failure to comply with her requirements to the Loyalists and to British credi-

---

lan Co., 1972), 168. The agreement between Britain and Spain is discussed below in the next chapter. Their final treaty is printed in *The Remembrancer* 16 (1783): 329–33.

20. Richard B. Morris, "The Durable Significance of the Treaty of 1783," in Hoffman and Albert, *Peace and the Peacemakers*, forthcoming.

tors gave Britain an excuse not to evacuate nine frontier posts within the United States, issues not resolved until 1794.

The agreement of November 30 was conditional, in theory not coming into effect until Britain and France had also reached agreement. In practice, the news of the preliminary agreement was almost universally regarded in America as the end of the war. (The Continental Congress was thereby left in an embarrassing position until two weeks later news arrived of a British agreement with France, Spain, and the Netherlands.)[21] It was thus a clear violation of the spirit, if not the letter, of Congress's instructions to the peace commissioners to consult the French before taking action. Franklin, knowing he would be outvoted by Jay and Adams, had urged his colleagues to do so. Once the preliminary agreement was signed, Franklin apologized for the American "breach of etiquette" and with astonishing nerve requested—and received—a further loan of six million livres tournois from the French government.[22]

Vergennes and Rayneval were amazed by the extent of Shelburne's concessions to the Americans.[23] France had little interest in who received the American West or, for that matter, whether the Americans shared fishing rights in the *British* zone of Newfoundland. In one sense the agreement advanced the peace France so urgently needed by putting additional pressure on Spain. In a more immediate sense, however, the American betrayal of the French alliance endangered the process of peacemaking by unraveling a complex agreement between Britain, Spain, and France laboriously knitted by Vergennes. I next will examine how Britain and her other enemies finally negotiated a settlement and brought to an end the War for American Independence.

21. William C. Stinchcombe, *The American Revolution and the French Alliance* (Syracuse, N.Y.: Syracuse University Press, 1969), 197–99.

22. Dull, *Franklin the Diplomat*, 60–61. Franklin's actual expression in his apology was for "neglecting a point of *bienséance.*"

23. Dull, *French Navy and American Independence*, 325.

CHAPTER 19

The European Settlement

As we have seen, Shelburne moved at the end of July 1782 to reach a settlement with the United States. Within the next two weeks he also moved to unfreeze the negotiations with France. He met with Admiral de Grasse, who had been sent to England as a prisoner of war after the Battle of the Saintes. According to the admiral's later testimony, Shelburne announced to him that he was willing to grant unconditional independence to the United States, to refrain from further conquests from the Netherlands and satisfy her wishes by accepting the principles of the League of Armed Neutrality, and to permit Spain to have West Florida and either Gibraltar or Minorca. Supposedly he was also willing to satisfy virtually all of France's war aims: restitution of the Caribbean island of Saint Lucia (captured by Britain in 1778), retention by France of two West Indian islands she had captured, an end to prohibitions on France's fortifying Dunkirk, improved fishing rights off Newfoundland, a colonial establishment in Africa to support the slave trade to the West Indies, and a return to France's position in India of 1763 or 1748. De Grasse was released from captivity and on August 15 arrived in Paris with the report of his conversation with Shelburne.[1]

1. Jonathan R. Dull, "Vergennes, Rayneval and the Diplomacy of Trust," in Ronald Hoffman and Peter J. Albert, eds., *Peace and the Peacemakers: The Treaty of 1783* (Charlottesville: University Press of Virginia, forthcoming). Shelburne's account of the meeting differs considerably: Sir John Fortescue, ed., *The Correspondence of King George the Third from 1760 to December 1783*, 6 vols. (London: Macmillan and Co., 1927–28), 6:99.

Vergennes and the French council of state had ample reason to welcome a British peace initiative. Over the summer the news from Russia and the Crimea had grown increasingly ominous, while simultaneously evidence mounted that the French war effort against Britain was disintegrating. The ships lost off the Saintes could be replaced, but for France and Spain to retain the military initiative it was necessary to attempt another attack on Jamaica. Elaborate plans were made for them to send massive reinforcements from Europe as soon as the attack on Gibraltar was over. Now news arrived that de Grasse's successor had agreed to a temporary dispersal of forces already in the Caribbean, meaning that the British would hold an interior position between the various components of the invasion flotilla. It also was becoming apparent that the French navy lacked the experienced officers and crews to man its increased number of warships; in a skirmish off the coast a new ship of the line surrendered to the British with hardly a fight. As Vergennes told his ambassador in Madrid: "The English have to some degree regenerated their navy while ours has been used up. Construction has not been at all equivalent to consumption; the supply of good sailors is exhausted and the officers show a lassitude in war which contrasts in a disadvantageous way with the energy which not only the sailors but the entire English nation eagerly manifests." Finally, in both Spain and France there was the increasing danger of state bankruptcy, which could cut off the flow of food and supplies from private business contractors to the armed forces.[2]

However anxious he was for peace, Vergennes distrusted Shelburne, whose reputation for duplicity (whether deserved or undeserved) was unsurpassed in British politics. In order to play for time, he asked de Grasse to thank Shelburne for his courteous treatment and tell him that, although his proposals seemed capable of leading to peace, King Louis XVI needed to consult King Charles of Spain before responding. In order to ascertain Shel-

2. Jonathan R. Dull, *The French Navy and American Independence: A Study of Arms and Diplomacy, 1774–1787* (Princeton, N.J.: Princeton University Press, 1975), 278–80, 297–302; quotation is from pp. 316–317.

burne's sincerity, a representative would have to be sent to meet with him; Spanish approval of the mission was solicited and received in early September.

Vergennes chose Gérard de Rayneval to go to England. The undersecretary of state was familiar with both the western lands question and the Newfoundland fishery issue. More importantly, he and his fellow undersecretary P.-M. Hennin were Vergennes's most trusted and knowledgeable subordinates. Rayneval's instructions were clear. His mission was to establish the accuracy of de Grasse's report. If Shelburne disavowed the proposals he was said to have made, Rayneval was to return immediately home. If, however, Shelburne acknowledged their accuracy, Rayneval could discuss them unofficially; this should take no more than eight to ten days. In theory the mission was simple, even for a diplomat who had not served outside the French court for eight years and whose previous service had been limited to Danzig and a few minor German courts. In fact, Rayneval's mission became the hinge on which turned the entire future of the peace negotiations; he later admitted that had he foreseen its delicacy he would not have had the courage to undertake it.[3]

The Rayneval-Shelburne discussions were held at Bowood, the chief minister's country estate. At their first meeting, September 13, Shelburne began by praising Vergennes and by speaking of the desire for peace which he, Shelburne, shared with King George III. When presented with de Grasse's memorandum, however, Shelburne denied having said what it reported. According to his orders, Rayneval should have broken off the discussions. Instead, when Shelburne volunteered to discuss the proposals anyway, the Frenchman remained. By that afternoon the discussions had become so detailed that maps were needed. Rayneval's flexibility had preserved the chance of breaking the diplomatic deadlock and ending the killing—on that very day the Spaniards unsuccessfully attacked Gibraltar. Furthermore, as

3. Ibid., 303–05. Rayneval's instructions are given in Henri Doniol, ed., *Histoire de la participation de la France à l'établissement des Etats-Unis d'Amérique: Correspondance diplomatique et documents*, 5 vols. and supplement (Paris: Imprimerie Nationale, 1886–99), 5:105–06.

Rayneval and Shelburne grew to trust each other, they established a bridge between the suspicious Vergennes and King
George III.

Shelburne was able to win Rayneval's confidence by arguing
that a reconciled France and Britain would become arbiters of
the peace of Europe. He claimed that in 1768, when he had resigned as secretary of state, he had wished to concert with France
a firm and decisive language toward Russia and Prussia so as to
prevent the partition of Poland. It is unlikely that Shelburne's
recollections were accurate—his main concern as the southern
secretary had been *French* expansion—but they were the perfect way to win over the former opponent of the Polish partition.
Rayneval remained in England for a week of discussions with
Shelburne and Foreign Secretary Grantham and then returned
to France convinced of Shelburne's sincerity.[4]

Vergennes was not wholly persuaded, but the hint of possible
help in eastern Europe was too tantalizing for him to resist. He
soon urged on Spain a quick peace so that they and Britain could
rescue the Turks (a cause to which the Spaniards showed su-
preme indifference). He also began a steady retreat on France's
own war demands, so as to concentrate on mediating a settlement between Britain and Spain. In so doing, he increased the
enmity of Naval Minister Castries, an advocate of French gains in
India, to which he had sent numerous ships and an expeditionary
corps. Castries sarcastically advised King Louis XVI to hold no
more meetings to discuss peace terms, as every meeting cost
France another colony.[5]

It was not until November that Spain moderated her peace demands. (She was motivated by the failure at Gibraltar and perhaps also by the resumption of the talks between Britain and the
United States.) The change in the Spanish diplomatic position,
however, was accompanied by a new demand on France. Ambassador Aranda brought a proposal to Vergennes. Spain would
transfer to France her large but undeveloped colony of Santo
Domingo (now the Dominican Republic), in return for which

4. For Rayneval's account of the meetings, see ibid., 5:603–26.
5. Dull, "Vergennes, Rayneval and the Diplomacy of Trust," forthcoming.

France would offer Britain an equivalent for Gibraltar (which would be given to Spain). Aranda suggested, to Vergennes's shock, that Corsica might be offered to Britain. If France refused to cooperate, it was clear that Spain would offer to trade Santo Domingo to Britain, endangering the enormously valuable adjoining French colony of St. Domingue.

France had little choice but to accept. Unless peace were made quickly, more years of war would be inevitable. Parliament was due to reconvene on November 26, after which Shelburne's political opponents would make it all the more difficult for him to negotiate. Moreover, a huge French and Spanish fleet was gathering at Cadiz to participate in the coming attack on Jamaica. Admiral d'Estaing, in spite of his failures in America, was named to command the fleet. The unfortunate admiral was ordered by the council of state to delay its sailing as long as possible and to attempt to convince the Spanish court of the dangers of the attack.[6]

Aranda was not the easiest of men with whom to deal (as Jay recently had learned), but he was a wise and experienced ambassador. At his suggestion Vergennes sent Rayneval back to bargain with Shelburne. When their discussions began on November 20, Shelburne was in a far stronger position than the French realized. His negotiators in Paris were in sight of an agreement with the Americans and, in spite of Shelburne's protestations to the French, by now King George III was eager to trade Gibraltar for gains in the West Indies.

Shelburne's terms were harsh. If Spain wanted to have Gibraltar she would not only have to return Minorca and West Florida but also give Britain Puerto Rico. If France wished, she could offer two of her Caribbean islands in place of Puerto Rico (either Guadeloupe and newly captured Dominica or Martinique and St. Lucia). Rayneval sent the new terms by messenger and then, with great foresight, rushed back to Versailles to argue for their acceptance. He arrived just in time to help Vergennes convince Aranda to accept the arrangement on behalf of Spain. It appears unlikely that Aranda had the formal authority to do so; his political superior and rival, Floridablanca, seems to have left to him

6. Dull, *French Navy and American Independence*, 317–19, 324.

the onus of surrendering Spain's conquests. In apparent agony, Aranda agreed to give up Minorca so as to prevent the rupture of negotiations. France would surrender Guadeloupe and Dominica, leaving West Florida as the only obstacle to the exchange of Gibraltar. Rayneval returned to England a third time, bringing Vergennes's oldest son as his secretary and as a personal gesture of French good faith.[7]

As Rayneval and his companion were on their way to England, the American and British negotiators reached agreement. The American settlement doomed the proposed exchange for Gibraltar. British public opinion would not accept the loss of Gibraltar and French acquisition of Santo Domingo on top of the concessions to the Americans, particularly since, with America effectively removed from the war, Britain could take from Spain and France whatever she wanted. Although Shelburne had managed to delay the reconvening of Parliament, he could not defy the British public.

Again Rayneval's courage and composure kept the negotiations alive. Unable to find an acceptable price for Gibraltar, Shelburne finally suggested that if Spain abandoned the attempt to obtain it she could retain West Florida as a war gain. Britain, moreover, would exchange East Florida for the Bahamas, recently captured by Bernardo de Gálvez.

The British offer, although welcome, was insufficient. Aranda was not prepared to give up either Minorca or the Floridas. Rayneval now firmly informed Shelburne and Grantham that without Minorca there could be no peace. With enormous reluctance they agreed to Rayneval's demand. The basis for an agreement with Spain had finally been reached.[8]

Obstacles to peace still remained. Aranda had to accept the arrangement, although technically he lacked the authority. Violating his orders proved easier for him the second time, particularly since d'Estaing and French ambassador Montmorin had convinced King Charles III to forgive his prior transgression. There was some confusion over which West Indian islands France

---

7. Dull, "Vergennes, Rayneval and the Diplomacy of Trust," forthcoming.
8. Ibid.

would receive; she finally settled for the return of St. Lucia and the retention of Tobago, and returned to Britain the remainder of her numerous Caribbean conquests. She also received improved fishing grounds off Newfoundland, the African colony of Senegal, and the right to fortify Dunkirk, although she was able to obtain virtually no gains in India. The final obstacle was the Dutch, whose commissioner, Brantsen, had no power to make concessions. Vergennes, negotiating on their behalf, was able to obtain for them the restitution of Trincomali in exchange for a small trading post in India. (He was perhaps aided by the news that a French force was en route to Ceylon to attack Trincomali.) Their claims for the rights of neutral shippers were ignored.[9]

On January 20, 1783, an armistice and preliminary peace agreement with Britain was signed by the Americans, French, and Spaniards and on behalf of the Dutch. The hostilities were over and negotiations for a final treaty could be conducted at leisure. News of the armistice arrived at Cadiz in time to prevent d'Estaing's sailing, although it took several months for the news of peace to end the fighting in India.[10] During those months there were several developments that affected the final meaning of the War for American Independence.

9. Ibid.

10. Dull, *French Navy and American Independence*, 333–34.

CHAPTER 20

The Final Treaties and
Their Consequences

The peace agreement Shelburne had constructed against great opposition proved politically fatal to him. By a narrow majority the House of Commons in mid-February 1783 voted to censure the agreement. Shelburne resigned as chief minister, never again to serve in a British government.[1] He was succeeded by a strange coalition government formed by Lord North and Charles James Fox.

Although the new administration did not repudiate the preliminary peace agreements, Shelburne's fall doomed any chances that the final peace treaty would incorporate better terms for the United States, such as privileges for her trade. Although Fox appointed as British negotiator Franklin's old friend David Hartley, the true mood of the British public was revealed by the decision to exclude American shipping from the British West Indies.[2] Doomed, too, were Franklin's hopes of using the final treaty as a vehicle for proclaiming the rights of noncombatants and limiting

---

1. John M. Norris, *Shelburne and Reform* (London: Macmillan and Co.; New York: St. Martin's Press, 1963), 240–70, 295–307; John Cannon, *The Fox-North Coalition: Crisis of the Constitution, 1782–4* (Cambridge: Cambridge University Press, 1969), 38–64.

2. Charles R. Ritcheson, *Aftermath of Revolution: British Policy toward the United States, 1783–1795* (Dallas: Southern Methodist University Press, 1969), 6–7; Vincent T. Harlow, *The Founding of the Second British Empire, 1763–1793*, vol. 1: *Discovery and Revolution* (London: Longmans, Green and Co., 1952), 448–92.

the scope of future wars.[3] The final treaty was signed at Paris on
September 3, 1783, and in substance merely restated the terms
agreed upon the previous November.[4] On the same day the
French and Spanish treaties were signed in Versailles; they too
were unchanged. The Dutch signed a preliminary agreement;
their final treaty with Britain was signed the following May 20.

Shelburne's departure from office ended whatever chance had
existed for a joint effort on behalf of the Turks. Shelburne's successors had no interest in cooperating with France, and for several years Britain played little part in European diplomacy except
for commercial negotiations. In April 1783 Empress Catherine II
of Russia announced the annexation of the Crimea. Vergennes
desperately sought help from Britain, Prussia, or Austria, but his
efforts were futile. The Turks had little choice but to accept their
losses; they were fortunate that Austrian caution prevented Russia from attempting to take more. Vergennes's only consolation
was that his urging of restraint on the Turks helped to prevent
war.[5]

The American war had given Russia the chance to expand her
trade, boost her prestige, and finally to improve her position in
the balance of power. As the Dutch had learned in a previous
war, it is the onlookers who stand to profit from a war (or, rather,
one should say an eighteenth-century war). What happened to
those states which participated directly in the war?

Ironically, the European state that ultimately benefited most

3. For Franklin's hopes, see Francis P. Wharton, *The Revolutionary Diplomatic Correspondence of the United States*, 6 vols. (Washington, D.C.: Government Printing Office, 1889), 5:606. The negotiations leading to the final treaties
are discussed in Richard B. Morris, *The Peacemakers: The Great Powers and
American Independence* (New York, Evanston and London: Harper & Row,
1965), 426–37.

4. The final treaty is printed in ibid., 461–65, the definitive treaty with
France in *The Remembrancer* 16 (1783): 321–25, the preliminary articles with the
Netherlands in ibid., 336–37.

5. M. S. Anderson, "The Great Powers and the Russian Annexation of the
Crimea, 1783–4," *Slavonic and East European Review* 37 (1958–59): 17–41;
Alan W. Fisher, *The Russian Annexation of the Crimea, 1772–1783* (Cambridge:
Cambridge University Press, 1970), 128–52; Orville T. Murphy, *Charles Grav-
ier, Comte de Vergennes: French Diplomacy in the Age of Revolution, 1719–1787*
(Albany: State University of New York Press, 1982), 333–43.

from the war was Britain. Her crisis of confidence and even her withdrawal from European diplomacy were only temporary. Freed from the lengthy and debilitating American crisis and war, she was soon rejuvenated. Within a short time Fox and North were succeeded by a brilliant chief minister, Shelburne's protégé, William Pitt the Younger (son of the former chief minister). Pitt reformed government finances and administration (although not elections to the House of Commons) and rebuilt the British navy. The British economy revived, fueled in part by innovations in the cotton industry that we now see as the beginnings of the Industrial Revolution. Far from being fatal to Britain, the loss of America marked the beginning of her period of greatest power.[6]

The results were just the opposite for France—her apparent victory was really a defeat. Americans continued to trade predominantly with Britain, British power and prosperity soon were greater than before the war, and the British government appeared less likely than ever to cooperate with France in continental diplomacy. Vergennes even negotiated a commercial treaty with Britain in 1786 in the hope of improving relations; but in its few years of existence it brought few benefits, commercial or diplomatic (although it was not fully tested).[7] The crisis in eastern Europe had merely been postponed for a few years; in 1787 the long-dreaded Austro-Russian war against the Turks finally began. By then France was helpless to intervene; the government, its debts swollen by the one billion livres the war had cost, was almost bankrupt.[8] The threat of bankruptcy finally forced the reluctant King Louis XVI to call the Estates General,

6. See John Ehrman, *The Younger Pitt*, vol. 1: *The Years of Acclaim* (London: Constable and Co., 1969), and Ritcheson, *Aftermath of Revolution*, 3–32, 128–29.

7. Murphy, *Charles Gravier, Comte de Vergennes*, 432–58. For detailed discussions, see John Ehrman, *The British Government and Commercial Negotiations with Europe, 1783–1793* (Cambridge: Cambridge University Press, 1962), and Marie Martenis Donaghay, "The Anglo-French Negotiations of 1786–1787" (Ph.D. diss., University of Virginia, 1970).

8. Jonathan R. Dull, *The French Navy and American Independence: A Study of Arms and Diplomacy, 1774–1787* (Princeton, N.J.: Princeton University Press, 1975), 345–50; for a comparable estimate but very different conclusions, see Robert D. Harris, "French Finances and the American War," *Journal of Modern History* 48 (1976): 233–58.

the French equivalent of Parliament, which had not met for 175 years. Soon France had its own revolution.

For the Netherlands the war it had hoped to avoid brought only humiliation. It demonstrated the ineffectiveness of Dutch institutions and the inability of the Netherlands to command foreign respect. It also helped to discredit the stadholder and speed a reform movement that swept Dutch political life. That reform movement was soon checked—the stadholder received the help of Prussian troops in 1787 to restore his power—but Dutch political life was permanently changed.[9]

For Spain the war meant a reprieve for her endangered empire in the Western Hemisphere. The reprieve was only temporary; as Floridablanca and other Spanish statesmen had feared, as neighbors the Americans were as dangerous as the British had been. In 1803 the United States acquired Louisiana, by 1821 all of Florida; within another decade almost the entire Spanish colonial empire, swept by revolution, was lost. Only Minorca remained as a permanent gain in exchange for the bloodshed and the diversion of Spanish resources.

What the war meant above all for the United States was independence. That independence was far from complete in economic terms. For many decades the United States would be economically dependent on Britain. During the immediate postwar period Britain restricted American access to the British West Indies, severely damaged American shipping, and surpassed all her foreign competitors combined in American trade. Even postwar British manufactured exports to the United States almost equaled prewar totals.[10]

American political independence even seemed likely to be short-lived. Few foreign statesmen expected the Americn union to endure. The mutual jealousy of her states, the weakness of her institutions, and the character of her citizenry seemed to promise little hope that the United States would ever become a world power, even if it had the good fortune to survive. Congress could neither prevent the states from passing laws discriminating

---

9. Simon Schama, *Patriots and Liberators: Revolution in the Netherlands, 1780–1813* (New York: Alfred A. Knopf, 1977), 64–135.

10. Ritcheson, *Aftermath of Revolution*, 3–87, 188, 363–71, 374–75.

against foreign countries nor compel the payment of debts to British merchants as required by the treaty of 1783. This and the continued American ill-treatment of Loyalists prompted Britain to retaliate by refusing to evacuate her remaining posts within the United States. Congress lacked the military forces to attack frontier Indian tribes, let alone the British-held posts.[11]

The adoption of the Federal Constitution of 1787 did not immediately resolve America's foreign-policy problems. With the danger of internal disintegration greatly reduced, the United States, however, could draw on formidable diplomatic assets. Her resources (especially her surplus of food),[12] military potential, and proximity to the West Indies made her a useful ally or a troublesome opponent. Her distance from Europe and hostile terrain made her difficult to invade, and her great potential as a market for manufactured goods made Britain, at any rate, anxious to maintain peace and friendship. It was not until after her own Industrial Revolution and the great growth of her population, however, that the United States became a great power.

American survival in the postwar world was not entirely due to good fortune. It was also, in part, a product of the same resiliency that helped the United States to survive its birth. America, however, must take care when celebrating the past not to overglorify her own accomplishments. As Americans have learned in recent years, the United States is neither invincible in war nor necessarily wiser, better, or more ethical than other countries. Her victory in the war for her independence depended on a heavy dose of foreign help and abundant good luck. Ironically, that foreign help was extended for reasons having little to do with America and brought few benefits to the countries which extended it. For the diplomatic historian, the moral of the American Revolution thus may be the unpredictability, the expense, and the danger of war.

11. For a survey of postwar American foreign relations, see Frederick W. Marks, III, *Independence on Trial: Foreign Affairs and the Making of the Constitution* (Baton Rouge: Louisiana State University Press, 1973).

12. For the importance of this trade to the American economy, see John H. Coatsworth, "American Trade with European Colonies in the Caribbean and South America, 1790–1812," *William and Mary Quarterly*, 3rd ser., 24 (1967): 243–66.

APPENDIX 1

The Franco-American
Treaty of Alliance

*From a dual-language copy in the
National Archives, Washington, D.C.*

TREATY OF ALLIANCE EVENTUAL AND DEFENSIVE

The most Christian King and the United States of North America, to wit,
New Hampshire, Massachusetts Bay, Rhode Island, Connecticut, New
York, New Jersey, Pennsylvania, Delaware, Maryland, Virginia, North
Carolina, South Carolina & Georgia, having this day concluded a Treaty
of Amity & Commerce for the reciprocal advantage of their Subjects and
Citizens, have thought it necessary to take into consideration the means
of strengthening those engagements and of rendering them useful to the
safety and tranquility of the two parties; particularly in case Great-
Britain in resentment of that connection and of the good correspondence
which is the object of the said Treaty, should break the peace with
France either by direct hostilities or by hindering her Commerce and
navigation in a manner contrary to the rights of nations and the peace
subsisting between the two Crowns: And his Majesty and the said United
States having resolved in that case to join their Councils and efforts
against the enterprizes of their common enemy, the respective plenipotentiaries empowered to concert the clauses and conditions proper to
fulfil the said intentions, have after the most mature deliberation, concluded and determined on the following Articles.

Article 1

If war should break out between France & Great Britain during the con-
tinuance of the present war between the United States and England, his
Majesty and the said United States shall make it a common cause and aid
each other mutually with their good Offices, their counsels and their
forces according to the exigence of conjunctures, as becomes good and
faithful Allies.

Art 2d

The essential and direct end of the present defensive Alliance is to maintain effectually the liberty, sovereignty and independence absolute and unlimited of the said United States as well in matters of government as of Commerce.

Art 3d

The two contracting parties shall each on its own part and in the manner it may judge most proper make all the efforts in its power against their common enemy in order to attain the end proposed.

Art 4th

The contracting parties agree that in case either of them should form any particuar enterprize in which the concurrence of the other may be desired, the party whose concurrence is desired shall readily and with good faith join to act in concert for that purpose as far as circumstances and its own particular situation will permit, and in that case they shall regulate by a particular convention the quantity and kind of succour to be furnished and the time & manner of its being brought into action, as well as the advantages which are to be its compensation.

Art 5th

If the United States should think fit to attempt the reduction of the British power remaining in the northern parts of America or the islands of Bermudas, those Countries or islands in case of success shall be confederated with or dependent upon the said United States.

Art 6th

The most Christian King renounces forever the possession of the Islands of Bermudas as well as of any part of the Continent of North America which before the Treaty of Paris in 1763 or in virtue of that Treaty were acknowledged to belong to the Crown of Great Britain or to the United States heretofore called British Colonies or which are at this time or have lately been under the power of the King and Crown of Great Britain.

Art 7th

If his Most Christian Majesty shall think proper to attack any of the islands situated in the Gulph of Mexico or near the Gulph, which are at present under the power of Great Britain, all the said isles in case of success shall appertain to the Crown of France.

Art 8th

Neither of the two parties shall conclude either truce or peace with Great Britain without the formal consent of the other first obtained, and they mutually engage not to lay down their arms until the independence of the United States shall have been formally or tacitly assured by the Treaty or Treaties that shall terminate the War.

Art 9th

The contracting parties declare that being resolved to fulfil each on its own part the clauses and conditions of the present Treaty of Alliance according to its own power and circumstances, there shall be no after claim of compensation on one side or the other, whatever may be the event of the War.

Art 10

The most Christian King and the United States agree to invite or admit other powers who may have received injuries from England to make common cause with them and to accede to the present alliance under such conditions as shall be freely agreed to and settled between all the parties.

Art 11

The two parties guarantee mutually from the present time and forever against all other powers, to wit, the United States to his most Christian Majesty the present possessions of the Crown of France in America as well as those which it may acquire by the future Treaty of peace; and his most Christian Majesty guarantees on his part to the United States their liberty, sovereignty and independence absolute and unlimited as well in matters of government as commerce and also their possessions and the additions or conquests that their Confederation may obtain during the War from any of the dominions now or heretofore possessed by Great Britain in North America conformable to the 5th and 6th Articles above written, the whole as their possession shall be fixed and assured to the said States at the moment of the cessation of their present War with England.

Art 12

In order to fix more precisely the sense & application of the preceding Article, the contracting parties declare that in case of a rupture between France & England the reciprocal guarantee declared in the said Article shall have its full force and effect the moment such war shall break out and if such rupture shall not take place the mutual obligations of the said guarantee shall not commence until the moment of the cessation of the present war between the United States and England shall have ascertained their possessions.

Art 13

The present Treaty shall be ratified on both sides and the ratifications shall be exchanged in the space of six months or sooner if possible.

If faith whereof the respective plenipotentiaries, to wit, on the part of the most Christian King Conrad Alexander Gérard, royal syndic of the City of Strasbourgh and Secretary of his Majesty's Council of State, and on the part of the United States Benjamin Franklin deputy of the general Congress from the State of Pennsylvania & president of the Convention of the said State, Silas Deane heretofore deputy from the State of Connecticut, and Arthur Lee Counsellor at Law have signed the above Articles both in the french & english Languages, declaring nevertheless that the present treaty was originally composed & concluded in the french language and they have hereunto affixed their seals.

Done at Paris this 6th day of February, one thousand seven hundred and seventy eight.

[signed] C. A. Gérard, B. Franklin, Silas Deane, Arthur Lee

ACT SEPARATE & SECRET

The most Christian King declares in consequence of the intimate Union which subsists between him and the King of Spain that in concluding with the United States of America this Treaty of Amity and Commerce and that of eventual and defensive Alliance his Majesty hath intended and intends to reserve expressly as he reserves by this present separate and secret act to his said Catholic Majesty the power of acceding to the said Treaties and to participate in their stipulations at such time as he shall judge proper. It being well understood nevertheless that if any of the stipulations of the said Treaties are not agreeable to the King of Spain his Catholic Majesty may propose other conditions analogous to the principal aim of the Alliance and conformable to the rules of equality reciprocity and Friendship. The deputies of the United States in the name of their Constituents accept the present declaration in its full extent, and the deputy of the said States who is fully empowered to treat with Spain promises to sign on the first requisition of his Catholic Majesty the act or acts necessary to communicate to him the stipulations of the treaties above written; and the said deputy shall endeavour in good

faith the adjustment of the points in which the King of Spain may propose any alteration conformable to the principles of equality, reciprocity
and perfect amity; he the said deputy not doubting but that the person
or persons empowered by his Catholic Majesty to treat with the United
States will do the same with regard to any alterations of the same kind
that may be thought necessary by the said Plenipotentiary of the United
States. In faith whereof the respective plenipotentiaries have signed the
present separate and secret article and affixed to the same their seals.

Done at Paris this sixth day of February, one thousand seven hundred
& seventy eight.

[signed] C. A. Gérard, B. Franklin, Silas Deane, Arthur Lee

APPENDIX 2

Preliminary Terms of Peace between Britain and The United States, November 30, 1782

[Copy, National Archives, Washington, D.C.]

Articles agreed upon, by and between Richard Oswald, Esquire, the Commissioner of his Britannic Majesty for treating of Peace with the Commissioners of the United States of America, in Behalf of his said Majesty on the one Part, and John Adams, Benjamin Franklin, John Jay, and Henry Laurens, four of the Commissioners of the said States for treating of Peace with the Commissioner of his said Majesty on their Behalf on the other Part: to be inserted in, and to constitute the Treaty of Peace proposed to be concluded between the Crown of Great Britain and the said United States; but which Treaty is not to be concluded until Terms of a Peace shall be agreed upon between Great Britain and France, and his Britannic Majesty shall be ready to conclude such Treaty accordingly.

Whereas reciprocal Advantages and mutual Convenience are found by Experience to form the only permanent Foundation of Peace and Friendship between States, it is agreed to form the Articles of the Proposed Treaty on such Principles of liberal Equity and Reciprocity as that partial Advantages, (those Seeds of discord) being excluded, such a beneficial and satisfactory Intercourse between the two Countries may be established as to promise and secure, to both, perpetual Peace and Harmony.

Article 1st

His Brittanic majesty acknowledges the said United States, Vizt: New Hampshire, Massachusetts Bay, Rhode Island and Providence Plantations, Connecticut, New York, New Jersey, Pennsylvania, Delaware,

Maryland, Virginia, North Carolina, South Carolina, & Georgia to be free, sovereign, and independent States; that he treats with them as such; and for himself, his Heirs and Successors, relinquishes all Claims to the Government, Propriety, and Territorial Rights of the same, and every Part thereof; and that all Disputes which might arise in future on the Subject of the Boundaries of the said United States may be prevented it is hereby agreed and declared that the following are and shall be their Boundaries, Vizt.

Art 2d

From the northwest Angle of Nova Scotia, vizt, that Angle which is formed by a Line drawn due North from the Source of St. Croix River to the Highlands along the said Highlands which divide those Rivers that empty themselves into the River St. Lawrence from those that fall into the Atlantic Ocean to the Northwesternmost Head of Connecticut River, thence down along the Middle of that River to the 45° of North Latitude, from thence by a Line due West on said Latitude until it strikes the River Iroquois or Cataraquy, thence along the Middle of said River into Lake Ontario, through the Middle of said Lake until it strikes the Communication by Water between that Lake and Lake Erie, thence along the Middle of said Communication into Lake Erie, through the Middle of said Lake until it arrives at the Water Communication between that Lake and Lake Huron, thence along the Middle of such Water Communication into the Lake Huron, thence through the Middle of said Lake to the Water Communication between that Lake and Lake Superior, thence through Lake Superior northward of the Isles Royal & Phelipeaux to the Long Lake; thence through the Middle of said Long Lake and the Water Communications between it and the Lake of the Woods to the said Lake of the Woods, thence through the said Lake to the most Northwestern Point thereof and from thence on a due West Course to the River Mississippi; thence by a Line to be drawn along the Middle of the said River Mississippi until it shall intersect the Northernmost Part of the 31° of North Latitude.

South by a Line to be drawn due East from the Termination of the Line last mentioned, in the Latitude of 31° North of the Equator to the Middle of the River Appalachicola or Catahouche, thence along the Middle thereof to its Junction with the Flynt River, thence strait to the Head of St. Mary's River, and thence down along the Middle of St. Mary's River to the Atlantic Ocean.

East by a Line to be drawn along the Middle of the River St. Croix from its Mouth in the Bay of Fundy to its Source, and from its Source di-

rectly North to the aforesaid Highlands which divide the Rivers that fall
into the Atlantic Ocean from those which fall into the River St.
Laurence; comprehending all islands within twenty Leagues of any Part
of the Shores of the United States and lying between Lines to be drawn
due East from the Points where the aforesaid Boundaries between Nova
Scotia on the one Part and East Florida on the other shall respectively
touch the Bay of Fundy and the Atlantic Ocean excepting such Islands as
now are, or heretofore have been, within the Limits of the said Province
of Nova Scotia.

Art 3d

It is agreed that the People of the United States shall continue to enjoy
unmolested the Right to take Fish of every Kind on the Grand Bank and
on all the other Banks of Newfoundland; also in the Gulph of St. Laurence and at all other Places in the Sea where the Inhabitants of both
Countries used at any Time heretofore to fish; and also that the Inhabitants of the United States shall have Liberty to take Fish of every Kind on
such Part of the Coast of Newfoundland as British Fishermen shall use
(but not to dry or cure the same on that Island) And also on the Coasts,
Bays, and Creeks of all other of his Britannic Majesty's Dominions in
America and that the American Fishermen shall have Liberty to dry and
cure Fish in any of the unsettled Bays, Harbors, and Creeks of Nova
Scotia, Magdalene Islands and Labradore so long as the same shall remain unsettled; but so soon as the same or either of them shall be settled
it shall not be lawful for the said Fishermen to dry or cure Fish at such
Settlement without a previous Agreement for that Purpose with the Inhabitants, Proprietors or Possessors of the Ground.

Art 4th

It is agreed that Creditors on either side shall meet with no lawful Im-
pediment to the Recovery of the full Value in Sterling Money of all bona
fide Debts heretofore contracted.

Art 5th

It is agreed that the Congress shall earnestly recommend it to the Legis-
latures of the respective States to provide for the Restitution of all Estates, Rights & Properties which have been confiscated belonging to real
British Subjects; and also of the Estates, Rights and Properties of Persons resident in Districts in the Possession of his Majesty's Arms and
who have not borne Arms against the said United States; and that Persons of any other Description shall have free Liberty to go to any Part or

Parts of any of the thirteen United States and therein to remain twelve Months unmolested in their Endeavors to obtain the Restitution of such of their Estates, Rights and Properties as may have been confiscated; and that Congress shall also earnestly recommend to the several States a Reconsideration and Revision of all Acts or Laws regarding the Premises, so as to render the said Laws or Acts perfectly consistent not only with Justice and Equity but with that Spirit of Conciliation which on the Return of the Blessings of Peace should universally prevail and that Congress should also earnestly recommend to the several States that the Estates, Rights & Properties of such last mentioned Persons shall be restored to them, they refunding to any Persons who may be now in Possession the bona fide Price (where any has been given) which such Persons may have paid on purchasing any of the said Lands, Rights or Properties since the Confiscation.

And it is agreed that all persons who have any Interest in confiscated Lands either by Debts, Marriage Settlements or otherwise shall meet with no lawful Impediments in the Prosecution of their just Rights.

Art 6th

That there shall be no future Confiscations made nor any Prosecutions commenced against any Person or Persons for or by Reason of the Part which he or they may have taken in the present War and that no Person shall on that Account suffer any future Loss or Damage either in his Person, Liberty or Property and that those who may be now in Confinement on such Charges at the Time of the Ratification of the Treaty in America shall be immediately set at Liberty and the Prosecutions so commenced be discontinued.

Art 7th

There shall be a firm and perpetual Peace between his britannic Majesty and the said States and between the Subjects of the one and the Citizens of the other; Wherefore all Hostilities both by Sea and Land shall then immediately cease, all Prisoners on both Sides shall be set at Liberty, and his Britannic Majesty shall with all convenient speed and without causing any Destruction or carrying away any Negroes or other Property of the American Inhabitants withdraw all his Armies, Garrisons and Fleets from the said United States, and from every Port, Place and Harbor within the same, leaving in all Fortifications the American Artillery that may be therein; and shall also order and cause all Archives, Records, Deeds and Papers belonging to any of the said States or their Citizens, which in the Course of the War may have fallen into the Hands of his Officers to be forthwith restored and delivered to the proper States and Persons to whom they belong.

Art 8th

The Navigation of the River Mississippi from its Source to the Ocean shall forever remain free & open to the Subjects of Great Britain and the Citizens of the United States.

Art 9th

In Case it should so happen that any Place or Territory belonging to Great Britain or to the United States should be conquered by the Arms of either from the other before the Arrival of these Articles in America it is agreed that the same shall be restored without Difficulty and without requiring any Compensation.

Done at Paris, November 30th 1782.

John Jay		Richard Oswald
Henry Laurens	[signed]	John Adams
		Benja Franklin

Witness Caleb Whitefoord, Secy. to the British Commission
[signed] W. T. Franklin Secy. to the am. Commission

Separate Article

It is hereby understood and agreed that in Case Great Britain at the Conclusion of the present War shall recover or be put in Possession of West Florida, the Line of North Boundary between the said Province and the United States shall be a Line drawn from the Mouth of the River Yazsous where it unites with the Missisippi due East to the River Appalachicola.

Done at Paris the thirtieth Day of November, one thousand seven hundred and Eighty two.

> [signed] Richard Oswald
> John Adams
> Benja Franklin
> John Jay
> Henry Laurens

[signed] Attest. Caleb Whitefoord, Secy. to the British Commission
Attest. W. T. Franklin, Secy. to the Am. Commission

BIBLIOGRAPHY

Abarca, Ramón E. "Classical Diplomacy and Bourbon 'Revanche' Strategy, 1763–1770." *Review of Politics* 32 (1970): 313–37. Of some interest, but harmed by the narrowness of its focus. Another article with the same failing is Margaret Cotter Morison, "The Duc de Choiseul and the Invasion of England, 1768–1770," *Transactions of the Royal Historical Society*, 3rd ser., 4 (1910): 83–115.

Abernethy, Thomas Perkins. "Commercial Activities of Silas Deane in France." *American Historical Review* 39 (1933–34): 477–85. A cursory and inaccurate exposé of Deane's supposed profiteering in France.

———. "The Origin of the Franklin-Lee Imbroglio." *North Carolina Historical Review* 15 (1938): 41–52. Cites documents out of context and puts the worst possible interpretation on the motivations and actions of those unfriendly to Arthur and William Lee.

Acomb, Frances. *Anglophobia in France, 1763–1789: An Essay in the History of Constitutionalism and Nationalism.* Durham, N.C.: Duke University Press, 1950. Contains a 20-page sketch of the views different components of French public opinion held about the American-British conflict.

Affaires de l'Angleterre et de l'Amérique. 15 vols. Antwerp [Paris]: publisher unlisted [Ministère des affaires étrangères], 1776–79. This journal, secretly published by the French government, was issued at intervals of one to several weeks. A guide to its erratic system of numbering issues and pages is Paul Leicester Ford, "Affaires de l'Angleterre et de l'Amérique," *Pennsylvania Magazine of History and Biography* 13 (1889): 222–26. For a study of its contents, see Gilbert Chinard, "Adventures in a Library," *Huntington Library Bulletin*, 2nd ser., 8 (March 1952): 225–36.

Aiton, Arthur S. "Spain and the Family Compact, 1770–1773." In A. Curtis Wilgus, ed., *Hispanic American Essays: A Memorial to James*

Alexander Robertson. Chapel Hill: University of North Carolina Press, 1942: 135–49. An interesting article that describes the deterioration of the Franco-Spanish alliance during Aiguillon's ministry (1771–74).

Alberts, Robert C. *The Golden Voyage: The Life and Times of William Bingham, 1752–1804*. Boston: Houghton-Mifflin Co., 1969. Bingham was American commercial agent at Martinique and corresponded with American diplomats in Europe.

Alcázar Molina, Cayetano. *El conde de Floridablanca (Notes para su estudio)*. Madrid: Sucesores de Rivadeneyra, 1929. This short book discusses other aspects of Floridablanca's diplomatic career but not his role in the American war. I have not had the opportunity to consult Jacques J. Engerrand, "The Anglo-French Policy of Floridablanca (1777–1783)," Ph.D. diss., University of Michigan, 1935.

Alden, John R. *Stephen Sayre: American Revolutionary Adventurer*. Baton Rouge and London: Louisiana State University Press, 1983. Sayre served as secretary to Arthur Lee's unsuccessful mission to Berlin and thereafter masqueraded at a variety of European courts as an American diplomat. Alden's biography, although scholarly, takes him more seriously than he deserves.

Aldridge, Alfred Owen. *Franklin and His French Contemporaries*. New York: New York University Press, 1957. A thorough discussion of Franklin's reputation in France, although it is based chiefly on the written record. It is complemented by James Leith, "Le Culte de Franklin avant et pendant la Révolution Française." *Annales Historiques de la Révolution Française* 48 (1976): 543–71.

————. "Jacques Barbeu-Dubourg, a French Disciple of Benjamin Franklin." *Proceedings of the American Philosophical Society* 95 (1951): 331–92. Barbeu-Dubourg was an important early link between the French and American governments, but this study is too uncritical of him to be as useful as it might.

Allen, David Grayson et al., eds. *Diary of John Quincy Adams*. 2 vols. to date. Cambridge, Mass. and London: Belknap Press of Harvard University Press, 1981–. Provides some details about the unsuccessful American wartime mission to Russia.

Alsop, Susan Mary. *Yankees at the Court: The First Americans in Paris*. Garden City, N.Y.: Doubleday and Co., 1982. An entertaining book for a nonscholarly audience.

Anderson, M. S. "Great Britain and the Russian Fleet, 1769–70." *Slavonic and East European Review* 31 (1952–53): 148–63. Criticizes British policy during the 1768–74 Russo-Turkish war; see also Anderson's article "Great Britain and the Growth of the Russian Navy in the Eighteenth Century," *Mariner's Mirror* 42 (1953): 132–46.

———. "Great Britain and the Russo-Turkish War of 1768–74." *English Historical Review* 69 (1954): 39–58. Very good overview of Britain's vacillating policy during the war.

———. "The Great Powers and the Russian Annexation of the Crimea, 1783–4." *Slavonic and East European Review* 37 (1958–59): 17–41. France's American triumph was followed by this defeat; this excellent article describes her attempts to forestall Russia. See also Fisher, Alan W., below.

Andrews, Charles M. "A Note on the Franklin-Deane Mission to France." *Yale University Library Gazette 2* (1927–28): 53–68. Contains a previously unpublished portion of Silas Deane's testimony before Congress and two previously unpublished letters.

Anson, Sir William, ed. *Autobiography and Political Correspondence of Augustus Henry, Third Duke of Grafton*. London: John Murray, 1898. Grafton was one of the more inept British secretaries of state of the prewar period.

Arneth, Alfred d', and Flammermont, Jules, eds. *Correspondance secrète du comte de Mercy-Argenteau avec l'empereur Joseph II et le prince de Kaunitz*. 2 vols. Paris: Imprimerie Nationale, 1889–91. Mercy-Argenteau was the ambassador at the French court for Maria Theresa and her son Emperor Joseph; Kaunitz was the Austrian foreign minister.

———, and Geffroy, A., eds. *Marie-Antoinette: Correspondance secrète entre Marie-Thérèse et le cte. de Mercy-Argenteau, avec les lettres de Marie-Thérèse et de Marie-Antoinette*. 3 vols. Paris: Firmin Didot frères, fils, 1874–75. Mercy-Argenteau served as confidant for Marie-Antoinette, wife of King Louis XVI and daughter of Maria Theresa.

Ascoli, Peter M. "The French Press and the American Revolution: The Battle of Saratoga." *Proceedings of the Fifth Annual Meeting of the Western Society for French History*, pp. 46–55. Santa Barbara, Calif.: privately printed, 1978. Describes French public enthusiasm at the news of Saratoga.

Atwood, Rodney. *The Hessians: Mercenaries from Hessen-Kassel in the American Revolution*. Cambridge and elsewhere: Cambridge University Press, 1980. Of value to social and diplomatic historians as well as military historians, this excellent monograph discusses the largest single contingent of German auxiliaries. Still useful for the other contingents is Max von Eelking, *The German Allied Troops in the North American War of Independence, 1776–1783*, trans. J. G. Rosengarten (Albany: Joel Munsell's Sons, 1893).

Augur, Helen. *The Secret War of Independence*. New York: Duell, Sloan and Pearce; Boston: Little, Brown and Co., 1955. A bit superior to popularized history, it occasionally presents new discoveries and insights, such as Franklin's understanding of maritime commerce. It should be used cautiously, however, because it also contains unsubstantiated generalizations, speculation, and some errors.

Ayling, Stanley Edward. *The Elder Pitt, Earl of Chatham*. London: Collins, 1976. A good introduction to Pitt and his diplomacy. Another recent biography is Peter Douglas Brown, *William Pitt, Earl of Chatham, the Great Commoner* (London: George Allen & Unwin, 1978). For Pitt's correspondence, see William S. Taylor and John H. Pringle, eds., *Correspondence of William Pitt, Earl of Chatham*, 4 vols. (London: John Murray, 1838–40).

Barker, G. F. Russell, ed. *Horace Walpole: Memoirs of the Reign of King George the Third*. 4 vols. London: Lawrence and Bullen, 1894. Of some interest for British politics but has little on diplomacy. See also A. Francis Steuart, ed., *The Last Journals of Horace Walpole during the Reign of George III, from 1771–1783*, 2 vols. (London and New York: John Lane, 1910) and Wilmarth S. Lewis et al., eds., *The Yale Edition of Horace Walpole's Correspondence*, 48 vols. (New Haven and London: Yale University Press, 1937–83).

Barral de Montferrat, Horace-Dominique de. *Dix ans de paix armée entre la France et l'Angleterre, 1783–93*. Paris: E. Plon, Nourrit, 1893. An introduction to postwar Franco-British relations. Only the first volume of the planned work was published.

Barrow, Thomas. "The American Revolution as a Colonial War for Independence." *William and Mary Quarterly*, 3rd ser., 25 (1968): 452–64. Barrow's provocative way of considering the American Revolution provides an interesting perspective on its diplomacy.

Barton, H. A. "Sweden and the War of American Independence." *William and Mary Quarterly*, 3rd ser., 23 (1966): 408–30. A sophisticated introduction to both governmental and popular attitudes toward the American Revolution; also provides bibliographical information.

Bashkina, Nina N. et al., eds. *The United States and Russia: The Beginning of Relations, 1765–1815*. Washington, D.C.: United States Department of State, ca. 1980. This superbly edited collection of documents (in English or English translation) was a joint Soviet-

American project. Approximately one hundred of the documents date from prior to the final peace treaty of 1783.

Bemis, Samuel Flagg, ed., *The American Secretaries of State and Their Diplomacy*. Vol. 1. New York: Alfred A. Knopf, 1928. Contains a rather out-of-date survey of Revolutionary diplomacy by James Brown Scott (pp. 3–111) and a brief sketch of Robert R. Livingston's tenure as the first American secretary of state by Milledge L. Bonham, Jr. (pp. 113–89).

————. "British Secret Service and the French-American Alliance," *American Historical Review* 29 (1923–24): 474–95. This brief article on Edward Bancroft and his fellow spies is less thoroughly researched but more balanced than the article by Boyd cited below. It, however, does avoid some of the more difficult questions, such as Deane's relationship with Bancroft. See also Bemis's "Secret Intelligence, 1777: Two Documents," *Huntington Library Quarterly* 24 (1960–61): 233–49.

————. "Canada and the Peace Settlement of 1782–3." *Canadian Historical Review* 14 (1933): 265–84. Discounts the possibility of the United States' obtaining Canada by the peace treaty. Like the rest of Bemis's work, it is marred by his excessive suspicion of Vergennes and the French government.

————. *The Diplomacy of the American Revolution*. Rev. ed. Bloomington: Indiana University Press, 1957. Slightly revised from the original edition of 1935, it is succinct and wide-ranging but by now vastly out of date.

————. *The Hussey-Cumberland Mission and American Independence*. Princeton, N.J.: Princeton University Press, 1931. Treats with far more seriousness than they are worth the supposedly secret British-Spanish negotiations of 1780.

————. "The Rayneval Memoranda of 1782 on Western Boundaries and Some Comments on the French Historian Doniol." *Proceedings of the American Antiquarian Society* 47 (1937): 15–92. By discussing out of its context the French attempt to mediate between the United States and Spain, Bemis helped contribute to the myth of French duplicity toward America.

Bendiner, Elmer. *The Virgin Diplomats*. New York: Alfred A. Knopf, 1976. Amusing and unpretentious, although not to be taken very seriously as history.

Bernard, Paul P. *Joseph II and Bavaria: Two Eighteenth-Century Attempts at German Unification*. The Hague: Martinus Nijhoff, 1965. Describes the other diplomatic crisis of 1778, the Austrian attempt to absorb much of Bavaria. Other books on the subject include Georges Grosjean, *La Politique rhénane de Vergennes* (Paris: Société d'édition "Les belles-lettres," 1925); Paul Oursel, *La Diplomatie de la France sous Louis XVI: Succession de Bavière et Paix de Teschen* (Paris: Plon-Nourrit, 1921); and Harold W. V. Temperley, *Frederic the Great and Kaiser Joseph: An Episode of War and Diplomacy in the Eighteenth Century*, 2nd ed. (London: Frank Cass and Co., 1968).

Bernardy, Amy A. "La missione di Beniamino Franklin a Parigi nei dispacci degli ambasciatori veneziani in Francia (1776–1786)." *Archivio storico italiano* 78 (1920): 237–62. Provides extracts from the correspondence of the Venetian ambassador; major emphasis is on the postwar period.

Blart, Louis. *Les Rapports de la France et de l'Espagne après le pacte de famille, jusqu'à la fin du ministère du duc de Choiseul.* Paris: Felix Alcan, 1915. Blart's book is interesting and well annotated but too narrowly focused on Franco-Spanish relations to give a balanced appraisal of Choiseul's aims.

Bolkhovitinov, Nikolaĭ. *The Beginnings of Russian-American Relations, 1775–1815.* Trans. Elena Levin. Cambridge, Mass.: Harvard University Press, 1975. An informative survey by a contemporary Soviet historian.

——. *Russia and the American Revolution.* Trans. C. Jay Smith. Tallahassee, Fla.: Diplomatic Press, 1976. A somewhat expanded version of the opening chapters of Bolkhovitinov's earlier work; it provides some data not elsewhere readily available but is somewhat weak on the diplomatic context of Russian policy.

Bonneville de Marsangy, Louis. *Le Chevalier de Vergennes, son ambassade à Constantinople.* 2 vols. *Le Comte de Vergennes, son ambassade en Suède, 1771–1774.* Paris: Plon, Nourrit, 1894, 1898. Somewhat outdated but still the most detailed biography of Vergennes prior to his assumption of office as French foreign minister.

Bourguet, Alfred. *Etudes sur la politique étrangère du duc de Choiseul.* Paris: Plon-Nourrit, 1907. Essays on Choiseul's Austrian, Dutch, and English policies. See also Bourguet's *Le duc de Choiseul et l'alliance espagnole* (Paris: Plon-Nourrit, 1906).

Boutry, Maurice. "L'Ambassade de Prince Louis de Rohan à Vienne (1772–1774)." *Revue d'histoire diplomatique* 17 (1903): 216–60. Rohan's was a vital post during the diplomatic crisis over Poland; this is a most interesting article.

Boyd, Julian P. et al., eds. *The Papers of Thomas Jefferson.* 21 vols. to date. Princeton, N.J.: Princeton University Press, 1950–. Jefferson's first diplomatic mission lies outside the period of the Revolution, but the earlier volumes of Boyd's magnificent edition contain considerable material relative to Revolutionary diplomacy. The standard biography of Jefferson is Dumas Malone, *Jefferson and His Time*, 6 vols. (Boston: Little, Brown and Co., 1948–81).

———. "Silas Deane: Death by a Kindly Teacher of Treason?" *William and Mary Quarterly*, 3rd ser., 16 (1959): 165–87, 319–42, 515–50. Traces the activities of Edward Bancroft who, the author suggests, may have poisoned Silas Deane. Although this article is enormously imaginative and superbly written, it also is speculative and sometimes erroneous. For refutations from a medical perspective of its central premise, see William Stinchcombe, "A Note on Silas Deane's Death," *William and Mary Quarterly*, 3rd ser., 32 (1975): 619–24, and Dennis Kent Anderson and Godfrey Tryggve Anderson, "The Death of Silas Deane: Another Opinion," *New England Quarterly* 57 (1984): 98–105.

Brant, Irving. *James Madison: The Nationalist, 1780–7*. Indianapolis and New York: Bobbs-Merrill Co., 1948. A charming and scholarly work which, because of congressional delegate Madison's involvement in foreign-policy decisions, is of great interest to diplomatic historians. See also William T. Hutchinson et al., eds., *The Papers of James Madison*, 15 vols. to date (Chicago and Charlottesville: University of Chicago Press, University Press of Virginia, 1962–).

Broglie, Albert, duc de. *The King's Secret: Being the Secret Correspondence of Louis XV with His Diplomatic Agents, from 1752 to 1774*. English trans. unidentified. 2 vols. London, Paris, and New York: Cassell, Petter and Galpin, 1879. An important book in spite of its inaccuracies and biases, written by a descendant of the count de Broglie, who headed Louis XV's secret diplomatic service.

Brown, Marvin L. *American Independence through Prussian Eyes; A Neutral View of the Peace Negotiations of 1782–1783: Selections from the Prussian Diplomatic Correspondence*. Durham, N.C.: Duke University Press, 1959. An English translation of excerpts from the Prussian diplomatic correspondence; too narrowly defined a topic to be of much worth to diplomatic historians.

Brown, Weldon A. *Empire or Independence: A Study in the Failure of Reconciliation, 1774–1783*. University, La.: Louisiana State University Press, 1941. Details British attempts to negotiate with the Americans an end to the Revolution. Two related articles are Nathan R. Einhorn, "The Reception of the British Peace Offer of

1778," *Pennsylvania History* 16 (1949): 191–214, and Reginald E. Rabb, "The Role of William Eden in the British Peace Commission of 1778," *Historian* 20 (1957–58): 153–78.

Browning, Reed. *The Duke of Newcastle*. New Haven and London: Yale University Press, 1975. A modern biography of a politician and statesman who was involved in British foreign relations from the early 1720s to early 1760s.

Burlingame, Roger. *Benjamin Franklin, Envoy Extraordinary*. New York: Coward-McCann, 1967. A popularized account of Franklin's services in London and Paris.

Burnett, Edmund Cody. *The Continental Congress*. New York: Macmillan, 1941. A useful straightforward history of congressional proceedings.

————, ed. *Letters of Members of the Continental Congress*. 8 vols. Washington, D.C.: Carnegie Institution, 1921–36. Contains extracts of more than 6,000 letters, minutes, and instructions, some of which concern foreign affairs. This edition is gradually being superceded by that of Paul Smith, cited below.

Burns, Richard Dean, ed. *Guide to American Foreign Relations since 1700*. Santa Barbara, Calif. and Oxford, Eng.: ABC-Clio, 1983. This magnificent annotated bibliography replaces, albeit not completely, Samuel Flagg Bemis and Grace Gardner Griffin, eds., *Guide to the Diplomatic History of the United States, 1775–1921* (Washington, D.C.: Government Printing Office, 1935). Those planning research on Revolutionary diplomacy should consult the chapters on colonial diplomacy by Lawrence Kaplan et al. and on Revolutionary history by William Stinchcombe.

Butler, John P., comp. *Index, The Papers of the Continental Congress, 1774–1789*. 5 vols. Washington, D.C.: Government Printing Office, 1978. The papers of the Continental Congress consist of some 50,000 documents, which have been reproduced on 220 reels of microfilm. This index is an invaluable aid in their use.

Butler, Rohan. *Choiseul*. Vol. 1, *Father and Son, 1719–1754*. Oxford: Clarendon Press, 1980. A thousand-page study of Choiseul's youth and early military career; in spite of the author's massive research it is a disappointing book because of his bias in favor of Choiseul.

Butterfield, Herbert. "Review Article: British Foreign Policy, 1762–5." *Historical Journal* 6 (1963): 131–40. An excellent critique of the British diplomacy of the period.

Butterfield, Lyman H., ed. *Diary and Autobiography of John Adams*. 4 vols. Cambridge, Mass.: Belknap Press of Harvard University

Press, 1961. Adams, so willing to expose his feelings, is a biographer's dream, and this source, if used carefully, is a valuable source for the study of his diplomatic activity. Also of some use are the four volumes published to date of Lyman H. Butterfield and Marc Friedlaender, eds., *Adams Family Correspondence* (Cambridge, Mass.: Belknap Press of Harvard University Press, 1963–).

Calmettes, Fernand, ed. *Mémoires du duc de Choiseul, 1719–1785.* Paris: Plon-Nourrit, 1904. A fascinating source, but one that must be used with extreme caution, as Choiseul was not one to question his own accomplishments.

Carter, Alice Clare. *Neutrality or Commitment: The Evolution of Dutch Foreign Policy, 1667–1795.* London: Edward Arnold, 1975. A concise introduction to seventeenth- and eighteenth-century Dutch diplomacy.

Castries, René de la Croix, duc de. *La France et l'indépendance américaine: Le livre du bicentenaire de l'indépendance.* Paris: Librairie Académique Perrin, 1975. Rather unoriginal and uninteresting. Castries also wrote "Le Pacte de famille et la guerre de l'Indépendance américaine," *Revue d'histoire diplomatique* 75 (1961): 294–306.

Chambrun, Charles. *A l'école d'un diplomate, Vergennes.* Paris: Plon, 1944. Has little of value to say.

Chase, Eugene Parker, ed. *Our Revolutionary Forefathers: The Letters of François, Marquis de Barbé-Marbois during His Residence in the United States as Secretary of the French Legation, 1779–1785.* New York: Duffield & Co., 1929. The title is misleading—this is a translation of Barbe-Marbois's diary and contains little of interest to diplomatic historians.

Chinard, Gilbert, ed. *The Treaties of 1778, and Allied Documents.* Baltimore: Johns Hopkins Press, 1928. Provides the texts of the draft treaty of 1776 and the treaties of 1778 and a historical introduction.

Clark, George L. *Silas Deane, a Connecticut Leader in the American Revolution.* New York: G. P. Putnam's Sons, 1913. Uncritical and unscholarly. Until an adequate biography of Deane appears, use the article by Goldstein cited below and Christopher Collier, *Roger Sherman's Connecticut: Yankee Politics and the American Revolution* (Middletown, Conn.: Wesleyan University Press, 1971), which deals with him in passing.

Clark, William Bell. *Ben Franklin's Privateers: A Naval Epic of the American Revolution.* Baton Rouge: Louisiana State University Press, 1956. As American minister in France, Franklin devoted

enormous effort to aiding American prisoners of war and effecting
their release; Clark details his efforts to obtain British prisoners to
offer in exchange for them.

———. "In Defense of Thomas Digges." *Pennsylvania Magazine of History and Biography* 77 (1953): 381–438. A good introduction to a
minor but controversial contact of the American mission, who was
involved in prisoner relief. His papers have been published: Robert
H. Elias and Eugene D. Finch, eds., *Letters of Thomas Attwood
Digges (1742–1821)* (Columbia: University of South Carolina Press,
1982).

———. "John the Painter." *Pennsylvania Magazine of History and Biography* 63 (1939): 1–23. An account of one of Deane's most lunatic
undertakings, the hiring of a pyromaniac to burn British dockyards.

———. *Lambert Wickes, Sea Raider and Diplomat: The Story of a Naval Captain of the Revolution*. New Haven: Yale University Press,
1932. A valuable account of American naval and diplomatic activities in France in 1776–77, but to be used only with extreme caution
because of Clark's tendency to go beyond his evidence.

———, and Morgan, William James, eds. *Naval Documents of the
American Revolution*. 8 vols. to date. Washington, D.C.: Department of the Navy, 1964–. Prints some documents relating to the
work of the American mission in France. The series to date extends
only to mid-1777.

Coe, Samuel Gwynn. *The Mission of William Carmichael to Spain*. Baltimore: Johns Hopkins University, 1926. A published dissertation
about an important but relatively neglected figure. See also Floyd
B. Streeter, "The Diplomatic Career of William Carmichael,"
Maryland Historical Magazine 8 (1913): 119–40. Neither author is
very probing.

Conn, Stetson. *Gibraltar in British Diplomacy in the Eighteenth Century*. New Haven: Yale University Press, 1942. A good book, although it is always somewhat misleading to deal with one diplomatic issue in isolation. A more current military and diplomatic
history of Gibraltar is George Hills, *Rock of Contention: A History
of Gibraltar* (London: Robert Hale and Co., 1974).

Conrotte, Manuel. *La intervención de España en la independencia de
los Estados Unidos de la América del Norte*. Madrid: Victoriano
Suárez, 1920. A brief general history of the Spanish participation in
the war.

Copeland, Thomas W. et al., eds. *The Correspondence of Edmund
Burke*. 9 vols. Cambridge: Cambridge University Press; Chicago:

University of Chicago Press, 1958–70. Burke took a great interest in European as well as American and imperial affairs (being a strong opponent of the Polish partition). See also Paul Langford et al., eds., *The Writings and Speeches of Edmund Burke*, 2 vols. to date (Oxford: Clarendon Press, 1980–).

Coquelle, P. *L'Alliance franco-hollandaise contre l'Angleterre, 1735–1788*. Paris: Plon-Nourrit, 1902. A survey of Franco-Dutch relations. See also the author's article "Le Cabinet secret de Louis XV en Hollande," *Revue d'histoire diplomatique* 15 (1901): 275–92.

Cortada, James W., ed. *A Bibliographic Guide to Spanish Diplomatic History, 1460–1977*. Westport, Conn.: Greenwood Press, 1977. Chapter 12 provides a 15-page list of books and articles on Spanish diplomacy between 1759 and 1788.

Corwin, Edward S. *French Policy and the American Alliance of 1778*. Princeton, N.J.: Princeton University Press, 1916. The work of one of the most perceptive of all American diplomatic historians, it has become outdated because of its reliance on published sources. The opening chapters are the best; a slightly different version of them was published as "The French Objective in the American Revolution," *American Historical Review* 21 (1915–16): 33–61. A somewhat inferior book written in the same era is James Breck Perkins, *France in the American Revolution* (London: Constable and Co.; Boston and New York: Houghton Mifflin Co., 1911).

Crankshaw, Edward. *Maria Theresa*. New York: Viking Press, 1969. An excellent biography which contains an extensive bibliography of works in German about the Austrian ruler.

Cresson, William Penn. *Francis Dana, a Puritan Diplomat at the Court of Catherine the Great*. New York: Dial Press, 1930. Not very reliable, but it quotes extensively from Dana's journal of his mission to Russia.

Crout, Robert Rhodes. "The Diplomacy of Trade: The Influence of Commercial Considerations on French Involvement in the Anglo-american War of Independence, 1775–78." Ph.D. diss., University of Georgia, 1977. An extremely provocative work, although it may overestimate the importance of commercial considerations in the making of French foreign policy.

———. "In Search of a 'Just and Lasting Peace': The Treaty of 1783, Louis XVI, Vergennes, and the Regeneration of the Realm." *International History Review* 5 (1983): 364–98. Particularly valuable for its discussion of Louis XVI's views about foreign policy.

Currey, Cecil B. *Code Number 72 / Ben Franklin: Patriot or Spy?* En-

glewood Cliffs, N.J.: Prentice-Hall, 1972. A work worthy of the
John Birch Society, which argues on the basis of innuendo that
Franklin was a British double agent.

Dangerfield, George. *Chancellor Robert R. Livingston of New York,
1746–1813*. New York: Harcourt, Brace and Co., 1960. An excellent biography of America's first secretary of state.

Danvila y Collado, Manuel. *Reinado de Carlos III*. 6 vols. Madrid: El
Progresso editorial, 1891–96. This multivolume biography pro-
vides a detailed account of the Spanish king's diplomacy. Recent
English biographies tend to be superficial—examples are Anthony
H. Hull, *Charles III and the Revival of Spain* (Washington, D.C.:
University Press of America, 1981), and Sir Charles Petrie, *King
Charles III of Spain: An Enlightened Despot* (London: Constable
and Co., 1971). An exception is Richard Herr's superb *The Eighteenth-Century Revolution in Spain* (Princeton, N.J.: Princeton University Press, 1958), which discusses at length his domestic policy
but not diplomacy.

Davies, Godfrey, and Tinling, Marion. "The Independence of America:
Six Unpublished Items on the Treaty in 1782–1783." *Huntington
Library Quarterly* 12 (1948–49): 213–20. Taken from the papers of
Shelburne's home and colonial secretary.

Davies, Kenneth Gordon, ed. *Documents of the American Revolution*.
21 vols. Shannon, Ire.: Irish University Press, 1972–81. Provides
transcripts of thousands of British colonial office documents relating
to American affairs, 1770–83.

Deacon, Richard. *A History of the British Secret Service*. London:
Frederick Muller, 1969. The chapter on the American Revolution is
of little value.

DeConde, Alexander. "Historians, the War of American Independence,
and the Persistence of the Exceptionalist Ideal." *International History Review* 5 (1983): 399–430. Traces the way historians have dealt
with the 1783 Treaty of Paris. The subject is also discussed in Jerald
A. Combs, *American Diplomatic History: Two Centuries of Changing Interpretations* (Berkeley, Los Angeles, and London: University of California Press, 1983).

Derry, John W. *Charles James Fox*. London: B. T. Batsford, 1972. Contains a chapter on the Shelburne-Fox dispute but neglects Fox's
European diplomacy.

Dippel, Horst. *Germany and the American Revolution, 1770–1800: A
Sociohistorical Investigation of Late Eighteenth-Century Political
Thinking*. Trans. Bernard A. Uhlendorf. Chapel Hill: University of

North Carolina Press, 1977. A monumental study, marred only by Dippel's tendency to overgeneralize from limited data.

————. "Prussia's English Policy after the Seven Years' War." *Central European History* 4 (1971): 195–214. A brilliant article that reveals Frederick II's caution and unwillingness to alienate Britain. It is a useful corrective to the many studies of Prussian policy which treat Frederick as pro-American in sympathy.

Doniol, Henry, ed. *Histoire de la participation de la France à l'établissement des Etats-Unis d'Amérique: Correspondance diplomatique et documents.* 5 vols. and supplement. Paris: Imprimerie Nationale, 1886–99. This massive documentary history published by the French government is very useful for those unable to do archival research, but it should be used with care. The documents have been selected to establish a particular set of theories, which are sometimes at variance with evidence not herein included.

————. *Politiques d'autrefois: Le comte de Vergennes et P. M. Hennin, 1749–1787.* Paris: Armand Colin, 1898. Reprint of a lengthy and interesting article about Vergennes and the organization of the French foreign ministry which first appeared in the *Revue d'histoire diplomatique* 7 (1893): 528–60.

Dull, Jonathan R. *Franklin the Diplomat: The French Mission.* Philadelphia: American Philosophical Society, 1982 (*Transactions* 72, pt. 1). I have attempted to complement Gerald Stourzh's book on Franklin as a diplomatic thinker (cited below) by discussing his work as a practicing diplomat. I have elaborated on some of the themes in this book in "Benjamin Franklin and the Nature of American Diplomacy," *International History Review* 5 (1983): 346–63.

————. *The French Navy and American Independence: A Study of Arms and Diplomacy, 1774–1787.* Princeton, N.J.: Princeton University Press, 1975. Studies the interrelationship between the naval and diplomatic history of the American Revolution. My bibliography contains a number of items not discussed in the bibliography of the present book, particularly works on naval and colonial history and tangential items in diplomatic history, such as archival guides.

Dumouriez, Charles-François Dupérier. *Mémoires du Général Dumouriez pour servir à l'histoire de la Convention nationale.* 2 vols. Paris: Firmin-Didot frères, 1862–63. Dumouriez played an exalted role in the Polish rebellion and a less exalted one in a plot to restore the Franco-Prussian alliance; use his memoirs with caution.

Dyck, Harvey L. "Pondering the Russian Fact: Kaunitz and the Catherinian Empire in the 1770s." *Canadian Slavonic Papers* 22 (1980):

451–69. Provocative article on the motivation for Austria's alliance with Russia.

Echeverria, Durand. *Mirage in the West: A History of the French Image of American Society to 1815*. Princeton, N.J.: Princeton University Press, 1957. A scholarly and graceful account of the American impact on France.

Edler, Friedrich. *The Dutch Republic and the American Revolution*. Baltimore: Johns Hopkins University Press, 1911 (*John Hopkins University Studies in Historical and Political Science*, ser. 29, no. 2). Deficient but still the best introduction in English to its subject. See also Francis P. Renaut, *Les Provinces-Unies et la guerre d'Amérique (1775–1784): De la neutralité à la belligérance (1775–1780)* (Paris: Graouli, 1924). The most thorough history of Dutch foreign policy is in Dutch: Herman Theodor Colenbrander, *De patriottentijd, hoofdzakelijk naar buitenlandsche bescheiden,* vol. 1, *1776–1784* (The Hague: Martinus Nijhoff, 1897).

Ehrman, John. *The Younger Pitt*. Vol. 1, *The Years of Acclaim*. London: Constable and Co., 1969. Pitt the Younger was a member of the Shelburne administration. In addition to this superlative biography (a second volume of which was published in 1983), Ehrman is the author of *The British Government and Commercial Negotiations with Europe, 1783–1793* (Cambridge: Cambridge University Press, 1962).

Einstein, Lewis. *Divided Loyalties: Americans in England during the War of Independence*. London: Cobden-Sanderson, 1933. Einstein's opening chapter deals with Americans in the British secret service. His work is sometimes superficial or inaccurate, but he has worked diligently in primary sources and uncovered some interesting details.

Evans, William B. "John Adams' Opinion of Benjamin Franklin." *Pennsylvania Magazine of History and Biography* 92 (1968): 220–38. A solid if somewhat unimaginative article.

Fagniez, G. "La politique de Vergennes et la diplomatie de Breteuil, 1774–1787." *Revue Historique* 140 (May-August 1922): 1–25, 161–207. A study of Vergennes's Austrian policy, based on the correspondence of the French ambassador in Vienna.

Fauchille, Paul. *La Diplomatie française et la ligue des neutres de 1780 (1776–1783)*. Paris: A. Durand et Pedone-Lauriel, 1893. Based chiefly on French diplomatic documents, this lengthy book traces the interrelationship of French diplomacy and trade policy.

Faure, Edgar. *La disgrâce de Turgot, 12 mai 1776*. Paris: Gallimard,

1961. Provides information on Anglo-French relations during the first year of the American Revolution.

Faÿ, Bernard. *The Revolutionary Spirit in France and America*. Trans. Ramon Guthrie. New York: Harcourt, Brace and Co., 1927. Inaccurate and outdated—consult instead the work by Durand Echeverria cited above.

Ferguson, E. James. *The Power of the Purse: A History of American Public Finance, 1776–1790*. Chapel Hill: University of North Carolina Press, 1961. A masterful book that helps explain the French role in financing the Revolution, Deane's business activities, and other topics relevant to Revolutionary diplomacy. See also Clarence L. Ver Steeg, *Robert Morris, Revolutionary Financier: With an Analysis of His Earlier Career* (Philadelphia: University of Pennsylvania Press, 1954), and E. James Ferguson, John Catanzariti et al., eds., *The Papers of Robert Morris, 1781–1784*, 6 vols. to date (Pittsburgh: University of Pittsburgh Press, 1973–).

Fisher, Alan W. *The Russian Annexation of the Crimea, 1772–1783*. Cambridge: Cambridge University Press, 1970. A concise account of the ongoing diplomatic crisis that rivaled the American war for Europe's attention.

Fitzmaurice, Lord Edmond. *Life of William, Earl of Shelburne, Afterwards First Marquis of Lansdowne with Extracts from His Papers and Correspondence*. Rev. ed. 2 vols. London: Macmillan and Co., 1912. A detailed but biased study, which contains relatively little about Shelburne's diplomacy. It is of use chiefly for the documents it prints.

Fohlen, Claude. "The Commercial Failure of France in America." In Nancy L. Roelker and Charles K. Warner, eds. *Two Hundred Years of Franco-American Relations: The Bicentennial Colloquium of the Society for French Historical Studies*, pp. 93–119. Worcester, Mass.: Heffernan Press, 1983. Analyzes the failure of France to break the British dominance of American trade. See also John F. Stover, "French-American Trade during the Confederation, 1781–1789," *North Carolina Historical Review* 35 (1958): 399–414, and Edmund Buron, "Statistics on Franco-American Trade, 1778–1806," *Journal of Economic and Business History* 4 (1931–32): 571–82.

——, and Godechot, Jacques, eds. *La Révolution Américaine et L'Europe*. Paris: Centre National de la Recherche Scientifique, 1979 (Colloque international no. 577). Among the papers from this colloquium are three on diplomacy: an attack on Vergennes for his supposed duplicity toward America (Jacob Osinga), a discussion of the breakdown of the Franco-American alliance (Peter P. Hill), and an analysis of Jefferson's attitude toward France (Lawrence Kaplan, author of a book on the same subject).

Ford, Worthington Chauncey et al., eds. *Journals of the Continental Congress, 1774–1789.* 35 vols. Washington, D.C.: Government Printing Office, 1904–76. The official record of the sessions of the Continental Congress. The first 34 volumes are textual and were produced by the Library of Congress between 1904 and 1937; the last volume, a cumulative index, was done by the National Archives and Records Service.

————, ed. *Letters of William Lee, Sheriff and Alderman of London; Commercial Agent of the Continental Congress in France; and Minister to the Courts of Vienna and Berlin, 1766–1783.* 3 vols. Brooklyn: Historical Printing Club, 1891. A model documentary edition for its time, and still useful.

Fortescue, Sir John. *The Correspondence of King George the Third from 1760 to December 1783.* 6 vols. London: Macmillan and Co., 1927–28. This collection of approximately 4,500 documents is basic to the understanding of British politics, diplomacy, and war strategy. There is a volume of corrections: L. B. Namier, *Additions and Corrections to Sir John Fortescue's Edition of the Correspondence of King George the Third (Vol. 1)* (Manchester, Eng.: Manchester University Press, 1937). For a recent sympathetic biography, see John Brooke, *King George III* (New York and elsewhere: McGraw-Hill, 1972).

Fraguier, Bertrand de. "Le duc d'Aiguillon et l'Angleterre (juin 1771–avril 1773)." *Revue d'histoire diplomatique* 26 (1912): 607–27. Until Michael Roberts's brilliant article on Great Britain and the Swedish Revolution (cited below), this was the standard account of the failed French attempt at reconciliation with Britain.

France: Commission des archives diplomatiques. *Receuil des instructions données aux ambassadeurs et ministres de France depuis les traites de Westphalie jusqu'à la révolution française.* 29 vols. to date. Paris: Germer Baillière and other publishers, 1884–. Ambassadors often were given very detailed instructions; this collection of them, arranged by countries, hence provides a capsule guide to French foreign policy.

Franklin, William Temple, ed. *Memoirs of the Life and Writings of Benjamin Franklin, LL.D.* 3 vols. London: Henry Colburn, 1818. This edition contains not only documents but also the commentary of the editor, Franklin's grandson, who had been secretary to the American mission in France.

Frederick II, king of Prussia. *Politische Correspondenz Friedrich's des Grossen*. 46 vols. and supplement. Berlin: Alexander Duncker and other publishers, 1879–1939. Although complete only through March 1782, this is one of the most important documentary sources for the diplomacy of the American Revolution. King Frederick's interpretation of events, however, is seldom objective.

Fruin, Robert, ed. *Dépêches van Thulemeyer, 1763–1788*. Amsterdam: Johannes Müller, 1912. A fascinating source, written in French—the diplomatic dispatches of the Prussian diplomatic representative in the Netherlands.

Gagliardo, John G. *Enlightened Despotism*. New York: Crowell, 1967. A valuable extended essay which shows the connection between the foreign and domestic policies of late-eighteenth-century European rulers.

———. *Reich and Nation: The Holy Roman Empire as Idea and Reality, 1763–1806*. Bloomington and London: Indiana University Press, 1980. Chiefly deals with political life within Germany, but also shows the diplomatic repercussions of developments within the Holy Roman Empire.

Georgel, Jean-François. *Mémoires pour servir à l'histoire des événemens de la fin du dix-huitième siècle depuis 1760 jusqu'en 1806– 1810*. 6 vols. Paris: Alexis Eymery et Delaunay, 1817–18. Georgel served with ambassador Rohan at the key post of Vienna during the Polish crisis.

Gephard, Ronald M., comp. *Revolutionary America, 1763–1789: A Bibliography*. 2 vols. Washington, D.C.: Library of Congress, 1984. Lists almost 15,000 titles, including several hundred dealing with diplomatic history; it is very useful, but in spite of its size, far from exhaustive.

Gilbert, Felix. *To the Farewell Address: Ideas of Early American Foreign Policy*. Princeton, N.J.: Princeton University Press, 1961. Gilbert argues that there was a fundamental tension in early American diplomacy between realism and idealism; this was an influential book and is still of considerable interest.

Gipson, Lawrence Henry. *The British Empire before the American Revolution*. 15 vols. Caldwell, Idaho and New York: Caxton Printers and Alfred A. Knopf, 1936–70. Written from a British perspective, this is an encyclopedic account of America's place within the British Empire. Gipson has written extensively about the causes of the

Revolution; for an introduction see his article "The American Revolution as an Aftermath of the Great War for Empire, 1754–1763," *Political Science Quarterly* 65 (1950): 86–104.

Goebel, Julius, Jr. *The Struggle for the Falkland Islands, A Study in Legal and Diplomatic History*. New Haven: Yale University Press, 1927. A detailed account of the major diplomatic crisis in western Europe in the decade preceding the American Revolution.

Goldstein, Kalman. "Silas Deane: Preparation for Rascality." *The Historian* 43 (1980–81): 75–97. Although it deals only with the period of Deane's life prior to his French mission, this superb article is invaluable for understanding the Connecticut politician and future diplomat.

Goodwin, Albert, ed. *The New Cambridge Modern History*. Vol. 8, *The American and French Revolutions, 1763–93*. Cambridge: Cambridge University Press, 1965. Like the preceding volume in the series (vol. 7, *The Old Regime, 1713–1763*, ed. J. O. Lindsay [Cambridge, 1963]), it contains a good, concise chapter on pre-French Revolutionary diplomacy.

Gottschalk, Louis. *Lafayette Comes to America*. Chicago: University of Chicago Press, 1935. Illuminates Deane's period as America's diplomatic representative in France. There is surprisingly little on French diplomacy or war strategy in the next volumes of Gottschalk's multivolume biography, *Lafayette Joins the American Army* (Chicago: University of Chicago Press, 1937) and *Lafayette and the Close of the American Revolution* (Chicago: University of Chicago Press, 1942).

Gough, John Francis, ed. *The Private Letters of Baron de Viomenil on Polish Affairs, with a Letter on the Siege of Yorktown*. Jersey City, N.J.: Collins Doan Co., 1935. Valuable source for French aid to the unsuccessful Polish rebels.

Grant, William L. "Canada versus Guadeloupe, an Episode of the Seven Years' War." *American Historical Review* 17 (1911–12): 735–43. Recounts the debate over whether Britain should keep Canada or the Caribbean island of Guadeloupe at the end of the Seven Years' War.

Greene, Jack P. "The Seven Years' War and the American Revolution: The Causal Relationship Reconsidered." *Journal of Imperial and Commonwealth History* 8, no. 2 (Jan. 1980): 85–105. An exceptionally sophisticated analysis of the ways in which the Seven Years' War changed relations between the American colonies and Britain. See also John M. Murrin, "The French and Indian War, the American Revolution, and the Counterfactual Hypothesis: Reflections on Lawrence Henry Gipson and John Shy," *Reviews in American History* 1 (1973): 307–18.

———, and Pole, J. R., eds. *Colonial British America: Essays in the New History of the Early Modern Era*. Baltimore and London: Johns Hopkins University Press, 1984. Of particular interest is the article by W. A. Speck, "The International and Imperial Context," pp. 384–407.

Griffiths, David M. "American Commercial Diplomacy in Russia, 1780 to 1783." *William and Mary Quarterly*, 3rd ser., 27 (1970): 379–410. A good introduction to the ill-considered mission of Francis Dana to Petersburg.

———. "Nikita Panin, Russian Diplomacy and the American Revolution." *Slavic Review* 28 (1969): 1–24. A very interesting article that examines the genesis and nature of the Russian attempt in 1780–81 to mediate an end to the war. See also Griffith's "An American Contribution to the Armed Neutrality of 1780," *Russian Review* 30 (1971): 164–72.

———. "The Rise and Fall of the Northern System: Court Politics and Foreign Policy in the First Half of Catherine II's Reign." *Canadian Slavic Studies* 4 (1970): 547–69. A brief study of N. I. Panin's diplomacy.

Guttridge, George Herbert. *David Hartley, M.P., an Advocate of Counciliation, 1774–1783*. Berkeley: University of California Press, 1926. (*University of California Publications in History* 14, no. 3.) A brief account of the public life of the British negotiator of the final peace treaty. New light on Hartley's career should be provided by Barbara Oberg's forthcoming edition of his correspondence. See also a pamphlet published by the University of Hull (1983): John Major, "Cementing the China Vase: David Hartley and America, 1774–1784."

Hale, Edward E., and Hale, Edward E., Jr. *Franklin in France*. 2 vols. Boston: Roberts Brothers, 1887–88. Although outdated, it does print some letters and documents not available elsewhere, including excerpts from the now missing journal of Jonathan Loring Austin. For Austin's journey to France with the news of Saratoga and his subsequent secret mission to England, see also the anonymous article in the *Boston Monthly Magazine* 2 (1826): 57–66.

Hall, Thadd E. *France and the Eighteenth-Century Corsican Question*. New York: New York University Press, 1971. Details Choiseul's one great success, the acquisition of Corsica.

Hammond, Robert. "La France et la Prusse, 1763–1769: Rétablisse-
    ment des rapports diplomatiques après la guerre de sept ans." *Re-
    vue Historique* 25 (May-August 1884): 69–82. In spite of its age an
    interesting article.
Hamon, Joseph. *Le Chevalier de Bonvouloir, premier émissaire secret
    de la France auprès du Congrès de Philadelphie avant l'indépen-
    dance américaine*. Paris: Jouve, 1953. A brief biography of the in-
    consequential young man who undertook what proved to be an
    enormously consequential secret mission.
Harlow, Vincent T. *The Founding of the Second British Empire, 1763–
    1793*. Vol. 1, *Discovery and Revolution*. London: Longmans,
    Green and Co., 1952. Harlow's perspective is unabashedly
    that of Shelburne and he has little appreciation of French policy,
    but this still contains the best available account of the peace
    negotiations.
Harris, Robert D. "French Finances and the American War, 1777–
    1783," *Journal of Modern History* 48 (1976): 233–58. A most inter-
    esting article, which downplays the connection between the Ameri-
    can war and the impending French governmental bankruptcy of
    1786–89. See also his *Necker, Reform Statesman of the Ancien Ré-
    gime* (Berkeley, Los Angeles, and London: University of California
    Press, 1979), and George V. Taylor, "The Paris Bourse on the Eve
    of the Revolution, 1781–1789," *American Historical Review* 67
    (1961–62): 951–77.
Henderson, H. James. *Party Politics in the Continental Congress*. New
    York: McGraw-Hill, 1974. Henderson's approach to congressional
    politics, foreign and domestic, is provocative but rather unsettling
    because his political "parties" are comprised of little more than a
    handful of congressional delegates. See also his "Congressional Fac-
    tionalism and the Attempt to Recall Benjamin Franklin," *William
    and Mary Quarterly*, 3rd ser., 27 (1970): 246–67.
Hendrick, Burton J. *The Lees of Virginia: Biography of a Family*. Bos-
    ton: Little, Brown and Co., 1935. Fair-minded but superficial col-
    lective biography of Arthur and William Lee and their family.
Herpin, Clare Adèle. *La Fin de XVIIIe siècle: le duc de Nivernais,
    1763–1798*. 4th ed. Paris: Calmann Lévy, 1891. Nivernais, who
    helped negotiate the 1763 treaty with Britain, was one of the most
    respected ambassadors of his time.
Hewins, William Albert Samuel, ed. *The Whitefoord Papers: Being the
    Correspondence and Other Manuscripts of Colonel Charles White-
    foord and Caleb Whitefoord, from 1739 to 1810*. Oxford: Clarendon

Press, 1898. Contains a few letters and anecdotes about the peace negotiations.

Hoffman, Paul P., ed. *The Lee Family Papers, 1742–1795*. 8 rolls of microfilm. Charlottesville: University of Virginia Library, 1966. Reproduces letters from the manuscript collections of the University of Virginia Library, Harvard University Library, and the American Philosophical Society—sometimes difficult to read but enormously useful. See also the printed editions of Ford (cited above) and Lee (below), as well as James Curtis Ballagh, *The Letters of Richard Henry Lee*, 2 vols. (New York: Macmillan Co., 1911–14).

Hoffman, Ronald, and Albert, Peter J., eds. *Diplomacy and Revolution: The Franco-American Alliance of 1778*. Charlottesville: University Press of Virginia, 1981. Contains essays on Vergennes (Orville T. Murphy and me), American feelings about the alliance (William Stinchcombe), the historiography of the alliance (Alexander De-Conde), and the alliance as compared to NATO (Lawrence Kaplan).

———, eds. *Peace and the Peacemakers: The Treaty of 1783*. Charlottesville: University Press of Virginia, forthcoming. Will contain essays on the American, British, and French negotiators (Gregg Lint, James H. Hutson, Esmond Wright, Charles R. Ritcheson, Bradford Perkins, and me) and the consequences of the peace (Marcus Cunliffe, Samuel F. Scott, and Richard B. Morris).

Hogge, George, ed. *The Journal and Correspondence of William, Lord Auckland*. 4 vols. London: R. Bentley, 1861–62. Lord Auckland was the later title of William Eden, in charge of the British secret service penetration of the American mission. Unfortunately this edition begins only in 1782 and is of little interest to students of the American Revolution.

Horn, David Bayne. *The British Diplomatic Service, 1689–1789*. Oxford: Clarendon Press, 1961. A thorough account of British diplomatic recruitment and practices.

———. *British Public Opinion and the First Partition of Poland*. Edinburgh and London: Oliver and Boyd, 1945. A short but useful book. Other works on the subject include Wolfgang Michael, *Englands Stellung zur ersten Theilung Polens* (Hamburg and Leipzig: L. Voss, 1890), W. F. Reddaway, "Great Britain and Poland, 1762–72," *Cambridge Historical Journal* 4 (1932–34): 223–62, Wladyslaw Konopczynski, "England and the First Partition of Poland," *Journal of Central European Affairs* 8 (1948): 1–23, and, contemporaneous with the events, John Lind, *Letters concerning the Present State of Poland* (London: T. Payne, 1773).

————. *Great Britain and Europe in the Eighteenth Century*. Oxford: Clarendon Press, 1967. Good introduction to eighteenth-century British diplomacy, arranged by countries rather than chronologically.

————, ed. *British Diplomatic Representatives, 1689–1789*. London: Royal Historical Society, 1932 (Camden third series, vol. 46). A useful guide to who was who (and where) in the British diplomatic service. For other countries, use Ludwig Bittner et al., eds. *Repertorium der diplomatischen vertreter aller Länder seit dem Westfälischen Frieden (1648)*, 3 vols. (Oldenburg, Germany and elsewhere: Gerhard Stalling, etc., 1936–65).

Hudson, Ruth. "The Strasbourg School of Law and Its Role in the French Intervention in the American Revolution." Ph.D. diss., Western Reserve University, 1947. Describes the roles of three Strasbourg graduates (including the brothers Gérard) in the French foreign ministry; perhaps most interesting is its discussion of the Franco-British propaganda war about who was responsible for the outbreak of hostilities.

Hutson, James H. *John Adams and the Diplomacy of the American Revolution*. Lexington: University Press of Kentucky, 1980. One of the best books yet published on Adams or American revolutionary diplomacy. An earlier version of its first chapter was published as "Intellectual Foundations of Early American Diplomacy," *Diplomatic History* 1 (1977): 1–19. Hutson also edited *Letters from a Distinguished American: Twelve Essays by John Adams on American Foreign Policy, 1780* (Washington, D.C.: Library of Congress, 1978).

————. "The Partition Treaty and the Declaration of American Independence." *Journal of American History* 58 (1971–72): 877–96. Argues, not wholly convincingly, that the timing of the Declaration of Independence was the result of American fears of a British bargain with France and Spain to divide the rebelling American colonies among themselves.

Idzerda, Stanley J., Crout, Robert R., et al., eds. *Lafayette in the Age of the American Revolution: Selected Letters and Papers, 1776–1790*. 5 vols. to date. Ithaca, N.Y. and London: Cornell University Press, 1977–. A splendid selected edition of Lafayette's correspondence. Letters written in French are given in both French and English.

Ingraham, Edward D., ed. *Papers in Relation to the Case of Silas Deane*. Philadelphia: Seventy-Six Society, 1855. Prints both Deane's and Arthur Lee's self-justifications to Congress.

Irvine, Dallas. "The Newfoundland Fisheries: A French Objective in the War of American Independence." *Canadian Historical Review* 13 (1932): 268–84. This article has been rebutted by Orville T. Murphy in his book cited below and, earlier, in "The Comte de Vergennes, the Newfoundland Fisheries, and the Peace Negotiation of 1783: A Reconsideration," *Canadian Historical Review* 46 (1965): 32–46.

Isham, Charles, ed. *The Deane Papers.* 5 vols. New York: New-York Historical Society, 1887–91 (*Collections of the New-York Historical Society*, vols. 19–23). One of the most basic documentary collections for Revolutionary diplomacy, even though it far from meets contemporary standards of historical editing. Somewhat less relevant is a supplementary volume, *The Deane Papers: Correspondence between Silas Deane, His Brothers and Their Business and Political Associates, 1771–1795* (Hartford: Connecticut Historical Society, 1930 [*Collections . . .* , vol. 23]).

Jacobson, Ljubow. *Russland und Frankreich in den ersten Regierungsjahren der Kaiserin Katharine II*. Berlin: Im-Ost-Europa Verlag, 1929. A 75-page book on Franco-Russian relations in the 1760s.

James, Coy Hilton, *Silas Deane—Patriot or Traitor?* East Lansing: Michigan State University Press, 1975. A superficial, biased, and inaccurate short biography.

Jarrett, Derek. *The Begetters of Revolution: England's Involvement with France, 1759–1789*. Totowa, N.J.: Rowman and Littlefield, 1973. Contains interesting discussions of politics and culture but is ill-informed about diplomacy.

Jobert, Ambroise. "Le Grand Frédéric et la Pologne (d'après un livre récent)." *Revue Historique* 203 (Jan.-June 1950): 225–33. A very critical summary of Frederick's role in the Polish partition.

Kammen, Michael G. *A Rope of Sand: The Colonial Agents, British Politics and the American Revolution*. Ithaca, N.Y.: Cornell University Press, 1968. An excellent collective biography and institutional study of the American colonial agents in London.

Kaplan, Herbert H. *The First Partition of Poland*. New York and London: Columbia University Press, 1962. A concise, although not always reliable, survey of the greatest diplomatic crisis of the decade before the American Revolution.

Kaplan, Lawrence S. "The American Revolution in an International Perspective: Views from Bicentennial Symposia." *International History Review* 1 (1979): 408–26. A useful survey of recent work. See also Kaplan's article "The Treaty of Paris, 1783: A Historiographical Challenge," *International History Review* 5 (1983): 431–42.

————. *Colonies into Nation: American Diplomacy, 1763–1801*. New York and London: Macmillan, 1972. By now needs some revision, but still probably the best introduction to eighteenth-century American diplomacy. A new survey of the period had been announced but not yet published when we went to press: Reginald Horsman, *The Diplomacy of the New Republic, 1776–1815* (Arlington Heights, Ill.: Harlan Davidson, 1985).

————, ed. *The American Revolution and "A Candid World."* Kent, Ohio: Kent State University Press, 1977. Contains articles on Empress Catherine's view of the American Revolution (David M. Griffiths), the drafting of the Model Treaty of 1776 (William C. Stinchcombe), American understanding of international law (Gregg Lint), the fate of the Franco-American alliance (Lawrence Kaplan), and British government (Carl B. Cone and Alan S. Brown), as well as an earlier draft of the article by Hutson cited above.

Kapp, Friedrich. *The Life of John Kalb, Major-General in the Revolutionary Army*. Trans. Charles Goepp. New York: privately printed, 1870. In 1768 Kalb undertook on behalf of Choiseul a secret mission to report on developments in America. See also Josephine F. Pacheco, "French Secret Agents in America, 1763–1778," Ph.D. diss., University of Chicago, 1951.

Kennett, Lee. *The French Forces in America, 1780–1783*. Westport, Conn. and London: Greenwood Press, 1977. The best introduction yet to the French expeditionary force. See also Howard C. Rice and Anne S. K. Brown, eds., *The American Campaigns of Rochambeau's Army, 1780, 1781, 1782, 1783*, 2 vols. (Princeton, N.J. and Providence, R.I.: Princeton University Press and Brown University Press, 1972).

Ketcham, Ralph L. "France and American Politics, 1763–1793." *Political Science Quarterly* 78 (1963): 198–223. A cursory survey based on published sources.

Klingelhofer, Herbert E. "Matthew Ridley's Diary during the Peace Negotiations of 1782." *William and Mary Quarterly*, 3rd ser., 20 (1963): 95–133. Gossipy and biased, but since Ridley was close to Jay, it provides otherwise unavailable information.

Konetze, Richard. *Die Politik des Grafen Aranda: Ein Beitrag zur Geschichte des spanisch-englischen Weltgegensatzes im 18. Jahrhundert*. Berlin: Emil Ebering, 1929. Aranda, the Spanish ambassador to the French court, held one of the key diplomatic posts in Europe during the American war. See also Miguel Gómez del Campillo, *El conde de Aranda en su embajada a Francia (años 1773–1787)* Madrid: Diana, 1945, and Marcelin Defourneaux, "Autour du 'Pacte de Famille': L'ambassade du comte d'Aranda en Pologne (1760–1762)," *Revue d'histoire diplomatique* 83 (1969): 20–45.

Krämer, F. J. L., ed. *Archives, ou correspondance inédite de la maison d'Orange-Nassau. Cinquième série (1766–1789).* 3 vols. Leyden: A. W. Sijthoff, 1910–15. This collection deals with both Dutch internal and external affairs; some documents are in French, others in Dutch.

Labande, L.-H., ed. *Un Diplomat français à la cour de Catherine II, 1775–1780: Journal intime du chevalier de Corberon.* 2 vols. Paris: Plon-Nourrit, 1901. Rather a disappointment: Corberon was not a very good ambassador, and his journal contains a gap from October 1777 to January 1779. For the period preceding Corberon's mission, see C. I. Andriescu, "La France et la politique orientale de Catherine II (d'après les rapports des ambassadeurs français à St. Petersbourg)," *Mélanges de l'Ecole roumaine en France* 5 (1927): 3–155.

Labaree, Leonard W., Willcox, William B., et al., eds. *The Papers of Benjamin Franklin.* 24 vols. to date. New Haven and London: Yale University Press, 1959–. Vol. 25 will contain the signing of the alliance. For the remainder of Franklin's mission to France, use: Albert Henry Smyth, ed., *The Writings of Benjamin Franklin,* 10 vols. (New York: Macmillan Co., 1907). I. Minis Hays, ed., *Calendar of the Papers of Benjamin Franklin in the Library of the American Philosophical Society,* 5 vols. (Philadelphia: American Philosophical Society, 1908); and Worthington Chauncey Ford, ed., *List of the Benjamin Franklin Papers in the Library of Congress* (Washington, D.C.: Government Printing Office, 1905).

La Feber, Walter. "Foreign Policies of a New Nation: Franklin, Madison and the 'Dream of a New Land to Fulfill with People in Self-Control,' 1750–1804." In William Appleman Williams, ed. *From Colony to Empire: Essays in the History of American Foreign Relations,* pp. 9–38. New York and elsewhere: John Wiley and Sons, 1972. Treats Franklin and Madison as advocates of American expansionism—a valid argument, but presented rather tritely.

Lanctot, Gustave. *Canada and the American Revolution, 1774–1783.* Trans. Margaret M. Cameron. Cambridge, Mass.: Harvard University Press, 1967. A good introduction to the American attempts to add Canada to the United States.

Langford, Paul. *The Eighteenth Century, 1688–1815.* In Malcolm Robinson, ed., *Modern British Foreign Policy,* vol. 3. London: Adam and Charles Black, 1976. The best survey I have yet encountered on 18th-century British diplomacy; exceptionally concise and smoothly written.

————. *The First Rockingham Administration, 1765–1766*. Oxford: Oxford University Press, 1973. An excellent study, which includes some discussion of the unsuccessful diplomacy of the Rockingham government. For the Rockinghamites, see also Ian R. Christie, "British Politics and the American Revolution," *Albion* 9 (1977): 205–26.

Laugier, Lucien. *Un Ministère réformateur sous Louis XV: Le Triumvirat (1770–1774)*. Paris: La Pensée Universelle, 1975. Includes the most detailed, although hardly the most impartial, account to date of Aiguillon's ministry. For Aiguillon's selection as foreign minister, see the work by Ozanam and Antoine cited below and Gabriel, duc de Choiseul, "Letter de M. le duc de Choiseul sur les Mémoires de Mme. Dubarry," *Revue de Paris* 4 (1829): 43–64.

Lee, Richard Henry. *Life of Arthur Lee, LL.D., Joint Commissioner of the United States to the Court of France, and Sole Commissioner to the Courts of Spain and Prussia, during the Revolutionary War*. 2 vols. Boston: Wells and Lilly, 1829. Chiefly of interest for the documents it contains, especially the selections from Lee's journals.

Legg, L. G. Wickham, ed. *British Diplomatic Instructions, 1689–1789*. Vol. 7, *France, part IV, 1745–1789*. London: Royal Society, 1934 (Camden third series, vol. 49). Contains some interesting documents about the British mission in France in 1777 and about the peace negotiations. Other volumes in the Camden third series provide instructions to other British diplomats; see especially James Frederick Chance, ed., vol. 3, *Denmark, 1689–1789* and vol. 5, *Sweden, 1727–1789* (London: Royal Society, 1928 [Camden third series, vols. 36, 39]).

Lodge, Sir Richard. *Great Britain and Prussia in the Eighteenth Century*. Oxford: Clarendon Press, 1928. By now out of date.

Lopez, Claude-Anne, "Benjamin Franklin, Lafayette, and the *Lafayette*." *Proceedings of the American Philosophical Society* 108 (1964): 181–223. An exhaustively researched article on Franklin's involvement in procuring uniforms and supplies for the American army. Lopez also is the author of an excellent book on Franklin's private life in France, *Mon Cher Papa: Franklin and the Ladies of Paris* (New Haven and London: Yale University Press, 1966).

Mackesy, Piers. *The War for America, 1775–1783*. Cambridge, Mass.: Harvard University Press, 1965. In addition to being the best overall history of the British war effort, this splendid book contains some discussion of British diplomacy.

Madariaga, Isabel de. *Britain, Russia, and the Armed Neutrality of 1780: Sir James Harris's Mission to St. Petersburg during the American Revolution.* New Haven: Yale University Press, 1962. Perhaps the best single book on British wartime diplomacy, this is a masterful study of an unsuccessful diplomatic mission.

————. *Russia in the Age of Catherine the Great.* New Haven and London: Yale University Press, 1981. An excellent, although sometimes demanding, survey of Catherine's reign.

————. "The Secret Austro-Russian Treaty of 1781." *Slavonic and East European Review* 38 (1959): 114–45. Treats one of the major European diplomatic developments of the period.

Malmesbury, James Howard Harris, third earl of, ed. *Diaries and Correspondence of James Harris, First Earl of Malmesbury.* 4 vols. London: Richard Bentley, 1844. Harris served in a series of key diplomatic posts. See also Madariaga's book about him and Alfred Cobban's somewhat inferior *Ambassadors and Secret Agents: The Diplomacy of the First Earl of Malmesbury at The Hague* (London: Jonathan Cape, 1954).

Manceron, Claude. *The French Revolution.* 4 vols. to date. Various translators. New York: Alfred A. Knopf, 1977– . Manceron's history begins with the accession of Louis XVI. His account of French court politics during the American war is vastly entertaining but not very profound.

Marks, Frederick W., III. *Independence on Trial: Foreign Affairs and the Making of the Constitution.* Baton Rouge: Louisiana State University Press, 1973. Argues that difficulties in implementing the Treaty of Paris of 1783 helped prompt the movement for constitutional reform. For a more optimistic appraisal of postwar America, see Merrill Jensen, *The New Nation: A History of the United States during the Confederation, 1781–1789* (New York: Alfred A. Knopf, 1950). Older works that deal with the postwar period include Samuel Flagg Bemis, *Jay's Treaty: A Study in Commerce and Diplomacy* (New York: Macmillan Co., 1923; rev. ed., New Haven: Yale University Press, 1962); Bemis's *Pinckney's Treaty: A Study of America's Advantage from Europe's Distress, 1783–1800* (Baltimore: Johns Hopkins Press, 1926; rev. ed., New Haven: Yale University Press, 1960); Arthur Preston Whitaker, *The Spanish-American Frontier, 1783–1795: The Westward Movement and the Spanish Retreat in the Mississippi Valley* (Boston and New York:

Houghton Mifflin Co., 1927); and Arthur Burr Darling, *Our Rising Empire, 1763–1803* (New Haven: Yale University Press, 1940).

Martange, Marie-Antoine Boüet de. *Correspondance inédite du Général-Major de Martange, aide de camp du prince Xavier de Saxe, Lieutenant Général des Armées (1756–1782)*. Paris: A. Picard et fils, 1898. Martange was sent by Aiguillon on a secret mission to England.

Mayer, Charles-Joseph. *Vie publique et privée de Charles Gravier, comte de Vergennes, ministre d'état*. Paris: Maradan, 1789. This biography, published two years after his death, contains copies of some of his financial records. See also Félix Vicq d'Azyr, *Eloge de M. le comte de Vergennes* (Paris: Clousier, 1788).

McCary, B. C. *The Causes of the French Intervention in the American Revolution*. Toulouse: Edouard Privat, 1928. A French minor thesis based on the sources published by Doniol.

McKay, Derek, and Scott, H. M. *The Rise of the Great Powers, 1648–1815*. London and New York: Longman Group, 1983. Fills the need for a concise, well-written, and accurate survey of eighteenth-century European diplomacy—a major accomplishment. An older survey convering much the same ground is Gaston Zeller, *Histoire des relations internationales*, vol. 3; *Les Temps modernes (Deuxième partie): Louis XIV à 1789* (Paris: Hachette, 1955).

Medina Encina, Purificación et al., eds. *Documentos relativos a la independencia de Norteamérica existentes en archivos españoles*. 8 vols. to date. Madrid: Ministerio de Asuntos Exteriores, 1976–. These invaluable research guides contain brief abstracts of documents in various archives relating to the American war and to Spanish-American relations through 1820. Use them in conjunction with Miguel Gómez del Campillo, ed. *Relaciones diplomáticas entre España y los Estados Unidos según los documentos del Archivo histórico nacional*, 2 vols. (Madrid: Consejo superior de investigaciones científicas, 1944–45).

Meng, John Joseph. "The Comte de Vergennes: European Phases of His American Diplomacy (1774–1780)." Ph.D. diss., Catholic University of America, 1932. Too adulatory of Vergennes to be of much use. Meng also wrote "Franco-American Diplomacy and the Treaty of Paris, 1783," *American Catholic Historical Society of Philadelphia Records* 44 (1933): 193–219, and "A Footnote to Secret Aid in the American Revolution," *American Historical Review* 43 (1937–38): 791–95.

———, ed. *Despatches and Instructions of Conrad Alexander Gérard, 1778–1780*. Baltimore: Johns Hopkins Press, 1939. A very valuable edition with annotation and a lengthy historical introduction; contains 10 dispatches from Vergennes and more than 120 from Gérard.

Miller, Daniel A. *Sir Joseph Yorke and Anglo-Dutch Relations, 1774–1780.* The Hague and Paris: Mouton, 1970. A somewhat cursory account of the diplomatic mission of the British minister to the Netherlands.

Monaghan, Frank. *John Jay, Defender of Liberty against Kings and Peoples.* New York and Indianapolis: Bobbs-Merrill Co., 1935. Jay deserves a more objective biography than this.

Morales Padrón, Francisco. *Spanish Help in American Independence.* Madrid: Publicaciones Españolas, 1952. A 45-page introduction to the topic.

Morgan, Edmund S. "The Puritan Ethic and the American Revolution." *William and Mary Quarterly,* 3rd ser., 24 (1967): 3–43. A brilliant article which examines the issues beneath the debate over Silas Deane's conduct in France.

Morison, Samuel Eliot. *John Paul Jones: A Sailor's Biography.* Boston and Toronto: Little, Brown and Co., 1959. Contains considerable discussion of the workings of the American mission in France, but Morison is really in his element only when dealing with Jones's activities afloat.

Morris, Richard B., ed. *John Jay, the Making of a Revolutionary: Unpublished Papers, 1745–1780; John Jay, the Winning of the Peace: Unpublished Papers, 1780–1784.* New York and elsewhere: Harper & Row, 1975, 1980. The major documentary source for Jay's congressional career and subsequent diplomatic activity. This edition supplements, but does not fully supplant, an earlier edition: Henry P. Johnston, ed., *The Correspondence and Public Papers of John Jay,* 4 vols. (New York and London: G. P. Putnam's Sons, 1890–93). See also Rebecca B. Gruver, "The Diplomacy of John Jay," Ph.D. diss., University of California, Berkeley, 1964.

———. *The Peacemakers: The Great Powers and American Independence.* New York, Evanston, and London: Harper & Row, 1965. Contains a great deal of information about diplomatic history between 1780 and the end of the war, but it must be used with care because of its anti-French and anti-Spanish bias. Morris directly criticizes the French alliance in his essay "The Diplomats and the Mythmakers," in Richard B. Morris, *The American Revolution Reconsidered* (New York, Evanston, and London: Harper & Row, 1967), 92–126.

Morton, Brian N. "Beaumarchais, Francy, Steuben, and Lafayette: An

Unpublished Correspondence or 'Feux de joye' at Valley Forge." *French Review* 49 (1976): 943–59. This article introduces us to the young man who served as a connecting link between three of the most famous Europeans involved in the American Revolution.

———. "'Roderigue Hortalez' to the Secret Committee: An Unpublished French Policy Statement of 1777." *French Review* 50 (1977): 875–90. Morton's discovery and elucidation of a disguised letter of September 1777 from the French government to Congress brought him a well-deserved literary prize.

———, and Spinelli, Donald C., eds. *Beaumarchais Correspondance.* 4 vols. to date. Paris: A.-G. Nizet, 1969–. A French-language edition. Biographical work on Beaumarchais prior to that of Morton has greatly inflated his importance to the American cause and cannot in general be recommended, although Roger Lafon, *Beaumarchais, le brillant armateur* (Paris: Société d'éditions géographiques, maritimes, et coloniales, 1928) has some useful information about arms shipments.

Muret, Pierre. *La Prépondérance anglaise (1715–1763).* 3rd ed. Paris: Presses Universitaires de France, 1949. Discusses Anglo-France relations in some detail.

Murphy, Orville T. *Charles Gravier, Comte de Vergennes: French Diplomacy in the Age of Revolution, 1719–1787.* Albany: State University of New York Press, 1982. A good introduction to Vergennes, although in general it is weakest on his policy in the American war. Murphy also is the author of a number of fine articles which largely have been herein incorporated.

Neeser, Robert Wilden, ed. *Letters and Papers Relating to the Cruises of Gustavus Conyngham, a Captain of the Continental Navy, 1777–1779.* New York: Naval History Society, 1915. Although the majority of its documents were previously published elsewhere, this is a useful collection dealing with a topic of considerable diplomatic impact.

Nicolson, Sir Harold. *The Evolution of Diplomatic Method.* New York: Macmillan Co., 1954. A witty and eloquent defense of pre-twentieth-century diplomatic practice, although it is not very scholarly.

Norris, John M. *Shelburne and Reform.* London: Macmillan and Co.; New York: St. Martin's Press, 1963. A useful supplement to Harlow's study of the peace negotiations. Another treatment of the political situation is John Cannon, *The Fox-North Coalition: Crisis of the Constitution, 1782–4.* (Cambridge: Cambridge University Press, 1969).

O'Donnell, William Emmett. *The Chevalier de la Luzerne, French Minister to the United States, 1779–1784.* Louvain: Bibliothèque de l'Université, 1938. A still-useful biography of the second French minister to the United States.

Oh, Wonyung Hyun. "Opinions of Continental American Leaders on International Relations, 1763–1775." Ph.D. diss., University of Washington, 1963. Dr. Oh's dissertation, while rather unfocused, does provide a useful compilation of newspaper articles, quotations from letters, and other sources dealing with foreign affairs.

Oliva, Lawrence Jay. *Misalliance: A Study of French Policy in Russia during the Seven Years' War.* New York: New York University Press, 1974. A fine book which helps explain the French difficulty in dealing with their intractable Russian problem.

Ozanam, Didier, and Antoine, Michel, eds. *Correspondance secrète du comte de Broglie avec Louis XV (1756–1774).* 2 vols. Paris: C. Klincksieck, 1956–61. Broglie headed a secret French diplomatic service coexisting with the official one, so his correspondence with King Louis XV is of great interest. Use this edition in conjunction with Edgard Boutaric, ed., *Correspondance secrète inédite de Louis XV sur la politique étrangère avec le comte de Broglie, Tercier, etc.,* 2 vols. (Paris: Henry Plon, 1866).

Pace, Antonio. *Benjamin Franklin and Italy.* Philadelphia: American Philosophical Society, 1958. Contains a chapter on American-Italian diplomatic relations, such as they were.

Palmer, Robert R. *The Age of the Democratic Revolution: A Political History of Europe and America, 1760–1800.* 2 vols. Princeton, N.J.: Princeton University Press, 1959–64. A work of rather inflated reputation which attempts to treat the American and French revolutions as interrelated phenomena. Other works on the foreign impact of the American Revolution include: Jacques Léon Godechot, *France and the Atlantic Revolution of the Eighteenth Century,* trans. Herbert H. Rowen (New York: Free Press, 1965); Richard B. Morris, *The Emerging Nations and the American Revolution* (New York: Harper & Row, 1970); Louis Gottschalk, "The Place of the American Revolution in the Causal Pattern of the French Revolution," in Esmond Wright, ed. *Causes and Consequences of the American Revolution* (Chicago: Quadrangle Books, 1966), 293–305; and a fine collection of essays, *The Impact of the American Revolution Abroad* (Washington, D.C.: Library of Congress, 1976).

Pares, Richard. "American versus Continental Warfare, 1739–1763." *English Historical Review* 51 (1936): 429–65. A very influential article describing the longstanding debate over British diplomacy and military efforts.

Phillips, Paul Chrisler. *The West in the Diplomacy of the American Revolution*. Urbana: University of Illinois Press, 1913. (*University of Illinois Studies in the Social Sciences* 2, nos. 2-3.) An excellent book for its time, but by now rather outdated.

Piccioni, Camille. *Les Prémiers Commis des affaires étrangères au XVIIe et au XVIIIe siècles*. Paris: E. de Boccard, 1928. Although inferior to Samoyault (below), it provides information about the evolution of the foreign ministry. See also Fréderic Masson, *Le Département des affaires étrangères pendant la Revolution, 1787–1804* (Paris: E. Plon, 1877), and A. Salomon, "Les Alsaciens employés au ministère des Affaires étrangères a Versailles au XVIIe et au XVIIIe siècles," *Revue d'histoire diplomatique* 45 (1931): 449–72.

Piggot, Sir Francis, and Omond, G. W. T. *Documentary History of the Armed Neutralities, 1780 and 1800*. London: University of London Press, 1919. A superb collection which contains 375 pages of documents in English or French dealing with the League of Armed Neutrality and other events of the American war; virtually every maritime state in Europe is represented in the collection.

Potts, Louis W. *Arthur Lee, a Virtuous Revolutionary*. Baton Rouge and London: Louisiana State University Press, 1981. A perceptive biography but not particularly original in its treatment of Lee's diplomacy. .

Prelinger, Catherine M. "Benjamin Franklin and the American Prisoners of War in England during the American Revolution." *William and Mary Quarterly*, 3rd ser., 32 (1975): 261–94. Skillful presentation of one of the most important activities of Franklin and his fellow American diplomats.

———. "Less Lucky than Lafayette: A Note on the French Applicants to Benjamin Franklin for Commissions in the American Army, 1776–1785." *Proceedings of the Fourth Annual Meeting of the Western Society for French History*, pp. 263–71. Santa Barbara, Calif.: privately printed, 1977. Although space limitations prevented publication of its supporting documentation, this is a scholarly analysis of French applications for American army officers' commissions.

Price, Jacob M. *France and the Chesapeake: A History of the French Tobacco Monopoly, 1674–1791, and of Its Relationship to the British and American Tobacco Trades*. 2 vols. Ann Arbor: University of Michigan Press, 1973. Tobacco shipments from America were the way Congress planned to pay the expenses of the American mission in France; Price's massive study of the tobacco trade discusses in detail the American commissioners' involvement in tobacco negotiations.

Rakove, Jack N. *The Beginnings of National Politics: An Interpretive History of the Continental Congress*. New York: Alfred A. Knopf, 1979. Rakove's narrative emphasizes the pragmatism and fluidity of congressional politics; he devotes considerable attention to foreign policy issues. Far narrower in focus is Joseph L. Davis, *Sectionalism in American Politics, 1774–1787* (Madison: University of Wisconsin Press, 1977).

Ramsey, John Fraser. "Anglo-French Relations, 1763–1770: A Study of Choiseul's Foreign Policy." *University of California Publications in History* 17 (1929–41): 143–263. A rather naïve defense of Choiseul as a man of peace.

Rashed, Zenab Esmat. *The Peace of Paris, 1763*. Liverpool, Eng.: Liverpool University Press, 1951. A scholarly and astute account of the British negotiation of the peace. See also Arthur S. Aiton, "The Diplomacy of the Louisiana Cession," *American Historical Review* 36 (1930–31): 701–20; Robert L. Gold, *Borderland Empires in Transition: The Triple-Nation Transfer of Florida* (Carbondale: Southern Illinois University Press, 1969); and Karl W. Schweizer, "William Pitt, Lord Bute, and the Peace Negotiations with France, May-September 1761," *Albion* 13 (1981): 262–75 (which has extensive and up-to-date bibliographical references).

Renaut, Francis P. *Le Pacte de famille et l'Amérique: La politique coloniale franco-espagnole de 1760 à 1792*. Paris: Leroux, 1922. Deals with an interesting topic, the effect of the Franco-Spanish alliance on the two states' colonial empires; but because of its lack of annotation it is of limited usefulness.

Rice, Geoffrey W. "Great Britain, the Manila Ransom and the First Falkland Islands Dispute with Spain, 1766." *International History Review* 2 (1980): 386–409. Argues that the British show of weakness had serious consequences.

Ritcheson, Charles R. *Aftermath of Revolution: British Policy toward the United States, 1783–1795*. Dallas, Tex.: Southern Methodist University Press, 1969. A witty, scholarly, and detailed presentation of the decline and revival of American-British postwar relations. See also J. Leitch Wright, Jr., *Britain and the American Frontier, 1783–1815* (Athens, Ga.: University of Georgia Press, 1975).

———. *British Politics and the American Revolution*. Norman: University of Oklahoma Press, 1954. An excellent introduction to British attempts through 1778 to resolve their American problem.

———. "The Earl of Shelburne and Peace with America, 1782–1783: Vision and Reality." *International History Review* 5 (1983): 322–45. An interesting article that challenges Harlow's view (cited above) of Shelburne as an idealist.

Ritter, Gerhard. *Frederick the Great: A Historical Profile*. Trans. Peter Paret. Berkeley and Los Angeles: University of California Press, 1968. A good introduction to the Prussian king, his wars, and his state.

Roberts, Michael. *British Diplomacy and Swedish Politics, 1758–1773*. Minneapolis: University of Minnesota Press, 1980. A book of awesome erudition and profound insight, written with style and wit. Although it is the study of a single British ambassador, it illuminates, as do few other books, the diplomacy of all Europe. A more limited approach to a part of Roberts's main topic is M. F. Metcalf, *Russia, England and Swedish Party Politics, 1762–1766* (Totowa, N.J.: Rowman and Littlefield, 1977).

———. "Great Britain and the Swedish Revolution, 1772–73." *Historical Journal* 7 (1964): 1–46. This magnificently researched and splendidly written article provides an explanation for France's bitterness toward Britain at the time of the American Revolution.

———. "Great Britain, Denmark and Russia, 1763–1770." In Ragnhild Hatton and M. S. Anderson, eds. *Studies in Diplomatic History: Essays in Memory of David Bayne Horn*. London, Longman, 1970, pp. 236–67. Describes the importance of relations with Denmark for British diplomacy. Other provocative articles on Danish foreign relations are Steward Oakley, "Gustavus III's Plans for War with Denmark in 1783–84," in ibid., pp. 268–86, and Lawrence J. Baack, "State Service in the Eighteenth Century: The Bernstorffs in Hanover and Denmark," *International History Review* 1 (1979): 323–48.

———. "Macartney in Russia." *English Historical Review*, supplement 7 (1974). Indispensable article for understanding the failure of British negotiations with Russia.

———. *Splendid Isolation, 1763–1780*. Reading, Eng.: University of Reading, 1970. A brilliant published lecture which argues that British isolation was inevitable unless Britain made unreasonable concessions to gain a Russian alliance.

Rodríguez, Mario. *La revolución americana de 1776 y el mundo hispánico: ensayos y documentos*. Madrid: Editorial Tecnos, 1976. A collection of essays and supporting documents, including chapters on the Spanish missions of Arthur Lee and John Jay.

Roider, Karl A., Jr. *Austria's Eastern Question, 1700–1790*. Princeton, N.J.: Princeton University Press, 1982. A concise history of one of the major issues in eighteenth-century (and subsequent) diplomacy. See also Franz A. J. Szabo, "Prince Kaunitz and the Balance of Power," *International History Review* 1 (1979): 399–408.

————. "William Lee, Our First Envoy in Vienna." *Virginia Magazine of History and Biography* 86 (1978): 163–68. Sketches Lee's May-July 1778 visit to Vienna.

Roosen, William James. *The Age of Louis XIV: The Rise of Modern Diplomacy*. Cambridge, Mass.: Schenkman Publishing Co., 1976. A useful introduction to seventeenth- and eighteenth-century diplomatic practices.

Rousseau, François. *Règne de Charles III d'Espagne (1759–1788)*. 2 vols. Paris: Plon-Nourrit, 1907. A very readable biography based on French diplomatic documents and published Spanish sources.

Ruigómez de Hernández, María Pilar. *El gobierno español del despotismo ilustrado ante la independencia de los Estados Unidos de América: una nueva estructura de la política internacional (1772–1783)*. Madrid: Ministerio de Asuntos Exteriores, 1978. An overview of the relationship between the Spanish government and the American Revolution.

Russell, Lord John, ed. *Memorials and Correspondence of Charles James Fox*. Vol. 4. London: Richard Bentley, 1857. Vital to the study of the peace negotiations.

Salomon, Robert. *La Politique orientale de Vergennes (1780–1784)*. Paris: Les Presses modernes, 1935. Describes the desperate French attempts to save the independence of the Crimea.

Samoyault, Jean-Pierre. *Les Bureaux du secrétariat d'état des affaires étrangères sous Louis XV*. Paris: A. Pedone, 1971. A detailed administrative history.

Sanders, Jennings B. *Evolution of Executive Departments of the Continental Congress, 1774–1789*. Chapel Hill: University of North Carolina Press, 1935. An administrative history that deals, among other topics, with the means devised by Congress to handle foreign affairs. See also George C. Wood, "Congressional Control of Foreign Relations during the American Revolution, 1774–1789" (Ph.D. diss., New York University, 1918), and Gaillard Hunt, *The Department of State of the United States: Its History and Functions* (New Haven, Conn.: Yale University Press, 1914), pp. 1–37.

Savelle, Max. "The Appearance of an American Attitude toward External Affairs, 1750–1775." *American Historical Review* 52 (1946–47):
655–66. A concise summary of changing American attitudes, particularly toward France.

———. "Colonial Origins of American Diplomatic Principles." *Pacific
Historical Review* 3 (1934): 334–50. Gives colonial examples of
American isolationism, interest in freedom of the seas, the use of international commissions to resolve disputes, and dislike of European involvement in American affairs.

———. *The Origins of American Diplomacy: The International History
of Angloamerica, 1492–1763*. New York: Macmillan, 1967. Savelle
spent much of his career studying the impact of America upon European diplomacy; see also his article "The American Balance of
Power and European Diplomacy, 1713–78," in Richard B. Morris,
ed., *The Era of the American Revolution: Studies Inscribed to
Evarts Boutell Greene* (New York: Columbia University Press,
1939), pp. 140–69.

Sbornik Imperatorskago russkago istoricheskago obshchestva [Collection of the Imperial Russian Historical Commission]. 148 vols. St.
Petersburg: Imperial Russian Historical Commission, 1867–1916.
This marvelous documentary collection contains a number of documents, many in English or French, dealing with foreign affairs. A
selection of the British ambassadors' correspondence of 1762–76,
for example, is in volumes 12 and 19. Empress Catherine's diplomatic correspondence is complete only through 1777; see vols. 48,
51, 57, 67, 87, 97, 118, 135 and 145.

Schaeper, Thomas J. "Pierre Penet: French Adventurer in the American
Revolution." *Daughters of the American Revolution Magazine* 117
(1983): 854–56. A good sketch of the merchant who played a brief
but significant role in the Revolution.

Schama, Simon. *Patriots and Liberators: Revolution in the Netherlands,
1780–1813*. New York: Alfred A. Knopf, 1977. A work of great erudition, which includes considerable discussion of the impact of the
American Revolution on Dutch intellectual and political life.

Schmidt, Knud Rahbek. "The Treaty of Commerce between Great Britain and Russia, 1766: A Study on the Development of Court Panin's
Northern System." *Scando-slavica* 1 (1954): 115–34. Schmidt's article is now rather dated; he wrote a related article in *Scando-slavica*
2 (1956): 134–48.

Schoenbrun, David. *Triumph in Paris: The Exploits of Benjamin Franklin*. New York: Harper & Row, 1976. Basically a reworking of some

of the latter chapters of Carl Van Doren, *Benjamin Franklin* (New
York: Garden City Publishing Co., 1941), the standard biography of
Franklin; of little scholarly interest.

Schulte Nordholt, Jan Willem. *The Dutch Republic and American Independence*. Trans. Herbert H. Rowen. Chapel Hill and London:
University of North Carolina Press, 1982. Less a diplomatic history
than a cultural history resembling the works of Dippel and Echeverria cited above. It, however, does have considerable information
about C. G. F. Dumas, who before Adams's arrival served as semi-
official American diplomatic representative in the Netherlands.

Schweizer, Karl W., and Leonard, Carol S. "Britain, Prussia, Russia and
the Galitzin Letter: A Reassessment." *Historical Journal* 26 (1983):
531–56. A very exciting article about the influence of Russia on the
breakup of the British-Prussian alliance in 1762. See also two other
articles by Schweizer: "Lord Bute, Newcastle, Prussia, and the
Hague Overtures: A Re-Examination, *Albion* 9 (1977): 72–97, and
"The Non-renewal of the Anglo-Prussian Subsidy Treaty, 1761–
1762: A Historical Revision," *Canadian Journal of History* 13
(1978): 384–96.

Scott, H. M. "Frederick II, the Ottoman Empire and the Origins of the
Russo-Prussian Alliance of April 1764." *European Studies Review* 7
(1977): 153–75. A revealing portrait of Frederick's diplomatic tactics.

————. "Great Britain, Poland and the Russian Alliance, 1763–1767."
Historical Journal 19 (1976): 53–74. An important article which argues that in 1763 Britain easily could have obtained a Russian alliance in exchange for a subsidy in Poland.

————. "The Importance of Bourbon Naval Reconstruction to the Strategy of Choiseul after the Seven Years' War." *International History
Review* 1 (1979): 17–35. An extremely valuable contribution to the
history of postwar Franco-British relations, which demonstrates the
failure of the French and Spanish naval rebuilding program and discusses its consequences.

———— "Review Article: British Foreign Policy in the Age of the American Revolution." *International History Review* 6 (1984): 113–25. A
superb historiographical article that not only provides a bibliography of recent work (including several British doctoral dissertations
not consulted for this book) but also discusses work still needed to
be done.

Scott, James Brown, ed. *The Armed Neutralities of 1780 and 1800: A
Collection of Official Documents, Preceded by the Views of Repre-*

sentative Publicists. New York: Oxford University Press, 1918. A more narrowly focused set of documents than those assembled by Piggot and Omond, cited above, it does contain a selection of writings about maritime rights and international law.

Ségur, Louis-Philippe, comte de. *Politique des cabinets de l'Europe*. 3 vols. 4th ed. Paris: Alexis Eymery, 1824–25. A diplomatic history of Europe by a former French ambassador to Russia. See also his superb autobiographical *Mémoires, ou souvenirs et anecdotes*, 3 vols. (Paris: Alexis Eymery, 1824–26). Ségur's mission marked a shift in Vergennes's tactics: see Frank Fox, "Negotiating with the Russians: Ambassador Ségur's Mission to Saint-Petersbourg, 1784–1789," *French Historical Studies* 7 (1971): 47–71.

Setser, Vernon G. "Did Americans Invent the Conditional Most-Favored-Nation Clause?" *Journal of Modern History* 5 (1933): 319–23. Gives the French credit for introducing into the 1778 Franco-American commercial treaty a modified version of reciprocal most-favored-nation commercial privileges. Setser is also the author of *The Commercial Reciprocity Policy of the United States 1774–1829* (Philadelphia: University of Pennsylvania Press, 1937).

Shaw, Peter. *The Character of John Adams*. Chapel Hill: University of North Carolina Press, 1976. A masterful biography, although overly speculative when it comes to diplomacy. It, like older biographies such as Page Smith, *John Adams* (2 vols.; Garden City, N.Y.: Doubleday & Co., 1962), lacks appreciation for the policy objectives of the foreign diplomats with whom Adams had to deal.

Simmons, R. C., and Thomas, P. D. G., eds. *Proceedings and Debates of the British Parliaments Respecting North America, 1754–1783*. 3 vols. to date. Millwood, N.Y. and elsewhere: Kraus International Publications, 1982–. This series prints extracts from the debates of the House of Commons and House of Lords. For a fuller record, see William Cobbett and Thomas C. Hansard, eds., *The Parliamentary History of England from the Earliest Period to 1803*, 36 vols. (London: T. C. Hansard, 1806–20). For 1774–80 there is also *The Parliamentary Register . . .* , 17 vols. (London: J. Almon, 1775–80), and for the preceding period, *The History, Debates and Proceedings of Both Houses of Parliament of Great Britain from the Year 1743 to the Year 1774*, 7 vols. (London: J. Debrett, 1792), and J. Wright, ed., *Sir Henry Cavendish's Debates of the House of Commons during the Thirteenth Parliament of Great Britain*, 2 vols. (London: Longman, Orme, Brown, Green and Longmans, 1841–43). The years 1780 and after are covered in *The Parliamentary Register . . .* , 45 vols. (London: J. Debrett, 1781–96).

Singh, John. *French Diplomacy in the Caribbean and the American Revolution*. Hicksville, N.Y.: Exposition Press, 1977. Actually deals primarily with Choiseul's preparations for war with Britain. On balance it is inferior to Pierre Henri Boulle, "The French Colonies and the Reform of their Administration during and following the Seven Years' War" (Ph.D. diss., University of California, Berkeley, 1968).

Smith, Charles C., ed. "Letters of Benjamin Vaughan to the Earl of Shelburne," *Massachusetts Historical Society Proceedings*, 2nd ser., 17 (1903): 406–38. Franklin's editor, Vaughan, served as Jay's contact with Shelburne; this article prints nine letters from October 1782 to January 1783.

Smith, D. E. Huger, ed. "The Mission of Col. John Laurens to Europe in 1781." *South Carolina Historical and Genealogical Magazine* 1 (1900): 13–41, 136–51, 213–22, 311–22; 2 (1901): 27–43, 108–25. Prints sixty documents relating to Laurens' mission.

Smith, Paul H., ed. *Letters of Delegates to Congress, 1774–1789.* 10 vols. to date. Washington, D.C.: Library of Congress, 1976–. Smith's massive collection, now complete through mid-1778, eventually will publish triple the letters that Burnett did; it reveals how individual congressional delegates felt about foreign affairs and gives details about the workings of Congress.

Sorel, Albert. *The Eastern Question in the Eighteenth Century: The Partition of Poland and the Treaty of Kainardji*. Trans. F. C. Bramwell. London: Methuen and Co., 1898. Although some of the details may not be accurate, this still may be the best introduction to European diplomacy in the years immediately preceding the American Revolution.

———. *Europe and the French Revolution: The Political Traditions of the Old Régime*. Trans. Alfred Cobban and J. W. Hunt. Garden City, N.Y.: Doubleday and Co., Anchor Books, 1971. Sorel arguably is the greatest of all diplomatic historians; this overview of eighteenth-century diplomacy, although written a century ago, can still be read with profit.

Sosin, Jack M. *Agents and Merchants: British Colonial Policy and the Origins of the American Revolution, 1763–1775*. Lincoln: University of Nebraska Press, 1965. Centered on British policymaking, it complements Kammen's book on the American colonial agents. Those interested in British colonial policy should also consult Franklin B. Wickwire, *British Subministers and Colonial America, 1763–1783* (Princeton, N.J.: Princeton University Press, 1966).

Spencer, Frank. "The Anglo-Prussian Breach of 1762: An Historical Revision." *History*, n.s. 41 (1956): 100–12. By now somewhat out of date. Spencer also is the author of "Lord Sandwich, Russian Masts and American Independence," *Mariner's Mirror* 44 (1958): 116–27.

————, ed. *The Fourth Earl of Sandwich: Diplomatic Correspondence, 1763–1765*. Manchester, Eng.: Manchester University Press, 1961. An extremely interesting selection from the papers of one of the more competent British secretaries of state plus a valuable introduction by the editor.

Steell, Willis. *Banjamin Franklin of Paris, 1776–1785*. New York: Minton, Balch and Co., 1938. A popularization with no particular merit.

Stephenson, Orlando W. "The Supply of Gunpowder in 1776." *American Historical Review* 30 (1924–25): 271–81. Analyzes French and other foreign gunpowder smuggling. See also J. Franklin Jameson, "St. Eustatius in the American Revolution," *American Historical Review* 8 (1902–03): 683–708.

Stevens, Benjamin Franklin, ed. *Facsimiles of Manuscripts in European Archives Relating to America, 1773–1783*. 25 vols. London: Privately printed, 1889–98. Actual photographic reproductions of thousands of documents relating to the Revolution. It is somewhat uneven in its coverage, best for Britain and for the years 1777–78. Stevens also collected documents relating to the peace negotiations that have not been published. The present work recently has been reissued by the Irish University Press.

Stiegung, Helle. *Ludvig XV:s Hemliga Diplomati och Sverige, 1752–1774*. Lund, Sweden: Skånska Centraltryckeriet, 1961. Contains a French summary and is a survey of the Swedish policy of Louis XV's secret diplomatic service.

Stinchcombe, William C. *The American Revolution and the French Alliance* Syracuse, N.Y.: Syracuse University Press, 1969. The standard history of the Franco-American alliance from an American standpoint.

————. "L'Alliance Franco-Américaine après l'Indépendance, rapports avec l'Europe après la Révolution américaine," *Actes du Colloque International de Sorèze 1976: Le Règne de Louis XVI et la Guerre d'Indépendance américaine* (1977), pp. 121–39. The only other diplomatic history paper given at this colloquium was a brief study by Georges Livet (pp. 141–86) of Gérard's mission to Philadelphia.

Stourzh, Gerald. *Benjamin Franklin and American Foreign Policy*. 2nd ed. Chicago and London: University of Chicago Press, 1969. An exceptionally penetrating and superbly written study of Franklin's beliefs and attitudes about issues of foreign policy.

Syrett, Harold C., ed. *The Papers of Alexander Hamilton*. 27 vols. New York and London: Columbia University Press, 1961–81. Hamilton's superbly edited papers are of interest to diplomatic historians even of the Revolution.

Taylor, Robert J., ed. *Papers of John Adams*. 6 vols. to date. Cambridge, Mass.: Belknap Press of Harvard University Press, 1977–. This magnificent edition is complete through the summer of 1778; for later years, use Charles Francis Adams, ed., *The Works of John Adams, Second President of the United States*, 10 vols. (Boston: Little, Brown and Co., 1856).

Thomas, Peter D. G. *Lord North*. London: Allen Lane, 1976. A very concise, scholarly, and readable account of North's political career.

Thomson, Mark A. *The Secretaries of State, 1681–1782*. Oxford: Clarendon Press, 1932. A brief institutional history of the Cabinet office responsible for the direction of British foreign affairs.

Tolles, Frederick B. "Franklin and the Pulteney Mission: An Episode in the Secret History of the American Revolution." *Huntington Library Quarterly* 17 (1953–54): 37–58. A somewhat scrambled account of an abortive 1778 diplomatic mission, which will be discussed in the forthcoming volume 26 of *The Papers of Benjamin Franklin*.

Townsend, Sara Bertha. *An American Soldier: The Life of John Laurens*. Raleigh, N.C.: Edwards and Broughton Co., 1958. An uncritical biography of the army officer and amateur diplomat.

Tracy, Nicholas. "The Administration of the Duke of Grafton and the French Invasion of Corsica." *Eighteenth-Century Studies* 8 (1974–75): 169–82. Describes the feeble British reaction to the French acquisition of Corsica.

———. "The Falkland Islands Crisis of 1770: Use of Naval Force." *English Historical Review* 90 (1975): 40–75. A good article about British policy but not a reliable guide to French intentions. The same can be said of two other of his articles, "British Assessments of French and Spanish Naval Reconstruction, 1763–1768," *Mariner's Mirror* 61 (1975): 73–85, and "Parry of a Threat to India, 1768–1774," *Mariner's Mirror* 59 (1973): 35–48.

———. "The Gunboat Diplomacy of the Government of George Grenville, 1764–1765: The Honduras, Turks Island and Gambian Incidents." *Historical Journal* 17 (1974): 711–31. A fine article describing a lesser known series of minor crises between Britain and the French and Spaniards.

Tucker, Robert W., and Hendrickson, David C. *The Fall of the First British Empire: Origins of the War of American Independence*. Baltimore: Johns Hopkins University Press, 1982. Argues that the Brit-

ish government brought on the Revolution by being *too* conciliatory; its discussion of British diplomacy is more orthodox.

Valentine, Alan. *Lord North.* 2 vols. Norman: University of Oklahoma
Press, 1967. This lengthy biography contains disappointingly little
about diplomacy.

Van Alstyne, Richard W. *Empire and Independence: The International
History of the American Revolution.* New York: John Wiley and
Sons, 1965. Reflects its excessive reliance on British source materi-
als by overstressing imperial rivalry as a diplomatic factor.

Van Doren, Carl. *Secret History of the American Revolution.* New York:
Viking Press, 1941. Contains a by now outdated chapter on
Wentworth, Eden, and the Carlisle commission.

Van Tyne, Claude H. "French Aid before the Alliance of 1778." *American Historical Review* 31 (1925–26): 20–40. Flawed by an insufficient understanding of Vergennes's policy objectives and con-
straints.

―――. "Influences Which Determined the French Government to
Make the Treaty with America, 1778." *American Historical Review*
21 (1915–16): 528–41. Presents an ably argued but to me uncon-
vincing brief that French policy was dictated by fear of a British reconciliation with America.

Varg, Paul A. *Foreign Policies of the Founding Fathers.* East Lansing:
Michigan State University Press, 1963. A general survey of American diplomacy from 1776 to 1815; the chapters on Revolutionary diplomacy are rather pedestrian.

Véou, Paul du, ed. "Un Chaiptre inedit des Mémoires de Barthélemy:
La Révolution suédois de 1772." *Revue des études historiques* 104
(1937): 269–303, 401–27. Contains Barthélemy's manuscript jour-
nal of the events of the Swedish Revolution. See also Jacques de
Dampierre, ed., *Mémoires de Barthélemy, 1768–1819* (Paris: Plon-
Nourritt, 1914).

Viner, Jacob. "Power versus Plenty as Objectives of Foreign Policy in
the Seventeenth and Eighteenth Centuries." *World Politics* 1
(1948): 1–30. An important article which argues that the two objectives were interrelated. See also Eli F. Heckscher, *Mercantilism,*
trans. Mendel Shapiro, 2 vols. (London: George Allen and Unwin,
1955).

Vucinich, Wayne S., ed. *Dubrovnik and the American Revolution:
Francesco Favi's Letters.* Palo Alto, Calif.: Ragusan Press, 1977.
Contains in English translation one hundred pages of extracts from
the 1778–83 correspondence of Francesco Favi, diplomatic repre-

sentative at the French court of the Adriatic city-state of Ragusa, now Dubrovnik, Yugoslavia. This edition also contains a historical introduction to both Favi and Ragusa.

Wallace, David Duncan. *The Life of Henry Laurens, with a Sketch of the Life of Lieutenant-Colonel John Laurens*. New York: G. P. Putnam's Sons, 1915. A hagiographic biography of the Revolutionary politician and diplomat. There is a superb new edition of Laurens's correspondence, but it has just reached the period of Laurens's service in the Revolution: Philip M. Hamer et al., eds. *The Papers of Henry Laurens*, 9 vols. to date (Columbia, S.C.: University of South Carolina Press, 1968–).

Ward, Sir A. W., and Gooch, G. P., eds. *The Cambridge History of British Foreign Policy, 1783–1919*. Vol. 1, *1783–1815*. Cambridge: Cambridge University Press, 1922. Ward's historical introduction covers the period before 1783 (pp. 1-140); there is also a chapter on British diplomacy from 1783 to 1792 (by J. H. Clapham, pp. 143–215).

Wharton, Francis, ed. *The Revolutionary Diplomatic Correspondence of the United States*. 6 vols. Washington, D.C.: Government Printing Office, 1889. In spite of antiquated editorial techniques, this massive series of documents is still valuable; eventually it will be largely, although not completely, superceded by documentary editions of the papers of Adams, Franklin, Jay, Laurens, and Morris and by Smith's *Letters of Delegates to Congress*.

Williams, William Appleman. "The Age of Mercantilism: An Interpretation of the American Political Economy, 1763 to 1828." *William and Mary Quarterly*, 3rd ser., 15 (1958): 419–37. Argues that the United States from its beginnings has continued the expansionist and imperialist traditions of Great Britain.

Winter, Pieter J. van. *American Finance and Dutch Investment, 1780–1805, with an Epilogue to 1840*. Adapted by James C. Riley. Trans. C. M. Geyl and I. Clephane. 2 vols. New York: Arno, 1977. Of some importance for those interested in Adams's mission to the Netherlands.

Witt, Cornélis-Henri de. *Thomas Jefferson: Etude historique sur la démocratie américaine*. Paris: Librairie Académique, Didier et Cie., 1861. Contains 160 pages of documents relating to Franco-American relations, including extracts from both Choiseul's and Vergennes's correspondence. It is more complete than the English translation, published as *Jefferson and the American Democracy: An Historical Study* (London, 1862).

Witte, Jehan, baron de, ed. *Journal de l'abbé de Véri*. 2 vols. Paris: Jules Tallandier, 1928–30. Véri's is the best of the court diaries of the early years of Louis XVI's reign; also useful is Emmanuel-Henri de Grouchy and Paul Cottin, eds., *Journal inédit du duc de Croÿ, 1718–1784*, 4 vols. (Paris: Ernest Flammarion, 1906–07).

Yela Utrilla, Juan F., ed. *España ante la independencia de los Estados Unidos*. 2 vols. Lérida, Spain: Gráficos Academia Mariana, 1925. A volume of text and another of diplomatic documents; the documents are very useful, but coverage varies from year to year.

INDEX

Adams, John: political, diplomatic views of, 11, 53, 118, 131; meets with Howe, 53; as commissioner to France, 101, 115; as peace commissioner, 117–18, 139, 148–51; in Netherlands, 118, 127, 131, 139, 149; North attempts to negotiate with, 127; and Dana, 130; and Austro-Russian mediation, 131

Adams, Samuel, 116

Adolphus Frederick (king of Sweden), 22, 25

Affaires de l'Angleterre et de l'Amérique, 79, 90

Aiguillon, Emmanuel-Armand Vignerot du Plessis-Richelieu, duke d', 36–38, 63

Aix-la-Chapelle: Treaty of (*1748*), 4–5; draft treaty signed in (*1778*), 102, 126

Alliance, Treaty of, 64, 92–94, 98, 100

America. *See* United States

American commissioners to France: appointment of, 10, 55; and Spain, 70, 78, 88; and Portugal, 70; and spies, 77–78; assemble, send supplies, 78, 87–88, 102; French distrust of, 78, 96; negotiate with France, 78–80, 88, 91–96; and American warships, 80–85; and dispute over port authority, 86–87, 101–02; financial difficulties of, 88; negotiate with British, 91–92; ac-

complishments of, 95–96, 102; publicly received at French court, 98

American peace commissioners, 117–19, 144–51

Amity and Commerce, Treaty of, 55, 78, 88, 92–94, 98, 100, 139, 149

Amsterdam, 69, 102, 126

Aranda, Pedro Pablo Abarca de Bolea, count de, 19, 78, 142, 155–57

Aranjuez, Treaty of, 109

Army, Austrian, 18

Army, British: strength of, 14, 43, 44; in American war, 43–44, 47, 54, 88, 95, 110, 117, 122; manning of, 46–47, 71; threat by, to West Indies, 57, 90, 145; supplying of, 68

Army, Continental: supplies for, 12, 50–51, 62, 78–79; military operations by, 44, 51, 88, 95, 114, 120; foreign officers in, applying to, 63, 66, 101; mutinies in, 119

Army, Dutch, 19, 46

Army, French: strength of, 16; reinforces West Indies, 49, 52, 57, 89, 118; officers of, in Continental Army, 63; threatens Britain, 98; in North America, 114–15, 117, 118, 119–20

Army, Prussian, 17

Army, Russian, 18

Army, Spanish, 19, 110–11, 118

Army, Turkish, 22

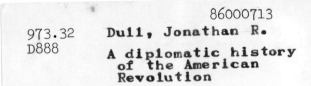
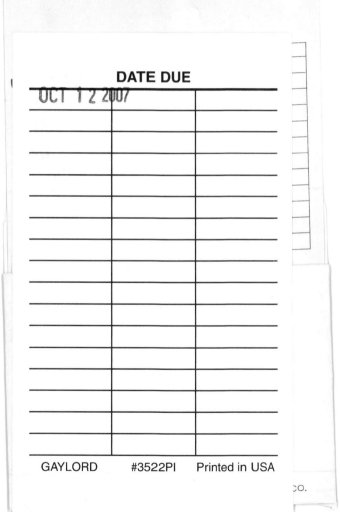